Spanish

An Essential Grammar

Spanish: An Essential Grammar is a concise and user-friendly reference guide to the most important aspects of Spanish.

It presents a fresh and accessible description of the language as it is spoken both in Europe and Latin America. The book sets out the complexities of Spanish in short, readable sections, and explanations are clear and free from jargon.

The *Grammar* is the ideal reference source for the learner and user of Spanish. It is suitable for either independent study or for students in schools, colleges, universities and adult classes of all types.

Features include:

- Clear distinctions between the essential and basic aspects of Spanish grammar and those that are more complex
- Full use of authentic examples
- Simple explanations of areas that customarily pose problems for English speakers
- Detailed contents list and index for easy access to information

Peter T. Bradley is Emeritus Professor of Latin American History and **Ian Mackenzie** is Senior Lecturer in Spanish, both at Newcastle University.

Routledge Essential Grammars

Essential Grammars are available for the following languages:

Chinese
Danish
Dutch
English
Finnish
Greek
Hungarian
Modern Hebrew
Norwegian
Polish
Portuguese
Spanish
Swedish
Thai
Urdu

Other titles of related interest published by Routledge:

Modern Spanish Grammar: A Practical Guide, Second Edition
By Juan Kattán-Ibarra and Christopher J. Pountain

Modern Spanish Grammar Workbook, Second Edition
By Juan Kattán-Ibarra and Irene Wilkie

Colloquial Spanish
By Untza Otaola Alday

Colloquial Spanish 2
By Untza Otaola Alday

Spanish

An Essential Grammar

 **Peter T. Bradley and
Ian Mackenzie**

 Routledge
Taylor & Francis Group

LONDON AND NEW YORK

First published 2004
by Routledge
2 Park Square, Milton Park, Abingdon, Oxon, OX14 4RN

Simultaneously published in the USA and Canada
by Routledge
270 Madison Ave, New York NY 10016

Routledge is an imprint of the Taylor & Francis Group

Transferred to Digital Printing 2010

Typeset in Sabon by
Florence Production Ltd, Stoodleigh, Devon.

British Library Cataloguing in Publication Data
A catalogue record for this book is available from the British Library

Library of Congress Cataloging in Publication Data
Bradley, Peter T., 1943–
   Spanish: an essential grammar/Peter T. Bradley and Ian Mackenzie.
      p. cm. – (Routledge Essential grammars)
    Includes index.
   1. Spanish language–Grammar. I. Mackenzie, I.E., 1965– II. Title.
   III. Series: Essential grammar.
   PC4112.B63 2004
   468.2'421–dc22   2003020645

ISBN 0–415–28642–5 (hbk)
ISBN 0–415–28643–3 (pbk)

Contents

Preface

Spanish, or *castellano* as native speakers often refer to it, now rivals English as the major world language. This state of affairs is largely the product of events that took place centuries ago.

By the late thirteenth century, in the wake of the Christian struggle to reconquer the Iberian Peninsula and expand the political influence of Castile, *castellano* had spread from the north to become established as the standard form of language in most of the Iberian Peninsula. However, whereas cities such as Toledo and later Madrid were centres of this standard language in spheres such as public administration and literature, around the thriving commercial centre of Seville in Andalusia, the language developed and spread with alternative distinctive norms such as *seseo* and *yeísmo*.

In 1492 the first written grammar of *castellano* was published and Christopher Columbus initiated a Spanish transoceanic maritime enterprise that would carry the language of the Iberian Peninsula throughout the world, and especially to what would become known as the Americas. It was during this process of imperial expansion in the sixteenth century that the language was more regularly described as *lengua española*, the language of Spain.

Today, the linguistic legacy of that past is more than 400 million speakers of Spanish in 23 countries, 19 of them in Latin America. Therefore, the vast majority of Spanish speakers live outside Spain, principally in Latin America. About one tenth of all speakers reside in the Iberian Peninsula, more than 102 million live in Mexico, which constitutes the largest national conglomeration of Spanish speakers, whilst those in the Canary Islands, Equatorial Guinea, Morocco and the Philippine Islands are also a testimony to the past. More recent emigration trends have planted Spanish speakers in Canada, and in the USA where there is an increasing awareness of the social and political significance of Hispanics. In January 2003, the US Census Bureau estimated that they are the largest and fastest growing minority numbering some 37 million or 13 per cent of the total population.

Largely due to its popularity as a second language, many more people speak English worldwide, but Spanish is the only other language that has a comparable international significance. Today, the vast majority of Spanish speakers throughout the world display characteristics of speech and writing that are reminiscent of features long ago established in Andalusia. Nowadays, this is usually attributed to the fact that the earliest explorers and settlers originated in that region, that later émigrés passed through it en route to the Canary Islands and the outposts of empire, whilst cities such as Seville and Cadiz dominated commercial enterprise in ships crewed by Andalusian seamen. If there is such a thing as standard Spanish, this book seeks to reflect the fact that today rather than being purely Peninsular it is intercontinental and especially American, but also that regional variation does not signify that it is undergoing a process of profound fragmentation.

Acknowledgement

The authors would like to acknowledge the invaluable assistance of Palma Roldán Núñez, who vetted and in many cases amended the examples used in this book.

Symbols

>   becomes, changes to
/   or, alternative forms or meanings
=   equivalent to
+   plus
× ×   unacceptable grammar
[SP]   word or phrase found usually (though not always exclusively) in Peninsular Spanish
[LA]   word or phrase found usually (though not always universally) in Latin America

Chapter 1

The alphabet, pronunciation, stress, spelling and punctuation

1.1 The alphabet

Due to recent changes, the composition of the Spanish alphabet today is more like English and other Romance languages. Because older reference works used a different system of classification, a few words of explanation may be helpful.

Until 1994, **ch** and **ll** were considered to be separate letters in the Spanish alphabet. Consequently, in dictionaries and word lists there were separate listings for words beginning with each of them, after **c** and **l** respectively. Likewise, this alphabetical order was observed when those letters occurred within words, with the result that **cocha** would be listed after all other words beginning with **coc-**, and **callada** after **calzo**. In 1994, under international pressure and the impact of computer sorting programs, the Association of Academies of Spanish adopted the internationally accepted standard of alphabetical order, no longer considering **ch** and **ll** to be separate letters. However, as a distinctive feature of the language, Spanish still considers **ñ** to be a separate letter. Dictionaries, therefore, still retain a separate listing for the few words beginning with **ñ** (after those beginning with **n**) and this order is preserved when **ñ** occurs within words (**caña** being listed after **canzonetista**).

1.2 Pronunciation

The only sure way of pronouncing Spanish correctly is to listen closely and try to imitate native speakers. However, a list of the Spanish letters together with their usual pronunciation is given in Table 1.1. This is offered as general guidance, drawing attention to instances where native speakers of English commonly make mistakes. Moreover, only the most important differences between Peninsular and Latin American Spanish are highlighted.

Table 1.1 The sounds of Spanish

Letter	Name	Pronunciation	Examples
a	a	as in *hat*, never *hate* nor *above*	**anagrama** – each **a** has the same sound
b	be	similar to English **b**; strongest after **n** or **m**, or following a pause weaker between vowels	**balsa, cambio haba**
c	ce	before **a**, **o**, **u** and consonants: as in *cat* before **e** and **i**: as *th* in *thin* in the centre and north of Spain and as s in *six* in Latin America and much of Andalusia (called **seseo**)	**casa, acta** **cena**
ch	che	as in *church*	**chacal, chacha**
d	de	strongest after **n** or **l**, or following a pause weaker between vowels or at the end of words, in some cases in Spain to the point of disappearance, e.g. **ado > ao** overall less strong than English *d* and pronounced with the tongue behind the top teeth and not on the ridge above the teeth, cf. *dead* and **dedo** 'finger'	**anda, balde** **viñedo, casado, Madrid, usted**
e	e	as in *egg*, not as *meet*, never silent as in English *pose*	**merece** – each **e** has the same sound
f	efe	as in English	**falta**
g	ge	before **a**, **o**, **u**: as in *go*, but less strong between vowels before **e** and **i**: like *ch* in Scottish *loch* (never as in *general*)	**gala, daga** **gente, giba**

2

Letter	Name	Pronunciation	Examples
		gu before **e** or **i** is pronounced like g in English *go* (the **u** is silent)	**guerrilla, guiño**
		gu before **a**, and **gü**, are pronounced like gw in *Gwen*	**averiguar, pingüe**
h	hache	silent	**hora**
i	i	as ee in *meet*, never as in *pit*	**pita**
j	jota	like **g** before **e** and **i**, i.e. as *ch* in Scottish *loch*	**jaca, migaja, reloj**
k	ka	mainly in foreign words, like c in English *cat*	**kilo**
l	ele	similar to *l* in English *clear*	**Lola, Lima**
ll	elle	for purists, like *lli* in English *million*, but today frequently softened to *y* as in English *yes*, especially in Andalusia and parts of Latin America (called **yeísmo**); in the River Plate and some other areas, close to *s* in *pleasure*	**calle, llevar**
m	eme	as *m* in English	**memo**
n	ene	as *n* in English	**nene**
ñ	eñe	more like *ny* in *canyon* than *ni* in *opinion*	**España, caña**
o	o	as the o in English *not*, a single sound, so never as in *vote*	**locomotor, ñoño** – each o has the same sound
p	pe	similar to English, but less aspirated; silent in the combinations **pt** and **ps**; sometimes dropped in writing from the combination **pt** (and occasionally from **ps**)	**Pedro** / **psicología** / **septiembre/setiembre**
q	cu	always followed by **u**; **qui** and **que** like *c* in *cat*; **qua** and **quo** as *quick*	**quema, saque** / **quásar, quórum**

3

Table 1.1 continued

Letter	Name	Pronunciation	Examples
r	ere	between vowels or after **b**, **c**, **d**, **g**, **p**, **t** – a single tap of the tongue at the front of the mouth, as in Scottish *pearl* at the beginning of words and after **l** or **n** – a trill or roll of the tongue	**caro, embrollo, agrio, potro** **rojo, alrededor, Enrique**
rr	erre	a trill or roll of the tongue when a prefix ending in a vowel is added to a word beginning with **r**, the **r > rr** care should be taken to distinguish between words such as **pero** 'but' and **perro** 'dog'	**carro** **para + rayos > pararrayos**
s	ese	generally as in *sit* rather than *rose*	**sesenta**
t	te	similar to English, but less aspirated like Spanish **d**, pronounced with the tongue against the top teeth and not the ridge above them, cf. English *total* and Spanish **total**	**tetera**
u	u	like *oo*, as in English *plume* and never *cube*; a single sound	**pluma, fuma, cubo**
v	uve	pronounced exactly like Spanish **b**, e.g. **tubo** and **tuvo**, **cabo** and **cavo** sound the same; never *v* in English *very* strongest after a pause, and after **n** weaker between vowels	**vino, enviar, ¡Vale! cava, bravo**
w	uve doble	rare, only in borrowed words, usually as in *wood* occasionally as **v/b**	**whisky, windsurf wáter**
x	equis	between vowels: as in *axis*	**taxi, éxito**

4

	before consonants: as s (especially in Spain)	explicar, extenso
	in Mexico: sometimes like Spanish **j**	**México, Oaxaca**
y	**i griega** at the beginning of words and between vowels: as in English *yet*, but in parts of Latin America, especially the River Plate and Chile, like s in *pleasure*	**yema, mayoría**
	at the end of a word and as the conjunction *y*: = Spanish **i**	rey
z	**zeta** or as *th* in *thin* in the centre and north of Spain	
	zeda as s in *six* in most of the Spanish-speaking world including Andalusia and Latin America (**seseo**)	**zorro, mazorca**
	apart from the name of the letter itself, **z** is very rare before **e** and **i**, being replaced by **c**, e.g. **feliz** but **felices**. Amongst the few exceptions are: **Nueva Zelanda, Zimbabwe, zigzag**	

Notes:

1 The letters of the alphabet are feminine, e.g. **la efe**. In contrast to most nouns, the names for letters use the feminine article **la** even when they begin with a stressed **a**, i.e. **la a, la hache** (cf. **el agua, el hacha**). The plurals add **-s**, with the exception of vowels, which add **-es**: **efes, aes, ees** (or **es**), **íes, oes, úes**.

2 Each Spanish vowel has a single sound, whereas English vowels may have different sounds in the same word, or may not even be pronounced at all, e.g. *Gibraltar, accommodation, trouble.* The vowel sounds themselves in Spanish are also single, and *never* diphthongs as in *hate, pure.*

3 Typical of Spanish is the fact that concurrent vowels at the end of one word and beginning of the next (even if separated by **h**) are run together, especially if they are the same: e.g. **está_aquí, mi_hijo, venga_usted, hasta_hoy.**

4 In general, double consonants are less common in Spanish than English (**ll** and **rr** are considered to be single elements in their own right). **Nn** exists in a few words, e.g. **ennegrecer, innato,** and **cc** only when each **c** has a different sound, e.g. **occidente, fracción.** Since there are no other double consonants, words such as **profesor, imposible,** or **difícil,** should pose no spelling problem for speakers of English.

5 Learners of Spanish need to take special care when in regions where **seseo** is the norm, since words with different spelling can have exactly the same pronunciation, e.g. **sebo** 'grease' and **cebo** 'bait', **casa** 'house' and **caza** 'hunt', **cegar** 'to blind', **segar** 'to reap/mow', **ves** 'you see' and **vez** 'time/occasion'.

5

1.3 Stress and written accents

The correct pronunciation of Spanish depends not only on being able to reproduce the correct sound for each letter, but on applying the correct emphasis to each syllable in individual words. Incorrect stress may mean that listeners have difficulty in understanding your meaning, and in some cases may even change the meaning of words.

1.3.1 Syllables: basic principles

For the purpose of identifying the syllables in Spanish words in order to understand stress and written accents, it is generally sufficient to know the following basic principles:

(a) syllables should end in a vowel as far as possible (so that a single consonant between vowels is attached to the vowel or vowels which follow it): **ta-ba-co, po-pu-lar**.
(b) combinations of consonants ending in -l or -r, as well as **ch**, cannot be split: **a-pli-car, re-gre-so, ca-lle, cu-cha-ra**.
(c) **s** does not belong to the same syllable as a following consonant: **cas-ta-ña, pos-tre**.

1.3.2 Stress: general principles

For purposes of identification only, stressed vowels are underlined.

1.3.2.1

When words end in a single vowel or the consonants **n** or **s**, the stress normally falls on the next to last syllable:

v_e_rde   **much_a_cho**   **n_o_ches**   **v_e_nden**   **vol_u_men**

1.3.2.2

When words end in consonants other than **n** or **s**, the stress normally falls on the last syllable:

Madr_i_d   **hospit_a_l**   **ten_a_z**   **viv_i_r**   **coñ_a_c**

1.3.2.3

When words are stressed in ways that do not conform to the above rules, the stress is indicated by a written acute accent:

cámara   chacolí   cólico   escáner   fácil   Perú

The correct use of the accent in Spanish is important, as a missing accent can completely change the meaning of a word: **llego** 'I arrive', **llegó** 'he/she arrived'.

Written acute accents

1   A written acute accent on a syllable always indicates that the stress is located on that syllable.

2   Words which are stressed on syllables other than the last or next to the last will always require a written accent: **enérgico, frívolo, válvula, miércoles**.

3   Care is required when forming the plural of words since normally the stress should remain in the same position whether the word is used in the singular or plural. In some cases, this may require either the addition or the removal of a written acute accent: **joven > jóvenes, interés > intereses**. See 2.1.4.1.

1.3.3   Stress on combinations of vowels

Fundamental to understanding what follows is the fact that vowels in Spanish are divided into two groups: strong vowels (**a, e,** and **o**) and weak vowels (**i** and **u**). For purposes of identification only, stressed vowels are underlined.

1.3.3.1

When two *strong* vowels are combined, they form two separate syllables:

ta-re-a   ca-er   o-a-sis   ca-o-ba   cre-en

1.3.3.2

When two *weak* vowels are combined they constitute a single syllable (a diphthong). When this syllable is stressed, the emphasis normally falls on the second of the vowels:

bui-tre   rui-dos   Piu-ra   diur-no   dis-tri-bui-do

1.3.3.3

When there is a combination of a strong vowel and one or two weak vowels they constitute a single syllable (a diphthong or triphthong) in the majority of cases:

his-to-ria far-ma-cia in-tem-pe-rie ha-blas-teis sim-po-sio

The stress falls on the strong vowel when the diphthong (or triphthong) is stressed:

pei-ne bri-ga-dier he-roi-co i-dio-ta gua-pa eu-ro liais

1.3.3.4

Words that do not conform to the principle that the combination of a strong vowel and one or two weak vowels forms a single syllable require the use of a written accent:

re-ís-teis frí-o pa-ís ba-úl con-ti-nú-o a-ba-dí-a ven-dí-ais

This case can be contrasted with that of words like **enviáis, evacuéis, metió, podéis** and **buscapiés**, which *do* conform to the principle that the combination of a strong vowel and one or two weak vowels forms a single syllable. The accent is required for an entirely different reason, namely that the stress falls on the final syllable, rather than the expected penultimate syllable (as per 1.3.2.1).

Notes:
1 Single syllable verb forms containing two vowels conform to the general rules and so do not require a written accent: **dio** 'he/she gave', **fui** 'I went'. Note, however, the exceptions **rió** 'he/she laughed', **huís** 'you (plural) flee', **huí** 'I fled'.

2 The Spanish Academy advises that there should be a written accent in cases where an **h** separates two vowels that are pronounced separately: **prohíbe, rehúso, retahíla, búho, ahínco, ahúmo, cohíbe**.

1.3.4 *Other uses of written acute accents*

Written acute accents are used to distinguish between the meanings of words with the same spelling:

si	if		sí	yes
mi	my		mí	me (after prepositions)

tu	your	**tú**	you (subject pronoun)
el	the	**él**	he, him (after prepositions)
se	himself, herself, itself, themselves	**sé**	I know, be (imperative of **ser**)
de	of	**dé**	he/she gives (present subjunctive)
te	you (object pronoun)	**té**	tea
aun	even	**aún**	still, yet
mas	but	**más**	more

For the use of accents on demonstrative pronouns, see Chapter 4. For the use of accents on interrogative and exclamatory words, see Chapter 27.

1.4   Spelling – capital letters

1.4.1   Cases where English has capitals but Spanish does not

1.4.1.1

With adjectives of national, regional and personal origin:

un vino peruano	a Peruvian wine
una fiesta andaluza	an Andalusian fiesta
un tema borgesiano	a Borgesian theme

1.4.1.2

With days of the week and months of the year:

los lunes	on Mondays
en mayo	in May

1.4.1.3

With nouns and adjectives referring to political and religious affiliation:

Es jefe de los conservadores.	He is leader of the Conservatives.
Esta creencia es de origen judío.	This belief is of Jewish origin.

1.4.1.4

In official titles:

los reyes de España	the King and Queen of Spain
el almirante Grau	Admiral Grau

1.4.1.5

In titles of plays, films and books:

Los ríos profundos de **Arguedas**	Arguedas's *Deep Rivers*

Note, however, the use of capitals for newspaper and magazine titles such as *El Comercio, El País, Ultima Hora.*

1.4.2 | *Acronyms and abbreviations*

Capitals in Spanish commonly form acronyms. It is also characteristic of Spanish to indicate the plural by a doubling of the capital letters:

la CGT (Confederación General del Trabajo)	the General Confederation of Workers
la ONU (Organización de Naciones Unidas)	UN (the United Nations)
las CCAA (Comunidades Autónomas)	the Autonomous Regions
las FFAA (Fuerzas Armadas)	the Armed Forces

Typical too of Spanish is the practice of forming nouns and adjectives from acronyms:

emerretista	a member of the **MRTA (Movimiento Revolucionario Túpac Amaru)**

1.5 Punctuation

Table 1.2 contains a list of common punctuation marks with notes on their use.

Table 1.2 Spanish punctuation marks

. **Punto** 'full stop' or 'period' – in most Spanish-speaking countries, with the notable exception of Mexico, this is used in numbers where English would have a comma: **5.651.242** '5,651,242'.

... **Puntos suspensivos** 'dots'

, **Coma** – in most Spanish-speaking countries, with the notable exception of Mexico, the **coma** is used to indicate decimals: **21,6** (**21 coma 6**) '21.6' (21 point 6).

: **Dos puntos** 'colon' – used after salutations in letters: **Mi querida Ana:** 'My dear Ana,'.

; **Punto y coma** 'semicolon'

¿ **Principio de interrogación** – unique to Spanish, it occurs not only at the beginning of sentences, but before interrogative phrases within sentences: **Dime, ¿quieres ir o no?** 'Tell me, do you want to go or not?'.

? **Fin de interrogación**

¡ **Principio de exclamación** or **admiración** – unique to Spanish, it occurs not only at the beginning of sentences, but before exclamations within sentences: **Me dijo, ¡hágalo ahora!** 'He said to me, "Do it now!"'.

! **Fin de exclamación** or **admiración**

« », **Comillas** 'inverted commas' – « » are still found in
' ' " " Spanish to begin and end short quotations within a sentence, or in other instances where English would use ' ' or " ". In the press, however, they are replaced today by " " or ' '.

- **Guión** 'hyphen' – less common than in English, since many compound words in Spanish are written as single words: **antirrobo** 'anti-theft', **francocanadiense** 'French-Canadian'.

Used to divide words at the end of a line.

Used to join nouns: **misiles superficie-aire** 'surface to air missiles'.

Used to form compound adjectives: **franco-alemán** 'Franco-German'.

—   **Raya** 'dash' – used to introduce reported speech, where English would use inverted commas.

( )   **Paréntesis** 'parentheses'

[ ]   **Paréntesis cuadrado/rectangular** 'square brackets'

Chapter 2

Nouns

In order to use nouns correctly in Spanish, we need to know their grammatical gender (which is usually arbitrary and unrelated to biological gender), and in the vast majority of cases their distinct singular and plural forms.

The three main groups of nouns in Spanish

Most Spanish nouns fall into one of the following categories:

1 Nouns that end in -o (**libro** 'book', **vino** 'wine').
2 Nouns that end in -a (**casa** 'house', **patata** 'potato').
3 Nouns that end in -e or a consonant (**nube** 'cloud', **tacón** 'heel').

Nouns ending in -o are almost always masculine, the majority of those ending in -a are feminine and those ending in -e or a consonant can be either gender.

2.1 Plural forms of nouns

The plural form of most Spanish nouns ends in -s.

2.1.1 *The plural of nouns ending in an unstressed vowel*

This is obtained by adding -s to the singular form:

| **la casa** | the house | **las casas** | the houses |
| **la tribu** | the tribe | **las tribus** | the tribes |

2.1.2 | *The plural of nouns ending in a consonant*

This is usually obtained by adding -es. This includes words of one syllable or a final *stressed* syllable ending in -s.

See 2.1.4.1 for other words ending in -s.

el olor	los olores	smell/s
el farol	los faroles	streetlight/s
el mes	los meses	month/s
el autobús	los autobuses	bus/buses

2.1.3 | *The plural of nouns ending in a stressed vowel*

This is usually obtained by adding -s, except when the singular form ends in -í:

el sofá	los sofás	sofa/s
el pie	los pies	foot/feet
el canapé	los canapés	sofa/s
el dominó	los dominós	domino/dominoes
el menú	los menús	menu/s

When the ending is -í, most common words create the plural by adding -es, although some add only -s:

el israelí	los israelíes	Israeli/s
el ají [LA]	los ajíes	chili pepper/s
el esquí	los esquís	ski/s

Note: Some words ending in -ú have plural forms in -úes: **tabú/tabúes** 'taboo/s', **bambú/bambúes** 'bamboo/s'.

2.1.4 | *Nouns which do not adopt a distinct plural form*

2.1.4.1

Nouns with a final *unstressed* syllable ending in -s, and those which end in -x do not change in the plural:

la crisis	**las crisis**	crisis/crises
el virus	**los virus**	virus/viruses
el fax	**los fax**	fax/faxes

Spelling changes as a result of forming plurals (see also 1.3.2)

1 Nouns which end in -z change this to -c before the plural ending -es: **voz > voces** 'voice/s' (see Table 1.1).
2 Nouns ending in -n or -s which have a written accent in the final syllable, will no longer require the written accent after adding -es: **avión > aviones** 'plane/s', **huracán > huracanes** 'hurricane/s', **botellín > botellines** 'small bottle/s', **andén > andenes** 'platform/s, pavement/s, sidewalk/s', **inglés > ingleses** 'Englishman/English people'.
3 Nouns containing combined vowels of which one is **í** or **ú**, retain the accent after adding -es: **raíz > raíces** 'root/s', **baúl > baúles** 'trunk/s'.
4 Nouns which end in -en will require a written accent to maintain the correct stress in the plural: **imagen > imágenes** 'image/s', **resumen > resúmenes** 'résumé/s', **dictamen > dictámenes** 'report/s'.
5 The following words have irregular plurals in that the stressed vowel (underlined) changes: **carácter > caracteres** 'character/s', **régimen > regímenes** 'regime/s, diet/s', **espécimen > especímenes** 'specimen/s'.

The plural of compound nouns

Compound words consisting of a verb or preposition and a plural noun have no distinct plural form:

el/los salvapantallas   screensaver/s

el/los paracaídas   parachute/s

In compounds forming single words in which the last element is not plural, a normal plural is formed:

el mirasol   **los mirasoles**   sunflower/s

In compound nouns formed from two separate nouns, only the first usually takes a normal plural form:

el barco vivienda   **los barcos vivienda**   houseboat/s

However, if the second noun can be regarded as qualifying the first, then both will be pluralized: **país miembro/países miembros** 'member country/countries', **documento maestro/documentos maestros** 'master document/s'. There is disagreement over the use of **clave**: **puntos clave** or **claves** 'key points'.

2.1.6 *The plural of foreign words*

The general trend is to form plurals only by the addition of -s, even if the word ends in a consonant. Some words of French origin at times drop the final -t:

el córner   **los córners**   corner/s (football)

el barman   **los barmans**   barman/barmen

el cabaret/cabaré   **los cabarets/cabarés**   cabaret/s

Some foreign words ending in consonants have, however, become incorporated into Spanish following the usual practice of adding -es, whereas in other cases two forms compete for acceptance:

el hotel   **los hoteles**   hotel/s

el gol   **los goles**   goal/s

el escáner/scanner   **los escáneres/scanners**   scanner/s

el club   **los clubs/clubes**   club/s

Words derived from Latin ending in -t or -um are found with and without the addition of -s, although an alternative recommended form in the case of -um is to replace this suffix with -o and treat the word as if it were Spanish:

el déficit	deficit	los déficit/s	deficits
el currículum	curriculum	los currículum/s	curricula
el currículo	curriculum	los currículos	curricula

2.1.7 | The plural of proper nouns

When used with the plural definite article, to designate a group collectively, proper nouns (or names) generally do not have a plural form (unless the name itself begins with los/las, as in **los Pirineos**):

Los Uribe de Colombia se encuentran en todo el mundo.
The Uribes of Colombia are found throughout the world.

In other cases plural forms are used, with the usual exception of names ending in -z or a final stressed syllable ending in -s:

Viven Velascos en todo el Perú.
Velascos live all over Peru.

Hay pocos Solís y Suárez en Suecia.
There are few Solíses and Suárezes in Sweden.

2.1.8 | Nouns which are always plural

Common are the following:

las afueras	outskirts	**las gafas, los anteojos** [LA]	spectacles
los alrededores	surroundings	**las tijeras**	scissors
los auriculares/ cascos	headphones	**las tinieblas**	dark(ness)
los celos	jealousy	**las vacaciones**	holidays
los comestibles	foodstuffs	**los víveres**	provisions
los espaguetis	spaghetti		

Nouns used both in the singular and plural include: el/los bigote/s 'moustache', el/los pantalón/pantalones 'trousers, pants', la/las nariz/narices 'nose', la/las escalera/s 'stairs'.

Note: El celo means 'zeal' and la escalera is also a 'ladder'.

2.1.9 | Mass (or uncountable) nouns

In Spanish there is a tendency to use certain nouns both as mass (i.e. uncountable) nouns or abstract nouns in the singular, and also as plural countable nouns. This contrasts with English which, for example, will not usually tolerate 'two breads' whereas in Spanish dos panes 'two loaves of bread' is normal. Other examples are:

el jabón	soap	**los jabones**	bars of soap
la tostada	toast	**las tostadas**	pieces/slices of toast
la amistad	friendship	**unas amistades**	some friends

Conversely, the English mass noun 'furniture' corresponds to a countable noun in Spanish:

Tenemos que cambiar los muebles.
We have to change the furniture.

2.2 Gender

Nouns in Spanish are generally assigned either to the masculine or feminine gender. Except in the case of nouns referring to persons or animals, the gender of a noun is unrelated to biological gender.

2.2.1 | Nouns referring to persons or animals

2.2.1.1

If a masculine noun ends in -o, often its feminine equivalent is derived by changing the -o into -a:

el abuelo	grandfather	**la abuela**	grandmother
el zorro	fox	**la zorra**	vixen

2.2.1.2

For many masculine nouns ending in a consonant, especially -or, -ón, -és
and -ín, the feminine equivalent is formed by adding -a:

el locutor	la locutora	announcer
el bailarín	la bailarina	dancer
el campeón	la campeona	champion
el marqués	la marquesa	marquis/marchioness

2.2.1.3

A few nouns add the feminine endings -esa or -isa after removing any final
vowel from the masculine form:

el alcalde	mayor	la alcaldesa	mayor's wife/mayoress
el poeta	poet	la poetisa	poetess

2.2.1.4

Other nouns form the feminine gender by the use of other typically feminine endings:

el actor	actor	la actriz	actress
el héroe	hero	la heroína	heroine

2.2.1.5 Nouns that can be masculine or feminine

In some instances the same word is used irrespective of gender, the definite
or indefinite articles alone making the distinction.

This is widely seen in nouns ending in -a (especially -ista) and in -e. It is
the safest option to choose for those ending in -nte. It is true also of some
nouns ending in a consonant and one or two ending in -o:

el/la futbolista	footballer	el/la intérprete	interpreter
el/la espía	spy	el/la cantante	singer
el/la joven	young man/woman	el/la piloto	pilot

Note: An exception is el monje/la monja 'monk/nun'.

Fixed gender nouns

Some nouns have a fixed gender regardless of the biological gender of the person they denote:

la persona	person	**la víctima**	victim
la estrella	(film) star	**la celebridad**	celebrity
el personaje	character	**el genio**	genius

This is true also of many nouns designating wild animals. Where a distinction needs to be made it is done through the addition of **macho** 'male' or **hembra** 'female', or by using the phrases **el macho de** or **la hembra de**:

el panda	panda	**las garzas macho**	male herons
la víbora	adder, viper	**el macho del tejón**	male badger

2.2.1.7 Gender and social change

During the final decades of the twentieth century, changing attitudes to the roles of women in society have initiated what has become an ongoing process of linguistic change. Consequently, it has become common practice to use feminine forms for job titles that hitherto existed only in the masculine form:

abogado	**abogada**	lawyer
catedrático	**catedrática**	professor
ministro	**ministra**	minister
ingeniero	**ingeniera**	engineer
juez	**jueza**	judge

2.2.1.8 Masculine plural for mixed gender groups

The masculine plural form of a noun bearing biological gender is used in reference to groups containing at least one male:

los niños	the children	**los alumnos**	the students
los señores	Mr and Mrs	**los esposos**	husband and wife

2.2.2 | *Determining gender from noun endings*

2.2.2.1 | Nouns ending in -o and -a

Those ending in -o are usually masculine, while those ending in -a are usually feminine, but there are exceptions:

(a) Many words ending in **-ista**, see 2.2.1.5 above.
(b) **La mano** 'hand', and abbreviated forms such as **la foto** 'photograph' (for **fotografía**), **la moto** 'motorcycle' (for **motocicleta**), and **la** [SP] **radio** (originally **radiodifusión**).
(c) **El día** 'day', **el mapa** 'map', **el planeta** 'planet', **el tranvía** 'tram'.
(d) Nouns ending in **-a** but referring to men: **el cura** 'priest', **el poeta** 'poet'.
(e) A large number of words ending in **-ma** (but not all) are masculine. The most common are shown in Table 2.1.

Table 2.1 Masculine nouns ending in *-ma*

el aroma	aroma	**el holograma**	hologram
el clima	climate	**el idioma**	language
el crucigrama	crossword	**el lema**	slogan
el diagrama	diagram	**el panorama**	panorama
el dilema	dilemma	**el pijama** [SP]	pyjamas
el diploma	diploma	**el poema**	poem
el dogma	dogma	**el problema**	problem
el drama	drama	**el programa**	program(me)
el emblema	emblem	**el síntoma**	symptom
el enigma	enigma	**el sistema**	system
el esquema	scheme	**el telegrama**	telegram
el estigma	stigma	**el tema**	theme/topic
el fantasma	ghost	**el trauma**	trauma

2.2.2.2 | Feminine endings other than *-a*

Nouns with the following endings are usually feminine: **-ad, -tud, -ción, -sión, -umbre** and **-ie**. Many of them are abstract nouns relating to concepts rather than persons or physical objects:

la caridad	charity	**la solicitud**	application
la acusación	accusation	**la decisión**	decision
la cumbre	summit	**la especie**	species

Notes:
1   El **pie** 'foot' is a common exception.

2   See also 2.2.1.4, and other words ending in **-triz: la matriz** 'uterus', 'master copy', **la cicatriz** 'scar'.

3   Words ending in **-is** need to be checked. The majority are feminine: **la crisis** 'crisis', **la tesis** 'thesis', but some common words are masculine: **el énfasis** 'emphasis', **el análisis** 'analysis'.

2.2.2.3 | Masculine endings other than *-o*

Nouns with the following endings are usually masculine: **-aje, -ambre, -án, -én, -or** and a stressed vowel:

el tatuaje	tattoo(ing)	**el fiambre**	cold meat
el gabán	overcoat	**el almacén**	warehouse/store
el interruptor	switch	**el pirulí**	lollipop

Note: Common exceptions are **la flor** 'flower', **la labor** 'labour', 'sewing' and **el hambre** 'hunger' (for use of **el** with feminine nouns, see 3.1.2).

2.2.3 | *Categories of nouns predictably masculine*

In the case of many proper nouns (or names), the gender is taken from an associated but unmentioned masculine noun.

2.2.3.1 |

Proper nouns designating a natural feature are typically masculine (due to unmentioned **río** 'river', **monte** 'mount', **lago** 'lake', **océano** 'ocean', etc.):

el **Amazonas**	the Amazon	el **Aconcagua**	Mt Aconcagua
el **Titicaca**	Lake Titicaca	el **Atlántico**	the Atlantic

Note: Exceptions occur when the name is based on a feminine noun: **la Sierra Nevada**.

2.2.3.2

Proper nouns relating to methods of transport are typically masculine (due to an unmentioned masculine noun such as **tren** 'train', **avión** 'plane', **coche/carro** [LA] 'car', **barco** 'boat/ship'):

el *AVE* (high-speed train)	el *Concord*	un *Citroën*	el *Santa Rosa*

2.2.3.3

Masculine also are paintings, wines, teams, colours, points of the compass, days and months (due to unmentioned masculine nouns such as **cuadro** 'painting', **vino** 'wine', **día** 'day' etc.):

un **Goya**	a painting by Goya	el **Rioja**	Rioja wine
el **Betis**	Seville football team	el **verde**	green
el **nordeste**	north east	el **miércoles**	Wednesday

2.2.3.4

Names of trees and shrubs (especially fruit-bearing ones) are normally masculine:

el **naranjo**	orange tree	el **castaño**	chestnut tree

Note: Conversely, some fruits are feminine: **naranja, castaña, oliva/aceituna** 'olive', but others are masculine like the tree: **limonero/limón** (lemon tree/fruit), **aguacate** (avocado tree and fruit). The 'fig' reverses the norm, **la higuera** being the tree and **el higo** the fruit.

2.2.4 Categories of nouns predictably feminine

These are rather more limited in number than their masculine counterparts. The categories are: letters of the alphabet, islands, companies and roads (due to an unmentioned feminine noun such as **letra** 'letter', **isla** 'island', **compañía** 'company', **carretera** 'road'):

las haches   the hs   **las Galápagos**   the Galapagos

la SEAT   SEAT   **la Panamericana**   the Pan-American highway

2.2.5 │ Names of countries, regions and towns

Place names ending in *unstressed* -a are feminine and the rest are masculine:

(el) Ecuador   Bolivia (fem.)   **Panamá** (masc.)   **Andalucía** (fem.)

el Sanlúcar   modern Sanlúcar   **la Huelva**   historic Huelva
moderno   **histórica**

For the use of articles with place names, see 3.2.2.1 and 3.2.2.2.

2.2.6 │ Nouns of dual gender with different meanings

Some nouns bear dual gender but change their meaning according to the gender used. The following are the most common:

Masculine		Feminine	
el capital	capital (money)	**la capital**	capital (city)
el cólera	cholera (sickness)	**la cólera**	anger
el cometa	comet	**la cometa**	kite
el corte	cut	**la corte**	(royal) court
el frente	front	**la frente**	forehead
el margen	margin	**la margen**	(river) bank
el orden	order (arrangement)	**la orden**	command, religious order
el Papa	the Pope	**la papa** [LA]	potato
el parte	dispatch, report	**la parte**	part, portion
el pendiente	earring	**la pendiente**	slope
el pez	fish (in water)	**la pez**	pitch, tar

A few feminine nouns signifying groups of persons may also refer to individual male or female members of that group:

Feminine		Masculine	
la guardia	guard (company), female guard	**el guardia**	male guard
la policía	the police (force), policewoman	**el policía**	policeman
la guía	guide (book), female guide	**el guía**	male guide
la vigía	lookout (post), female lookout	**el vigía**	watchman

In other instances nouns take a distinct masculine or feminine form to specify different meanings:

el banco	bank	**la banca**	banking system
el fruto	product (result)	**la fruta**	fruit (edible)
el bolso	handbag	**la bolsa**	plastic bag

2.2.7 Nouns of doubtful gender

(a) **Mar** 'sea': most users adopt the masculine gender. However, those whose lives are affected by the sea habitually use **la mar**. The feminine form is always used for some expressions: **la pleamar/bajamar** 'high/low tide', **en alta mar** 'on the high seas', **hacerse a la mar** 'to put to sea'.

(b) **Azúcar** 'sugar': widely used as masculine but occurs commonly with feminine adjectives in forms such as **azúcar blanca** 'white sugar', **extrafina** 'caster/or', **granulada** 'granulated'.

(c) **Arte** 'art': usually masculine in the singular, but always feminine in the plural: **las bellas artes** 'the fine arts'.

For regional variation of gender, see 30.6.2.

2.3 Collective nouns and agreement

Collective nouns are singular but refer to a group of people or things, e.g. **multitud** 'crowd', **mayoría** 'majority', **gente** 'people', **docena** 'dozen', **mitad** 'half'. When used on their own in Spanish, a verb in close proximity is usually singular (although it may be plural in English):

La mayoría no protestó.
The majority did not protest.

El gobierno no ha decidido.
The government has/have not decided.

When joined to a following plural noun by **de**, or when the verb is distant from the noun, the safest option for learners is to use a plural verb:

La mayoría de las casas son viejas.
The majority of the houses are old.

La gente se calló un momento al pasar el ataúd, luego siguieron charlando.
People stopped for a moment as the coffin passed, then they continued chattering.

Note: Usage by native speakers is not as clear-cut as the above guidance, and may be governed by factors such as consideration of whether it is logical to think of the group collectively (singular verb), or its parts individually (plural verb): **más de la mitad son refugiados** 'more than half are refugees'.

Chapter 3

Definite and indefinite articles

Articles in Spanish may be categorized as definite, indefinite and neuter. Definite articles are used before nouns to designate what is already known or specific, corresponding to English 'the'. The indefinite forms are used when the noun does not refer to a specific person, place or thing: English 'a' and 'an' in the singular, and 'some' in the plural.

3.1 Forms of the articles

The definite and indefinite articles vary in form to indicate gender and number. The forms are as follows:

	Masculine		Feminine	
	Singular	Plural	Singular	Plural
Definite article	el	los	la	las
Indefinite article	un	unos	una	unas

The neuter article is **lo**.

3.1.1 El used with a and de

When preceded by a or de, the e of the masculine singular form el is usually dropped, so that a + el > al and de + el > del:

al banco   to the bank   **del puerto**   from the port

When the article is an integral part of a title this contraction is not made, in writing at least:

Es reportera de *El Universo*.   She is a reporter on *El Universo*.

De/a + él

There is no contraction before the subject pronoun él: Esta copa es de él 'This glass is his'.

3.1.2 | **El *and* un *before feminine nouns***

Immediately before singular feminine nouns beginning with a *stressed* a or ha, the forms el and un are used. This does not change the gender of the noun and the plural form of the noun still demands **las** or **unas**:

el ancla oxidada the rusty anchor   **un águila blanca** a white eagle

el aula nueva y unas aulas viejas   the new classroom and some
old classrooms

Common words which fall into this category are: **agua** 'water', **alma** 'soul', **área** 'area', **arma** 'weapon', **asma** 'asthma', **haba** 'bean', **habla** 'language', **hambre** 'hunger'.

Exceptions include **La Haya** 'The Hague', **la 'a'** and **la 'hache'** 'the letter "a"' and 'the letter "h"', **la árabe** 'the Arab woman'.

When not to use el/un before feminine words

1   El and un are *not* used if the article is not immediately before the noun: **el arpa** 'the harp', but **la bella arpa del siglo XVI** 'the beautiful sixteenth-century harp'.
2   El and un are *not* used if initial a or ha are *not* stressed: **una alerta** 'alert', **la hamburguesa** 'hamburger'.
3   El and un are *not* used before other words such as adjectives or women's names beginning with stressed a: **una alta galería** 'a high gallery', **la Ana que conozco** 'the Ana I know'.

3.1.3 | El *used to form verbal nouns*

El is the required article before the infinitive of a verb used as a noun, see
17.6.

3.2 The definite article

Although there are very important differences in usage between English and
Spanish, in general terms the use of the definite article to refer to someone
or something specific is predictable from English:

Esto es jerez pero no el jerez que me gusta.
This is sherry but not the sherry that I like.

Juan trajo rosas y María tiró las flores que compró ayer.
Juan brought roses and María threw away the flowers she bought
yesterday.

3.2.1 | *Contexts in which the use of the definite article is
predominant*

3.2.1.1 | The definite article with generic nouns

In common with other Romance languages, Spanish requires the definite
article before a noun used to refer to an entire category of people or things
in general:

El plomo es un metal muy blando. Lead is a very soft metal.

Los vinos de Chile son magníficos. Chilean wines are splendid.

English does this only when a singular noun is used with a general meaning:

La jirafa es un animal extraño.
The giraffe is a strange animal = Giraffes are strange animals.

3.2.1.2 | The definite article with abstract nouns

The article is used with abstract nouns when they have a general sense:

Hay que reducir la pobreza en este país.
We have to reduce poverty in this country.

un aumento de la delicuencia   an increase in crime

But after verbs such as **tener** 'to have' and **faltar** 'to lack', the article is not used:

¡Hay que tener paciencia para hacer esto!
You need patience to do this!

Note: The article may be omitted when nouns occur in the form of a list: **Sinceridad, franqueza, y honradez son cualidades que le faltan** 'Sincerity, openness and honesty are qualities that he lacks'.

3.2.1.3 The definite article with terms for general concepts and practices

Unlike in English, the article in Spanish is used for any noun that refers to a general idea, phenomenon or practice. This category includes colours, diseases, games, fields of activity and even meals:

No me gusta el rojo como color.	I don't like red as a colour.
Casi se ha erradicado la viruela.	Smallpox has almost been eradicated.
Están jugando al béisbol.	They are playing baseball.
No sigo la política.	I don't follow politics.
¿A qué hora es la cena?	What time is dinner?

Note: The article is not used with colours after the prepositions **de** and **en**: **El cuarto está pintado de verde** 'The room is painted green'.

3.2.1.4 The definite article with days, seasons and years

The forms **el** and **los** are used with days of the week (often corresponding to English 'on'). **El** is used for single occasions and **los** for habitual practices:

Es el lunes cuando vamos.	It's on Monday that we are going.
No abren los sábados.	They don't open on Saturdays.
Vienen del sábado al lunes.	They are coming from Saturday until Monday.

However, the article is dropped after **ser** in sentences that merely identify what day of the week it is, or after **de** in sentences that refer to routine practices:

Hoy es viernes.	Today is Friday.
Trabajo de lunes a viernes.	I work from Monday to Friday.

The definite article is also used with names of seasons, except when **de** and a season combine to form an adjectival phrase. After the preposition **en** the definite article is optional before a season name:

El verano es la mejor época del año.	Summer is the best time of the year.
Ya ponen a la venta ropa de otoño.	They are already selling autumn clothes.
No vamos a la playa en (el) invierno.	We do not go to the beach in winter.

The definite article is usually not used in dating letters:

Domingo, 16 de enero de 1943	Sunday, 16 January 1943

3.2.1.5 The definite article with parts of the body, clothing and personal possessions

The definite article is used in situations where English would have a possessive adjective. See 5.5.

3.2.1.6 In place of a noun

The definite article occurs before adjectives, past participles, prepositions and relative clauses, to refer to a noun understood from the context. It agrees with the unexpressed noun in number and gender.

The article translates English 'the one(s)' or 'that', 'those':

El rubio me cae mal.	I don't like the blond one.
estos asuntos y los discutidos ayer	these matters and those discussed yesterday
La de tu casa es mejor.	The one at your house is better.
Las que se vendían en España eran más sabrosas.	The ones they were selling in Spain were tastier.

31

3.2.1.7 Definite article with numbers and numerical expressions

The definite article is used with numbered nouns and with certain expressions of rate, weight, measure and quantity:

a los 60 años	at 60 years of age
en la casa nº 3	in house no. 3
el 60 por ciento de la población	60 per cent of the population
dos veces al mes	twice a month
mil dólares la consulta	a thousand dollars per consultation

Note: With percentages the indefinite article is an alternative.

The definite article is omitted before the cardinal or ordinal number that follows a title:

Alfonso XIII (i.e. trece)	Alfonso the Thirteenth

3.2.1.8 The definite article with certain nouns

Unlike in English, the definite article is required in fixed combinations of noun and preposition:

en la cama/el espacio	in bed/space
ir a la escuela/a la iglesia/ al hospital	to go to school/church/hospital

3.2.1.9 The definite article with titles

The definite article is used with most titles unless the bearer of the title is being spoken to directly:

Les presento al comandante y a la señora de Paredes.
May I introduce Commander and Mrs Paredes?

–Buenos días doctor Sánchez.
'Hello Dr. Sánchez'.

Note: The article is not generally used with **don, doña, fray** 'brother' (religious), **san(to), santa** 'saint', **sor** 'sister' (religious): **Pertenece a don Miguel** 'It belongs to don Miguel'.

Informally, the definite article may be used with common nouns referring to relatives (but never in direct address):

La abuela está sentada en el jardín.
Granny is sitting in the garden.

3.2.1.10 The definite article with names of geographical features and locations

This includes unique features such as rivers, mountains, lakes, seas, oceans, straits, currents, volcanoes and deserts:

el Tajo	the Tagus	**el Teide**	Mt Teide
el golfo de Vizcaya	the Bay of Biscay	**el mar Adriático**	the Adriatic Sea
el Cotopaxi	Mt Cotopaxi	**el Atacama**	the Atacama Desert

We may also include el cielo 'heaven', el infierno 'hell', la Tierra 'Earth'

Streets and other forms of location are preceded by the definite article: la calle Alcalá 'Alcalá Street', el Parque María Luisa 'María Luisa Park'.

3.2.1.11 Names of teams

The definite article (usually masculine) is used before the names of sports teams:

el Betis   **el Sporting**   **el Barça**

3.2.2 Contexts in which omission of the definite article is predominant

3.2.2.1 Names of countries

The majority of countries do not take the definite article, unless the name is qualified by an adjective or adjectival phrase:

Millones de turistas visitan España.
Millions of tourists visit Spain.

Hay muchos vestigios de la España romana.
There are many remains from Roman Spain.

Note: If the qualifier forms part of a country's name the article is not used: **Irlanda del Norte** 'Northern Ireland'.

In addition, there is a tendency nowadays, especially amongst journalists, to drop the definite article before the names of countries that previously were preceded by it. This is particularly the case with masculine names:

(el) Brasil   **(el) Canadá**   **(el) Ecuador**   **(el) Irak**

(el) Japón   **(el) Pakistán**   **(el) Paraguay**   **(el) Uruguay**

Still bucking this trend are: **el Perú** (at least in the country itself), **el Congo**, **el Líbano** 'Lebanon' and **la India**.

In general, countries whose name is a descriptive title still retain the article:

los Países Bajos	the Netherlands	**el Reino Unido**	the United Kingdom
el Salvador	El Salvador	**la (República) Argentina**	Argentina

On the other hand, **Gran Bretaña** 'Great Britain' and **Arabia Saudí** 'Saudi Arabia' appear to have lost the article.

With **los Estados Unidos** (or **EEUU**) 'the United States', the article is generally omitted. When this is done an accompanying verb is used in the singular: **Estados Unidos apoya la última decisión** 'The USA supports the latest decision'.

3.2.2.2   Omission of the definite article with names of cities, regions and continents

As with countries (see 3.2.2.1) in general the article is not used unless the name is qualified:

Vive en Barcelona.   She lives in Barcelona.

la Barcelona de Gaudí   Gaudí's Barcelona

Some place names, however, contain a definite article that forms an integral part of the name, written with a capital letter in the case of towns and cities. Examples are:

La Habana	Havana	**La Coruña**	Corunna
El Callao	Callao	**La Mancha**	La Mancha

| 3.2.2.3 | Omission of the definite article with nouns in apposition |

In formal Spanish, the definite article is often omitted before a second noun which offers merely explanatory information about another one immediately preceding it:

Bogotá, capital de Colombia   Bogotá, the capital of Colombia

Raúl, marcador del gol   Raúl, the scorer of the goal

The article is however always retained before comparative and superlative phrases:

La Paz, la capital más alta del mundo
La Paz, the highest capital in the world

| 3.2.2.4 | Fixed phrases |

In many set phrases like the following the article is not used:

a orillas de   on the banks of   **a corto/**   in the short/
 largo plazo   long term

en manos de   in the hands of   **en nombre de**   in the name of

| 3.2.3 | *The definite article with names of languages* |

There are cases both of use and omission.

| 3.2.3.1 |

The definite article is *used* whenever reference is made to the language as a whole:

El vasco es una lengua de origen incierto.
Basque is a language of uncertain origin.

The definite article also occurs after **de** 'from/of' and certain other prepositions:

Esa palabra viene del alemán.   That word comes from German.

los problemas del ruso   the problems of Russian

Lo van a traducir al español.   They are going to translate it
 into Spanish.

Note: The article would generally not be used after **de** 'of' when the reference is *not* to the language as a whole: **un curso de inglés**, 'an English course'.

3.2.3.2

The definite article is *omitted* before unqualified names of languages after the preposition **en** 'in', and after the verbs **aprender** 'to learn', **hablar** 'to speak' and **saber** 'to know'.

This practice is common (but not obligatory) when stating other associated activities such as **entender** 'to understand', **enseñar** 'to teach', and **estudiar** 'to study':

Está escrito en quechua.	It is written in Quechua.
Está aprendiendo holandés y entiende (el) inglés.	He is learning Dutch and he understands English.

Note: The article may be inserted if an adverb separates the verb from the language name: **No hablo correctamente (el) portugués** 'I don't speak Portuguese correctly'.

A language name *always* requires an article (definite or indefinite) if it is qualified by a word or phrase:

en el francés antiguo	in old French
Habla un español tradicional.	She speaks a traditional sort of Spanish.

3.3 The indefinite article

3.3.1 *General use of the indefinite article*

In general terms, the use of the singular indefinite article (**un/una**) to refer to someone or something not yet known or not specifically identified is similar to English:

Un niño se me acercó.	A boy came up to me.

The plural forms **unos** and **unas** are used with plural nouns in a similar way (often translating English 'some'):

He comprado unos libros.	I've bought some books.

The plural forms must also be used with nouns which only exist in plural form (see 2.1.8), sometimes meaning 'a' or 'a pair':

unas vacaciones en Italia	a holiday in Italy
unas tijeras	a pair of scissors

3.3.2 The indefinite article with qualified abstract or mass nouns

The article is regularly used before an abstract or mass noun qualified by a following descriptive adjective or relative clause:

De aquella fuente sale un agua purísima.
That spring has very pure water.

Por la ventana entraba una luz que cegaba.
A blinding light came in through the window.

3.3.3 Omission of the indefinite article

There are a number of circumstances in which the indefinite article is omitted. If this omission results in a noun on its own appearing as the verb's subject, then this noun must follow the verb:

Caían gotas de lluvia en el tejado.	Rain drops were falling on the roof.
Sale humo del motor.	Smoke is coming from the engine.

3.3.3.1 Omission of the indefinite article before unqualified mass nouns

The singular indefinite article cannot be used to translate 'some' before unqualified mass nouns (compare 3.3.2):

Tráigame pan, vino y una botella de agua sin gas.
Bring me some bread, some red wine and a bottle of still water.

3.3.3.2 Unos/as omitted

Although in theory the plural forms **unos** and **unas** can be omitted in similar circumstances to English 'some', in practice they tend to be omitted *only* in cases in which the noun does not refer to particular persons or things (especially in sentences that describe habitual actions):

Por aquí pasan trenes cada cinco minutos.
Trains pass through here every five minutes.

Jorge repara televisiones.
Jorge repairs televisions.

Note: The omission of **unos/unas** before a noun that is the subject of the verb is uncommon. Compare English 'Scientists have identified the gene that determines eye colour' with Spanish <u>Unos</u> **científicos han identificado el gen que determina el color de los ojos.**

3.3.3.3 | *Unos/as* replaced by *algunos/as*

Unos and **unas** are sometimes replaced by the plural forms of the indefinite adjective **alguno** 'some':

Algunas madres se preocupan por eso.
Some mothers worry about that.

Depending on the context, **unos/as** may also be replaced by **ciertos/as** 'certain', **varios/as** 'several', **unos/as, cuantos/as** 'a number of', or **unos/as, pocos/as** 'a few'.

3.3.3.4 | Omission of the indefinite article with nouns classifying people, animals and things

Sometimes the indefinite article is not used before nouns that indicate profession, occupation, or religious and political affiliation.

This occurs after verbs like **ser** 'to be', **elegir** 'to elect', **hacerse** 'to become', **llamar** 'to call', **nombrar** 'to name', **calificar de** 'to describe as':

Ella es doctora y él es amo de casa.
She is a doctor and he is a househusband.

Lo calificaron de dictador.
They described him as a dictator.

Exceptions to this are cases where the noun is qualified:

Es conservador y además un conservador intransigente.
He is a Conservative and moreover a diehard Conservative.

3.3.3.5 | Omission of the indefinite article with nouns in apposition

Like the definite article (see 3.2.2.3), the indefinite article is often not used in formal Spanish before a second noun which offers merely explanatory information about another one immediately preceding it:

Pasamos la noche en Medinaceli, aldea ahora casi desierta.
We spent the night in Medinaceli, now an almost deserted village.

Trabaja como televendedora, empleo que odia.
She works as a telesales person, a job she hates.

3.3.3.6 | Omission of the indefinite article with certain indefinite adjectives and numerals

The indefinite article is omitted with **otro** 'another', **tal/semejante** 'such a', **medio** 'half a', **mil** 'a thousand', **cien(to)** 'a hundred', **qué** 'what a', and **cierto** 'a certain':

Hoy la vi con otro chico.   Today I saw her with another boy.

¡Qué imbécil es Paco!   What an idiot Paco is!

Note: For cases where the article is used with **cierto** and **tal/semejante**, see 9.15 and 9.16.

3.3.3.7 | Omission of the indefinite article after certain prepositions and phrases

The indefinite article is almost always omitted before nouns that follow **sin** 'without', and often after **con** 'with', 'wearing':

Salió sin chaqueta.   He went out without a jacket.

Nunca se le ve con sombrero.   You never see him wearing a hat.

Note: Exceptions are cases where the article is required specifically to emphasize 'one', e.g. **Me dejaron sin un (solo) peso** 'They left me without a (single) peso'.

When we place someone or something into a category or type, the indefinite article is also omitted after **como** 'as', 'like', **por** 'for', 'as', **a modo/manera de** 'as', 'by way of':

Como persona liberal no puedo apoyar esto.
As a liberal I can't support this.

Ella pasa por buena directora.   She passes for a good director.

| 3.3.3.8 | Omission of the indefinite article with common verb + noun combinations |

The indefinite article is often omitted after verbs such as **buscar** 'to look for', **emplear** 'to use', **encontrar** 'to find', **hay** 'there is/are', **llevar** 'to wear', **tener** 'to have':

Estamos buscando casa.	We are looking for a house.
No llevaba abrigo.	He wasn't wearing a coat.
No tienen garaje.	They don't have a garage.

Exceptions to the above, as with other uses of the articles, include contexts where the noun is qualified, and contexts where it is necessary to indicate 'one':

¿Hay una radio que funciona?	Is there a radio that works?
Encontró una rueda pero no la otra.	He found one wheel but not the other.

Use and omission of articles with more than one noun

Spanish is much less likely than English to omit an article before the second or subsequent nouns in a list (especially when the nouns are of different genders): **Los CDs y las cintas no están aquí** 'The CDs and tapes are not here'.

Spanish usage approximates to English only when the sequence consists of nouns of similar meaning that form part of a single idea: **El celo, dedicación y determinación de este estudiante son increíbles** 'The zeal, dedication and determination of this student are unbelievable'.

The safest option for foreign learners is to use the appropriate article with each noun.

3.4 The neuter article *lo*

This is used to refer to beliefs, concepts, thoughts, opinions or ideas that have no gender.

3.4.1 | Lo *with adjectives and past participles*

Lo may be used before a masculine singular adjective or past participle, to
state succinctly what is sometimes expressed in English by the use of an
adjective followed by a noun such as 'thing' or 'matter':

Lo más importante es informar al banco.
The most important thing is to inform the bank.

Todo lo mío está en esa maleta.
All that is mine is in that suitcase.

When used in this construction, the verb **ser** will be plural if what follows
is a plural noun:

Lo convenido ayer no son más que las líneas generales.
What was agreed yesterday was only the general outlines.

For **lo** with possessive adjectives see 5.3.

Notes:
1   **A + lo** + adjective or noun conveys the idea of **a la manera de** 'in the manner/style
    of': **a lo antiguo** 'in an old-fashioned way'.

2   **De + lo + más/menos** + adjective (or other comparative word) creates a superla-
    tive construction: **La lana de alpaca es de lo más fina que hay** 'Alpaca wool is
    very soft/one of the softest there is'.

3.4.2 | Lo + *adjective/past participle/adverb* + que

This common construction often corresponds to English 'how' + adjective
or adverb (sometimes with the force of an exclamation). An adjective or
past participle used in this way agrees with the noun to which it refers:

Hasta entonces no me había dado cuenta de lo alta que era.
Until then I hadn't realized how tall she was.

Hay que ver lo despacio que conduce.
You have to see how slowly he drives.

For the use of **qué** + adjective/adverb to translate 'how', see 27.4.1.

This construction is also preceded by **con, para** or **por**:

Con lo listo que es, y ¡mira qué mal ha hecho el examen!
He's so clever but look how badly he did in the exam!

Tiene bastantes canas para lo joven que es.
He has a lot of grey hairs for someone so young.

3.4.3 Lo + de + *noun*

This succinctly approximates to English 'the matter of', 'the business about':

Lo del agua es un problema grave.
The water situation is a serious problem.

3.4.4 Lo que

Approximates in English to 'the thing which', 'what':

Lo que nos sorprendió fue su dominio del inglés.
What surprised us was her excellent English.

For **lo que** and **lo cual** as relative pronouns see Chapter 25.

3.4.5 Lo *in idiomatic expressions*

Lo also occurs in a number of fixed phrases (usually involving **a**, **de** or **por**):

a lo mejor	perhaps	**por lo menos**	at least
por lo visto	apparently	**de lo contrario**	otherwise

Chapter 4

Demonstrative adjectives and pronouns

Demonstratives are the equivalent of English 'this'/'these' and 'that'/'those'. Spanish likewise uses the first of these two categories, but goes further by dividing the second category of 'that'/'those' into two. As a result, Spanish has three demonstratives rather than two.

Singular		Plural		Neuter
Masculine	Feminine	Masculine	Feminine	
este this	**esta** this	**estos** these	**estas** these	**esto** this
ese that	**esa** that	**esos** those	**esas** those	**eso** that
aquel that	**aquella** that	**aquellos** those	**aquellas** those	**aquello** that

The masculine and feminine forms can be used both as adjectives and as pronouns, while the neuter forms are pronouns only.

Native speakers still commonly use a written accent to distinguish the pronouns from the corresponding adjectives (e.g. éste 'this one' compared to **este libro** 'this book'). Since accented forms are no longer recommended they are not shown above or below.

4.1   Demonstrative adjectives

The adjectives are normally placed before the noun (as in English), and they agree with it in number and gender.

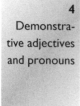

4.1.1 Este, esta, estos, estas

These are used to identify what is physically near to or is associated with the speaker:

Estas botas que acabo de limpiar.	These boots that I have just cleaned.

They also signify proximity in terms of time:

Lo voy a ver esta tarde.	I am going to see him this afternoon.

4.1.2 Ese, esa, esos, esas, *and* aquel, aquella, aquellos, aquellas

Both series of words translate English 'that'/'those'. However, Spanish establishes a distinction, by means of **ese** and its related forms, between what is connected with or known by the person being addressed and, by means of the **aquel** series, what is distant both from the speaker and the listener. Therefore, **ese** can signify 'that near you' or 'associated with you', whereas **aquel** tends to identify 'that distant from us both' or 'not associated with either of us'.

In practice, there may not always be such a clear-cut distinction in normal usage, and native speakers may alternate between the two forms, except in situations where the deliberate intention is to stress distance by the use of **aquel**:

ese pueblo donde estás	that village where you are
El documento está en aquel archivo en Madrid.	The document is in that archive in Madrid.

These two series of words make a similar distinction between a relatively recent past and one more distant:

esos días que pasamos juntos el verano pasado
those days we spent together last summer

En aquellos tiempos no existían armas de fuego.
In those days firearms did not exist.

4.1.3 | *Placing the demonstrative adjective after the noun*

Although its normal position is before the noun, the demonstrative adjective can also be used after it, especially in speech, in which case the noun is preceded by the definite article:

el libro ese   that book

los días aquellos   those days

Foreign speakers should take care in adopting this use, as it easily conveys a critical or dismissive attitude.

Demonstrative adjectives

1 Learners should take care not to confuse the masculine form of the demonstrative adjectives **este** and **ese** with the neuter pronouns **esto** and **eso**: **este libro** 'this book' and never ×**esto libro**×.

2 In contrast with English, demonstrative adjectives in Spanish are generally repeated before each noun, especially when they are nouns of different gender: **Este caballo y esta oveja viven juntos** 'This horse and sheep live together'.

3 Learners are recommended to *avoid* the practice of native speakers who use **este, ese** and **aquel** before feminine nouns beginning with a stressed **a** or **ha**: **este agua** 'this water'. See 3.1.2 on the correct use of the definite article in this situation.

4.2 Masculine and feminine demonstrative pronouns

The pronouns stand in place of a specific noun, expressed as 'this'/'that' (one), 'these'/'those' (ones), with which they agree in number and gender:

No me des esa papaya, prefiero esta.
Don't give me that papaya, I prefer this one.

Ese es el cuadro que más me gusta.
That's the picture I like most.

¿Cuál quieres: el de tu padre o aquel que vimos ayer?
Which one do you want: your father's or the one we saw yesterday?

The pronoun **este** is used with the meaning of 'the latter' ('this' – the last mentioned), and **aquel** 'the former' ('that' – mentioned earlier). They agree with nouns in number and gender as appropriate:

De las dos propuestas, esta es la más original y aquella la más práctica.
Of the two proposals, the latter is the most original and the former the most practical.

Note: The translation of 'those who' is not achieved by **esos** or **aquellos**, but by **los/las que**: **No perdona a los que lo critican** 'He does not forgive those who criticize him'.

4.3 Neuter demonstrative pronouns

These are used with the same meanings as the adjectives and pronouns above, but they refer to things which bear no gender, such as statements, actions, situations and items requiring identification:

Esto es una pesadilla.	This is a nightmare.
Todo aquello es bosque virgen.	All of that is virgin forest.
¿Qué es eso?	What is that?

Notes:

1 In speech these commonly occur in the pattern **esto/eso/aquello + de**. They convey the equivalent of English phrases like 'this matter', 'that business': **eso de no poder ver la tele** 'that business of not being able to watch TV'.

2 The phrase **y eso que** is used with the meaning of 'although', 'even though': **Decidió ir y eso que le dije que no** 'He decided to go even though I told him not to'.

3 Other common phrases are: **eso sí** 'yes indeed', 'of course', **eso no** 'certainly not', **eso es** 'that's it' or 'that's right', **eso sí que no** 'no way', **por eso** 'therefore' or 'for that reason'.

Chapter 5

Possessive adjectives

Possessive adjectives are used to indicate a relationship of possession or association, usually between a person and a thing. For example, the English word 'my' in the phrase 'my book' indicates that the book belongs to the person speaking. Each possessive adjective corresponds to a subject pronoun. For example, English 'my' is the possessive adjective for 'I' and 'your' is the possessive adjective for 'you'.

5.1 Possessive adjectives before the noun

The following forms are used before a noun, but another adjective may come between them and the noun:

Subject pronoun	Possessive adjective	
yo	**mi/mis**	my
tú, vos [LA]	**tu/tus**	your
él/ella/usted	**su/sus**	his/her/its/your
nosotros/-as	**nuestro/-os/-a/-as**	our
vosotros/-as [SP]	**vuestro/-os/-a/-as [SP]**	your
ellos/ellas/ustedes	**su/sus**	their/your

All the possessive adjectives agree in number, but only **nuestro** and **vuestro** [SP] have distinct feminine forms. The agreement is with the noun possessed (not with the possessor):

mis hijas	my daughters
nuestra maleta	our suitcase
¿Cantás (vos) tu propia canción?	Are you singing your own song?

Note: In contrast with English, the Spanish possessive adjective is repeated before each noun in a list, except where they refer to the same person or thing, or to parts of the same overall concept: **Tu primo y tu tío vivieron en Jaén** 'Your cousin and uncle lived in Jaén', but **mi colega y amigo, el Sr. Ortiz** 'my colleague and friend Mr Ortiz', **mis libros y artículos** 'my books and articles'.

5.2 Possessive adjectives after the noun

The following 'strong' or 'stressed' forms are used after a noun:

Subject pronoun	Possessive adjective	
yo	**mío/-os/-a/-as**	mine
tú, vos [LA]	**tuyo/-os/-a/-as**	yours
él/ella/usted	**suyo/-os/-a/-as**	his/hers/yours
nosotros/-as	**nuestro/-os/-a/-as**	ours
vosotros/-as [SP]	**vuestro/-os/-a/-as** [SP]	yours
ellos/ellas/ustedes	**suyo/-os/-a/-as**	theirs/yours

All the strong possessive adjectives agree in number and gender with the noun possessed. They can be used after a noun with meanings such as 'of mine', 'of yours':

| **unos libros míos** | some books of mine |
| **aquella propuesta tuya** | that proposal of yours |

After **ser** the indefinite article may be omitted before the noun unless the noun is qualified: **Es amigo nuestro** 'he's a friend of ours', but **Es un amigo nuestro que no conoces** 'he's a friend of ours you don't know'.

The strong forms may also be used without a noun, especially after **ser**. In this case they mean 'mine', 'yours' etc.:

| **Ese bolso es mío.** | That bag is mine. |
| **Vamos a abrirlos – son nuestros.** | Let's open them – they're ours. |

Note: The strong possessives are also used in the formulas **Muy señor mío** 'Dear Sir' and **Queridos amigos míos** 'Dear friends' (in correspondence), as well as in a number of set phrases such as **a costa mía** 'to my cost', **por culpa suya** 'because of him', **al lado mío** 'by my side'.

5.3   Definite and neuter articles with possessives

The possessive adjectives shown in 5.2 are used as pronouns when preceded by **el, la, los** or **las.** In this case the number and gender of both the article and the possessive adjective are determined by the noun to which reference is implicitly being made:

Necesito tu llave, ya que he perdido la mía.
I need your key as I've lost my own.

De las dos bicicletas, ¿cuál es la mejor? ¿La tuya o la de Andrea?
Of the two bicycles, which is the best? Yours or Andrea's?

The sequence neuter article **lo** + masculine singular possessive adjective often refers to something abstract rather than to a concrete noun:

Lo tuyo es impresionante.   That business of yours is amazing.

Note: The phrase **salirse con la suya** has a special meaning: **José siempre se sale con la suya** 'José always gets his own way'.

Mío or el mío?

1   Only the forms with the article (e.g. **el mío, el tuyo**) are capable of functioning as the subject or object of a verb, or as the object of a preposition: **El mío está aquí** 'Mine is here', **Han encontrado el tuyo** 'They have found yours', **Está debajo del nuestro** 'It's under ours'.

2   Both the forms with the article and the forms without the article can appear after the verb **ser.** However they mean different things. **Este libro es mío** says merely that this book belongs to me (with no prior assumption that any books did belong to me), while **Este libro es el mío** assumes some prior mention of a book belonging to me and now identifies **este libro** as that book.

5.4   Avoidance of ambiguity with *su/sus* and *suyo/a/os/as*

Although the context may preclude any possible ambiguity, the use of **su/sus** and **suyo/a/os/as** can be the cause of confusion because of the variety of their meanings: 'his', 'her(s)', 'your(s),' 'its', 'their(s)'. Such confusion can be avoided through the replacement of **su/sus** and **suyo/a/os/as** by **de** + the appropriate prepositional object pronoun (see Table 8.1):

los zapatos de ella	her shoes
la casa de ellos	their house

This formula can be adopted also to stress different possessors:

la bufanda de usted no la de él	your scarf not his

In Latin America **su/sus** and **suyo/a/os/as** are often assumed to refer to **usted** or **ustedes** and so are typically replaced by **de él, de ella** etc. when they mean 'his', 'her(s)' or 'their(s)'.

5.5   Parts of the body and personal effects

In contrast to English usage, it is usual in Spanish to use the definite article rather than a possessive adjective for parts of the body, clothing and personal possessions:

Ponte los zapatos.	Put your shoes on.
Enséñame las manos.	Show me your hands.
Tengo que depilarme las piernas.	I have to shave my legs.

See also 14.2(b).

However, a possessive adjective is required where its omission could lead to ambiguity:

¿Donde están mis zapatos?	Where are my shoes?

5.6   Possessive adjectives with adverbs and prepositions

Occasionally after an adverb or after a compound preposition, the sequence **de** + prepositional object pronoun (**mí, ti, él** etc.) is reduced to **mío, mía, tuyo, tuya** etc.

The possessive adjective usually takes the masculine singular form unless the adverb or preposition ends in an -a, in which case it takes the feminine singular form:

encima tuya = encima de ti	on top of you
alrededor nuestro = alrededor de nosotros	all around us

en contra suya = en contra de él/ella etc.	against him/her etc.
en torno suyo = en torno de él/ella etc.	all around him/her etc.

This is a feature of popular speech in the Iberian Peninsula and of widespread use in Latin America but, perhaps with the exception of **en torno,** it is frowned upon by some native speakers. It is perhaps best avoided in the initial stages by foreign learners, in favour of the construction with **de** + prepositional object pronoun.

Chapter 6

Adjectives

As in English, adjectives assign a property or characteristic to a noun. They can appear next to a noun, as in **un niño listo** 'a clever boy', or after verbs such as **ser/estar** 'to be', as in **El niño es listo** 'The boy is clever'.

Key differences between Spanish and English adjectives

1 Adjectives in English are invariable, whereas in Spanish they usually agree with nouns in gender and number: **un cojín <u>rojo</u>** 'a red cushion' but **unas camisetas <u>rojas</u>** 'some red T-shirts'.
2 Spanish adjectives are commonly placed after the noun rather than before: **una montaña <u>alta</u>** 'a high mountain'.

6.1 Gender

6.1.1 Adjectives ending in -o

If the masculine form ends in -o, the feminine form ends in -a:

blanco (masc.) **blanca** (fem.) white

6.1.2 Adjectives ending in -ón, -án, -ín and -or

Usually an -a is added to the masculine form to create the feminine:

llorón	**llorona**	crybaby
holgazán	**holgazana**	lazy
emprendedor	**emprendedora**	enterprising
parlanchín	**parlanchina**	chatty

Isolated exceptions without a distinct feminine form are: **marrón** 'brown', **afín** 'similar/related'.

A common group of exceptions ending in **-or**, without a distinct feminine form, is that comprising words which have a comparative sense:

anterior	previous	**mayor**	greater/ older	**posterior**	later
exterior	outer	**mejor**	better	**superior**	upper/ superior
inferior	lower/ inferior	**menor**	lesser/ younger	**ulterior**	further/ later
interior	inner	**peor**	worse		

Uniquely **superior** takes a feminine form for **la madre superiora** 'mother superior'.

6.1.3 Adjectives of nationality and regional origin

Those masculine forms ending in **-o** follow the pattern in 6.1.1, while those ending in a consonant add an **-a**:

chino	**china**	Chinese
francés	**francesa**	French
andaluz	**andaluza**	Andalusian

Other nationality adjectives (those that end in **-a**, **-ense**, **-í** or **-ú**) have the same form for both genders:

belga	Belgian	**canadiense**	Canadian
marroquí	Moroccan	**hindú**	Hindu/Indian

Su padre es belga y su madre canadiense.
Her father is Belgian and her mother Canadian.

6.1.4 Adjectives with no distinct feminine form

6.1.4.1

In general there are no different feminine forms for adjectives which do not fall into any of the three categories from 6.1.1 to 6.1.3.

This includes common adjectives ending in other consonants, or in the vowels -e and -a (such as the endings -ista and -ita):

feliz	happy	**fácil**	easy
cortés	polite	**triste**	sad
realista	realistic	**cosmopolita**	cosmopolitan

una chica feliz y cortés   a happy and polite girl

Note: A common exception is **burgués** 'middle class', with the feminine form **burguesa**.

6.1.4.2 | Adjectives of colour

Colours that are true adjectives usually follow the above guidelines:

una flor roja   a red flower   **una hoja verde**   a green leaf

However, when *nouns* are used to designate colour they are invariable, since their lone use represents the omission of the words (**de**) **color** or **color de**.

Amongst the most common are: **café** 'coffee-coloured', **cereza** 'cherry', **lila** 'lilac', **paja** 'straw-coloured', **rosa** 'pink', **turquesa** 'turquoise', **violeta** 'violet'.

un mantel naranja   an orange tablecloth

una camisa (de) color lila y malva   a lilac and mauve shirt

Furthermore, when compound colour adjectives are formed, these are also invariable in respect of gender, even if the individual adjectives used on their own have distinct feminine forms:

una gabardina azul marino   a navy blue raincoat

una corbata rojo oscuro   a dark red tie

Note: Single-word colour compounds formed from two adjectives follow the usual patterns for gender formation (e.g. **verdiblanco/a** 'greenish white', 'light green').

6.1.5 | *Gender agreement with nouns of mixed gender*

When an adjective relates to two or more nouns of the same gender, the adjective adopts the gender common to them, and is plural:

una camisa y una corbata bonitas   a nice shirt and tie

However, when the nouns are of mixed gender, the adjective is masculine and plural:

El sofá y la cama están sucios.   The sofa and the bed are dirty.

6.2 Singular and plural of adjectives

Most adjectives have distinct singular and plural forms and agree in number with their accompanying noun, or with the subject of the verb (if the verb is **ser, estar, parecer** etc.).

The plurals are generally formed as for nouns, by adding an -s to those ending in a vowel, and -es to those ending in a consonant. See 2.1.

6.2.1 Adjectives of colour

When nouns are used as adjectives of colour, such as those listed in 6.1.4.2, they are usually not only invariable for gender but also for number (although in speech and in Latin America this is not always the case):

unos guantes rosa   some pink gloves

rayos ultravioleta   ultraviolet rays

Similarly, compound colour adjectives are invariable for number:

blusas azul marino   navy blue blouses

ojos verde claro   light green eyes

6.2.2 Special cases of number agreement

6.2.2.1

When two or more nouns are considered to be a *single* item, the adjective qualifying them may be singular and in that case it agrees with the nearest noun:

Estudia lengua y cultura francesa.   He studies French language and culture.

el diseño y la moda italiana   Italian design and fashion

55

If the two nouns constitute *separate* items, the usual rule applies and the adjective is used in the plural:

una inteligencia y dedicación tremendas
tremendous intelligence and dedication

6.2.2.2

When a plural noun is qualified by adjectives which imply one of each, the adjectives are singular:

los embajadores peruano y ecuatoriano
the Peruvian and Ecuadorian ambassadors

6.2.2.3

When an adjective precedes two or more nouns, it usually adopts the gender and number of the first:

la extraña vida y aventuras de don Miguel
the strange life and adventures of don Miguel

6.2.2.4

When a compound adjective is formed with a hyphen, only the second of the adjectives agrees with the noun:

discusiones hispano-marroquíes
Hispano-Moroccan discussions

6.3 Shortening of adjectives

6.3.1

The adjectives **bueno** 'good' and **malo** 'bad', **primero** 'first' and **tercero** 'third', **uno** 'one', 'a', **alguno** 'some' and **ninguno** 'no' drop the final -o before *masculine singular* nouns.

In the case of **alguno** and **ninguno** a written accent is placed above the **u** in the shortened form:

un buen libro	a good book	**mal tiempo**	bad weather
el tercer día	the third day	**ningún hombre**	no man

Shortening occurs even if another adjective immediately follows before the noun:

el primer nuevo caso   the first new case

However, shortening does *not* occur when one of the above adjectives is joined to another adjective by a conjunction, or is otherwise separated from the noun:

el primero y último caso   the first and last case

6.3.2

The singular form **grande** 'big/large' is usually shortened to **gran** before nouns of *either* gender:

una gran pena a great   **un gran apetito** a great
sadness   appetite

However, **grande** is not shortened when preceded by **más** or **menos**, when used with another adjective to which it is linked by a conjunction, or is otherwise separated from the noun:

la más grande ocasión   the greatest occasion

el grande aunque   the great although unknown writer
desconocido escritor

6.3.3

The masculine form **Santo** 'Saint' is shortened to **San** except before names that begin with **To-** or **Do-**:

San Marcos   San Fernando   Santo Tomás   Santo Domingo

Santo is never shortened when it means 'holy': **el santo sacramento** 'the Holy Sacrament'.

6.4   Position of adjectives

Some adjectives have a fixed position in relation to their accompanying noun, while others enjoy a greater flexibility.

6.4.1 | Adjectives that have a fixed position

6.4.1.1

Adjectives that substitute for a noun phrase always *follow* their accompanying noun:

emisión televisiva	**emisión de la televisión**	television broadcast
giro bancario	**giro del banco**	bank transfer
estudios empresariales	**estudios sobre empresas**	business studies
delitos informáticos	**delitos de la informática**	computer crime

6.4.1.2

Adjectives that indicate nationality, regional origin, religious, ideological and political beliefs also usually *follow* their noun:

comida gallega	Galician cuisine
curas católicos	Catholic priests
costumbres democráticas	democratic practices

6.4.1.3

Numerals and indefinite adjectives (see Chapter 9) typically *precede* their noun:

tres amigos	three friends	**varias chicas**	several girls

6.4.1.4

Adjectives that do not assign a property to the associated noun always *precede* the noun. Examples are: **presunto** 'alleged', **mero** 'mere', **pleno** 'full', **dicho** 'the said', **denominado** 'so-called', and **supuesto/pretendido** 'supposed':

el presunto asesino	the alleged murderer
la mera intención	the mere intention
en pleno centro de la ciudad	right in the centre of the city

6.4.1.5

Some sequences of a noun with an adjective have developed a more or less *fixed* word order:

ideas fijas	fixed ideas	**sentido común**	common sense
mala suerte	bad luck	**largo plazo**	long term
rara vez	rarely	**hijo único**	only child

6.4.2 Adjectives that may be placed before or after the noun

6.4.2.1

Most adjectives other than those described in 6.4.1 can appear on either side of their noun, although the 'default position' is usually *after* the noun, as in **una montaña alta** 'a high mountain'. In this position the adjective receives more emphasis than the noun and marks out what is distinctive about the item referred to in contrast with others of its kind. In this usage the adjective is said to be *restrictive*, i.e. it restricts the reference of the noun.

In contrast, an adjective that is placed *before* its noun often denotes an incidental property or characteristic of the noun and so *does not restrict* the noun's reference.

Compare the two uses of **podridas** 'rotten' below:

Hay que cambiar las podridas maderas.
We have to replace the rotten wood.

Hay que cambiar las maderas podridas.
We have to replace the rotten wood.

In the first case, we need to replace *all* the wood, which incidentally is rotten. In the second case, we need to replace *only* those pieces of wood that are rotten. In other words, the adjective **podridas** is *not restrictive* when it comes before the noun **madera**, but *it is restrictive* (it contributes to identifying particular pieces of wood) when it comes after the noun.

Therefore the general rule is that adjectives *follow* the noun if they help to identify or pick out particular items within the category indicated by the noun, and they *precede* it when this is not the case.

For example, adjectives that express a subjective opinion or offer an emotional judgement commonly precede the noun, especially when used with the definite article or a possessive adjective:

la odiada/temida policía secreta	the hated/feared secret police
su oportuna intervención	your timely intervention
este maldito hotel	this wretched hotel
los gratos recuerdos que tenemos de España	the happy memories we have of Spain

In contrast, adjectives that describe categorically rather than subjectively generally follow the noun. Included among such adjectives are those that place items in technical, scientific or other classifications, and also those that assign characteristics such as colour, shape and condition:

un análisis sociológico	a sociological analysis
una cinta azul	a blue ribbon
una forma redonda	a round shape
una silla rota	a broken chair

Note: It is likely that an adjective qualified by an adverb is being used to qualify the noun objectively. Therefore placement after the noun is probably the safest option: **un cantante muy popular** 'a very popular singer', **ropa muy moderna** 'very trendy clothes'.

6.4.2.2

Some adjectives have different meanings depending on whether they come before or after a noun:

antiguo	la capital antigua	the ancient capital	la antigua capital	the former capital
medio	el hombre medio	the average man	medio vaso	half a glass
nuevo	una casa nueva	a brand-new house	una nueva casa	a new (another) house
numeroso	grupos numerosos	large groups	numerosos grupos	many groups
pobre	amigos pobres	poor friends	pobres amigos	unfortunate friends

puro	oro puro	pure gold	por pura casualidad	by sheer chance	
simple	una idea simple	a simple idea	un simple periodista	a mere journalist	
único	la única mujer	the only woman	una mujer única	a unique woman	
viejo	un colega viejo	an old colleague	un viejo colega	a long-standing colleague	

Translating English 'un' + adjective

6.4.2.3

With the adjectives **bueno** and **malo**, placement before the noun is more common unless the meaning is 'good'/'bad' in the moral sense:

una buena memoria	a good memory	**un niño malo**	a bad boy

6.4.2.4

With **grande** and **alto**, placement before the noun is more common when an abstract sense is intended:

una gran cantidad	a large amount	**una casa grande**	a big house
un alto cargo	a senior official	**una montaña alta**	a high mountain

6.5 Translating English 'un-' + adjective

The English prefix 'un-' negates the adjective to which it is applied: compare 'friendly' with its opposite 'unfriendly'. Spanish does not have a comparable prefix and so 'un-' is translated in a variety of ways, as follows:

(a) See 9.5.2 for the use of **poco** 'little'.
(b) See 17.2.5.1 for the use of **sin** 'without' + infinitive.
(c) See 24.1.2 for the use of **no** to negate an adjective.
(d) See 29.2.3 for the prefixes **in-, im-, ir-**.

6.6 Verb + adjective sequences

A very common construction in Spanish involves using an adjective in combination with a verb.

In one type of case, the adjective is linked with the verb's *subject* and so agrees with it in number and gender:

Ana compró el caballo entusiasmada.
Ana was thrilled to buy the horse.

Mi padre se casó joven.
My father married young.

In the second type of case, the adjective is linked with the verb's *object* and so agrees with that in number and gender.

Two word orders are possible: the adjective can be placed *either* after the verb *or* after the noun with which it is linked:

Toma muy caliente su café.	**Toma su café muy caliente.**	He takes his coffee very hot.
Tiene rota la pierna.	**Tiene la pierna rota.**	His leg is broken.

Chapter 7

Adverbs

Adverbs usually qualify verbs, adjectives (including past participles) and even other adverbs.

Se movían <u>lentamente</u>.	They moved slowly.
Es sumamente <u>inepto</u>.	He is completely inept.
Lo explicó admirablemente <u>bien</u>.	He explained it admirably well.

Adverbs both in English and Spanish may be divided into four broad categories, relating to manner, place, time, and degree or quantity.

In addition, adverbs like **afortunadamente** 'fortunately' or **necesariamente** 'necessarily' can be described as sentence adverbs, as they apply to the whole sentence rather than qualifying a single item such as a verb or an adjective.

As regards their form, adverbs in Spanish can be divided into those based on an adjective plus the ending **-mente**, e.g. **evidentemente** 'evidently' (see 7.1), and the remainder which have diverse forms, e.g. **despacio** 'slowly', **bien** 'well', **deprisa** 'quickly' (see 7.2).

Invariability of adverbs

Adverbs are invariable in form. They do not adopt distinct masculine and feminine forms or distinct singular and plural forms.

7.1   Adverbs ending in *-mente*

These are largely adverbs of manner, i.e. adverbs that say *how* an action is carried out.

They are formed by attaching the suffix -**mente** to the *feminine* form of the corresponding adjective or past participle (or to the invariable form if the adjective does not have a distinct feminine form). This corresponds to the English adverbial ending '-ly'.

lenta + mente	**lentamente**	slowly
decidida + mente	**decididamente**	resolutely
feliz + mente	**felizmente**	happily

However, not all adverbs in -**mente** are adverbs of manner:

Hablaron solamente dos personas. (quantity adverb)
Only two people spoke.

Posteriormente se casaron. (time adverb)
They got married later.

Políticamente ha sido un desastre. (sentence adverb)
Politically it's been a disaster

The suffix -**mente** can also be added, although not randomly, to the absolute superlative forms of adjectives (see 26.6.3):

clarísima + mente	**clarísimamente**	extremely clearly

7.1.1 Stress and written accents on adverbs ending in -mente

Both the -**mente** suffix and the adjective from which the adverb is derived are stressed independently. Therefore, an adjective that is normally written with an accent is also written with an accent when it is made into an adverb:

fácil + mente	**fácilmente**	easily

7.1.2 Two or more adverbs in succession

In written Spanish (and formal spoken Spanish), when two or more -**mente** adverbs are joined by link words such as **y**, **pero**, **o** or **ni**, the -**mente** suffix is omitted from all but the last adverb in the sequence:

Hablaron lenta y gravemente.
They spoke slowly and gravely.

7.2 Adverbs not ending in -mente

7.2.1 Adverbs of manner

These include items such as **bien** 'well', **mal** 'badly', **despacio** 'slowly', **deprisa** 'quickly', **así** 'like this/that', **mejor** 'better', **peor** 'worse':

No se puede entrar vestida así.
You can't go in dressed like that.

Mario nada despacio y mal.
Mario swims slowly and badly.

7.2.2 Adverbs of place

These state *where*. They can be both *positional* referring to a static location, and also *directional* indicating movement.

Comments on individual adverbs of place:

(a) **Aquí** 'here', **ahí** and **allí** 'there'. Their relative positions are best understood by relating them to demonstrative pronouns: **este aquí** 'this one here', **ese ahí** 'that one' (near the person addressed), and **aquel allí** 'that one over there' (further away from both speaker and addressee).

(b) **Acá** 'here' and **allá** 'there' are less common in Peninsular usage. They tend to express a less precise location than **aquí** and **allí**, or they indicate movement after **ir** 'to go' and **venir** 'to come'. However, in many parts of Latin America, especially southern South America, they have virtually replaced **aquí** and **allí**:

¡Ven acá!   Come here!

¡Ponlo en la papelera allá en el rincón!
Put it in the waste-paper basket over there in the corner!

Más allá means 'further away', 'beyond':

La casa está un poquito más allá.
The house a little bit further on.

(c) **Dentro/Adentro** 'inside' and **fuera/afuera** 'outside'. The longer forms are [LA] only, except when used with verbs of motion:

Tu padre está fuera [SP] **/afuera** [LA].
Your father is outside.

Los niños están dentro [SP] **/adentro** [LA].
The children are inside.

¡Ven adentro/afuera!   Come inside/outside!

(d) Detrás indicates position 'behind' and **atrás** directional movement 'behind' or 'backwards':

¿Has mirado detrás?   Have you looked behind?

Dio un paso atrás.   He took a step backwards.

(e) Delante indicates position 'in front', whereas **adelante** indicates directional movement 'forward(s)' or 'onward(s)':

El general marchaba delante. The general marched in front.

Decidió seguir adelante.   He decided to continue onwards.

(f) Directional movement is often indicated in Spanish by the use of a preposition (especially **por**) before the adverb of place:

Saltó por encima.   He jumped on top.

Se arrastró por debajo.   He crawled underneath.

hacia arriba/abajo   upwards/downwards

(g) An adverb of place can sometimes be placed after a noun to create an adverbial phrase:

cuesta arriba/abajo   uphill/downhill

río arriba/abajo   upstream/downstream

tierra adentro   inland

For the use of adverbs of place with **de** to form compound prepositions such as **delante de**, see Chapter 21.

7.2.3 | *Adverbs of time*

Comments on individual adverbs of time:

(a) **Ya** 'already' combines with a negative word to express the idea of 'no longer':

Ya no vive aquí.	He doesn't live here any more.
Nadie quiere estudiar ya.	No one wants to study any more.

Ya also has a variety of rhetorical uses, at times expressing a growing irritation or frustration:

¡Cállate ya!	Be quiet!
¡Ya era hora!	It's about time!
¡Ya empezamos!	Here we go again!

(b) Although both **entonces** and **luego** can mean 'then', they do so in different ways. **Entonces** means 'at that moment', whereas **luego** means 'next/afterwards':

Desde entonces no lo he vuelto a ver.
Since then I haven't seen him again.

Luego se mudaron a Córdoba.
They later moved to Córdoba.

(c) In Peninsular usage the form **recién** (from **recientemente** 'recently') is used exclusively before a past participle, with the meaning of 'newly', 'recently':

recién casado	newly wed	**recién llegado**	newly arrived

For Latin American usage of **recién**, see 30.6.3.9.

7.2.4 | Adverbs of degree or quantity

These include indefinite adjectives used as adverbs, such as **mucho** 'a lot', **poco** 'not much', **demasiado** 'too much', **bastante** 'enough' (for which, see Chapter 9), and the comparative words **más** 'more', **menos** 'less', **tan/tanto** 'so', 'so much' (for which, see Chapter 26).

In addition, this category includes items such as **muy** 'very', **casi** 'almost', **apenas** 'scarcely':

Apenas come.	He hardly eats anything.
Casi hemos terminado.	We have almost finished.

Note: **Apenas si** 'scarcely/barely' is found in literary Spanish: **Apenas si se reconocieron** 'They barely recognized one another'.

| 7.2.5 | *Adverbs meaning 'even'* |

These comprise an additional category of adverbs, which does not fit within the classification into manner, place, time and degree or quantity. Most frequently **hasta** or **incluso** can be used:

Hasta/incluso los abuelos bailaban.
Even the grandparents danced.

In negative sentences, **ni** or **ni siquiera** should be used: see 24.2.3.

With comparatives, **aún** or **todavía** should be used:

Es aún más difícil con un bebé en los brazos.
It's even more difficult with a baby in your arms.

7.3　Adverbial phrases

A number of fixed phrases such as the following have an adverbial function:

a ciegas	blindly/in the dark	**a veces**	sometimes
a escondidas	in secret	**de memoria**	from memory
a mano	by/at hand	**de noche**	at night
a menudo	often	**de repente**	suddenly/ perhaps [LA]
a pie	on foot	**en el acto**	on the spot
a propósito	on purpose	**en serio**	seriously

It is also common to replace an adverb ending in **-mente** by the use of **con** + abstract noun, or by **de (una) manera, de (un) modo, de forma, de carácter** + adjective:

Visita a sus padres con frecuencia.
He visits his parents frequently.

Prefiero hablar de (un) modo menos formal.
I prefer to speak less formally.

Esto me interesa de forma especial.
This is especially interesting to me.

7.4 Adjectives used as adverbs

The masculine singular form of the following adjectives may be used as adverbs of manner:

barato	cheap	**duro**	hard	**lento**	slow
caro	dear	**fatal**	terrible	**limpio**	clean
claro	clear	**fuerte**	strong	**rápido**	quick
directo	direct	**hondo**	deep		

¿Puedes ir un poco más rápido?	Can you go a bit faster?
Antonio canta fatal.	Antonio sings terribly.
Me agarró fuerte.	He grabbed me roughly.

For the use of an adjective in agreement with the subject or object of a verb, in instances where English would use an adverb, see 6.6.

Chapter 8

Personal pronouns

Personal pronouns are used either to refer to the participants in a conversation ('I/me', 'you', 'we/us') or in place of nouns or names (e.g. 'I can see *her*' instead of 'I can see *María*'). Despite being called personal pronouns, they can in the 3rd person refer also to animals, things or neuter concepts.

They exist for the following categories of use: as *subject* (e.g. English 'she' or 'we'), as *direct object* (e.g. 'her' or 'us'), as *indirect object* (e.g. 'to her' or 'to us') and *after prepositions* (e.g. 'behind her' or 'behind us'). Pronouns may also be used *reflexively* (e.g. English 'herself' or 'ourselves').

There are forms in each category which correspond to the 1st, 2nd and 3rd persons singular and plural. In addition, in Spanish the pronouns used to address other people vary depending on the appropriate degree of formality (e.g. **tú** is familiar whereas **usted** is generally polite).

Finally, differences of usage can be identified between Spain and Latin America, and even within Spain. A list of forms (excluding reflexives) is given in Table 8.1. For reflexive pronouns, see 8.4.

Accents on pronouns

1 Written accents are required on **mí** 'me', **tú** 'you' and **él** 'he' to distinguish them from the similarly spelled words **mi** 'my', **tu** 'your' and **el** 'the'. There is no written accent on **ti**, as there is no other similarly spelled word.

2 The direct and indirect object pronouns (or weak pronouns) can only be used in conjunction with a verb, whereas the subject pronouns and the prepositional object pronouns (or strong pronouns) can be used independently.

For example, you translate 'her' using **la** in **La he visto** 'I have seen her', but if 'her' is used in isolation, as in 'Who did you speak to?' 'To her', the form **ella** must be used:

–¿**Con quién hablaste?** –**Con ella.** (never ×**Con la**×).

Table 8.1 Subject and object pronouns

Person	Subject	Direct object	Indirect object	Prepositional object
Singular				
1st	**yo** (*I*)	**me** (*me*)	**me** (*to me*)	**mí** (*me*)
2nd	**tú** (*you*) familiar	**te** (*you*)	**te** (*to you*)	**ti** (*you*)
	usted (*you*) polite	**lo** (masc.) or **la** (fem.) (*you*)	**le** (*to you*)	**usted** (*you*)
	vos (*you*) familiar [LA]	**te** (*you*)	**te** (*to you*)	**vos** (*you*) [LA]
3rd	**él** (*he*)	**lo** (*him, it* masc.)	**le** (*to him/it*)	**él** (*him*)
	ella (*she*)	**la** (*her, it* fem.)	**le** (*to her/it*)	**ella** (*her*)
	ello (*it neuter*)	**lo** (*it neuter*)	**le** (*to it, neuter*)	**ello** (*it neuter*)
Plural				
1st	**nosotros** (*we*) masc.	**nos** (*us*)	**nos** (*to us*)	**nosotros** (*us*)
	nosotras (*we*) fem.	**nos** (*us*)	**nos** (*to us*)	**nosotras** (*us*)
2nd	**vosotros** (*you*) masc. familiar [SP]	**os** (*you*) [SP]	**os** (*to you*) [SP]	**vosotros** (*you*) [SP]
	vosotras (*you*) fem. familiar [SP]	**os** (*you*) [SP]	**os** (*to you*) [SP]	**vosotras** (*you*) [SP]
	ustedes (*you*) polite [SP and LA] familiar [LA]	**los** (masc.) or **las** (fem.) (*you*)	**les** (*to you*)	**ustedes** (*you*)
3rd	**ellos** (*they*) masc.	**los** (*them*)	**les** (*to them*)	**ellos** (*them*)
	ellas (*they*) fem.	**las** (*them*)	**les** (*to them*)	**ellas** (*them*)

Note: In central and northern Spain, **le** rather than **lo** is the preferred 3rd person singular direct object pronoun for reference to males.

8.1 Subject pronouns

8.1.1 Subject pronouns of the 2nd person

Contemporary Spanish retains the singular forms **tú**, **usted** and **vos** [LA], and the plural forms **vosotros/as** [SP] and **ustedes**, to cover the multiple meanings of English 'you'. Usted and ustedes (often abbreviated in writing to **Ud.**, **Vd.**, **Uds.** or **Vds.**) are used both in Spain and Latin America to signify a relationship that is formal, polite and respectful of the person to whom they are addressed. **Tú** and **vosotros** [SP], on the other hand, suggest familiarity, friendship, and equal social standing. **Vos** [LA] replaces this use in the *singular* in the River Plate region (especially in Argentina and Uruguay), and in Central America (excluding most of Mexico). Pockets of usage may also be found in the Andean countries. In addition, since **vosotros** [SP] is no longer found in Latin America, its place has been taken by **ustedes** [LA] to express familiarity and friendship. This also occurs in the Canary Islands and the west of Andalusia.

Usted and ustedes always take the 3rd person forms of the verb. For the verb forms associated with vos, see Chapter 10 and also 30.2.1.

> **¿Vosotros estáis de acuerdo?** [SP]
> Are you in agreement?
>
> **¿No podés hablar vos con Carlos?** [LA]
> Can't you talk to Carlos?
>
> **Pasen ustedes primero.** (polite or familiar [LA], polite [SP])
> Please go in first.

Since use of 2nd person subject pronouns can vary from region to region, foreign users are advised to err on the side of caution, i.e. use polite forms, until they have become familiar with regional practice.

8.1.2 Uses of subject pronouns

8.1.2.1 General uses

Subject pronouns in Spanish may be required for emphasis, to indicate a change in reference, or for clarity (e.g. where verb forms are not person-specific, as in **yo/él quería** 'I/he wanted').

An appropriate form of **mismo** 'myself', 'yourself' etc. can be added as appropriate for extra emphasis:

Tú y yo somos muy parecidos.
You and I are very much alike.

Usted mismo lo firmó.
You yourself signed it.

Yo puedo viajar hoy, pero él no podrá ir hasta mañana.
I can travel today, but he won't be able to go until tomorrow.

Subject pronouns can also be used on their own without a verb:

–¿Quién abrió la puerta?	'Who opened the door?'
–'Yo'.	'Me'.

Overuse of subject pronouns

In Spanish (unlike English) most verb endings are person-specific, therefore they alone indicate the verb's subject, e.g. **corremos** 'we run'. Consequently the use of subject pronouns in Spanish is less frequent than in English. Native speakers of English should take care not to overuse them.

8.1.2.2	Subject pronouns used with certain prepositions

The subject pronouns **tú** and **yo** are generally used, rather than the corresponding prepositional object pronouns (**mí** and **ti**), with the following: **entre** 'between', **excepto/salvo/menos** 'except', **hasta/incluso** 'even/including', **según** 'according to' and **como** 'as/like':

Entre tú y yo, creo que está chiflado.
Between you and me, I think he is barmy.

Care should be taken with **después** 'after' and **antes** 'before'. The phrase 'after you/me' is expressed in Spanish using **después de** + prepositional object pronoun, but the phrase 'before you/me' is expressed using **antes que** + subject pronoun:

Intentaré después de ti.	I'll have a go after you.
si terminas antes que yo	if you finish before me

Ello

Ello is a neuter pronoun (translated as 'it', 'this' or 'that') which refers back to something to which no gender can be ascribed, such as a statement or concept. As a subject pronoun it is rarely used in speech, being replaced normally by **esto** 'this' or **eso** 'that':

Ello/Esto dio paso a un largo periodo de inestabilidad.
This gave rise to a long period of instability.

8.1.2.4 Subject pronouns to translate 'it's me' etc.

The verb **ser** agrees in person and number with the subject pronoun:

Soy yo, Juan.   It's me, Juan.

Somos nosotros quienes   It's we who invited Maria.
invitamos a María.

8.2 Direct and indirect object pronouns

Direct and indirect object pronouns in Spanish are *weak* pronouns that can be used only in conjunction with verbs. Normally they precede finite verbs. Compare **Luis lo ha visto** with 'Luis has seen him' but see 8.5 on the position of pronouns.

The direct object corresponds to whoever or whatever receives the direct action of the verb ('him' in 'They kicked him'), while the indirect object corresponds to the beneficiary of the action ('me' in 'They gave it to me').

Forms of direct and indirect object pronouns

Direct and indirect object pronouns have identical forms except in the 3rd person (**lo, la, los, las** as opposed to **le** and **les**). **Usted** and **ustedes** correspond to 3rd person object pronouns, so the distinction also applies there.

8.2.1 | Direct object pronouns

No lo conozco muy bien.	I don't know him very well.
Me criticaron.	They criticized me.
Nos han visto.	They have seen us.

It should be noted that in the 3rd person the direct object pronoun agrees in gender (as well as number) with the item referred to:

Deja las cartas aquí y las subiré más tarde.
Leave the letters here and I'll take them upstairs later.

Like other pronouns that vary for gender, direct object pronouns are used in the masculine plural form to refer to groups containing both masculine and feminine components:

–¿Dónde están Ana y Eduardo? 'Where are Ana and Eduardo?'
–No los he visto. 'I haven't seen them.'

Notes:
1 The impersonal verb **haber** is sometimes used with a direct object pronoun to refer to an unexpressed noun, e.g. **Los hay en rojo** 'We have them in red'.

2 The pronoun los can be used to refer to **años** in situations such as the following: –Enrique cumple hoy cuarenta años. –No los aparenta ' "Enrique is forty today." "He doesn't look it" '.

8.2.2 | Uses of indirect object pronouns

For the indirect object with verbs like **gustar**, see 11.5.

8.2.2.1

Indirect object pronouns are most commonly used to indicate *to whom* something is given, directed or said:

Les trajo un regalo.	She brought them a present.
¿Qué te ha dicho?	What has he said to you?
Le dirigió la mirada.	She looked at him.

75

8.2.2.2

Indirect object pronouns can also indicate the person *for* whose benefit or gain something is done:

Le ha hecho un favor. She has done him a favour.

Te he fregado los platos. I've done the washing up for you.

8.2.2.3

Indirect object pronouns are found with impersonal expressions using **resultar** (less frequently **ser**) + adjective (such as **fácil** 'easy', **difícil** 'difficult', **imposible** 'impossible', **necesario** 'necessary').

The pronoun identifies the person to whom the expression applies:

Les resultó difícil adaptarse. It was difficult for them to adapt.

No nos será fácil resolver el It will not be easy for us to
conflicto. resolve the dispute.

8.2.2.4

Indirect object pronouns are further employed to refer to anyone *from* whom (rather than *to* whom) things are taken away:

Cómprale un billete de lotería a ese señor.
Buy a lottery ticket from that man.

¿Por qué me has quitado la revista?
Why did you take my magazine away?

8.2.3 Redundant use of indirect object pronouns

Indirect object pronouns are commonly used *in addition to* a noun functioning as the indirect object, especially if this refers to a person. This is sometimes called the redundant use:

Dile al mesero [LA] que traiga la comida.
Tell the waiter to bring the meal.

A Jorge no le gustó la película.
Jorge didn't like the film.

8.3   Prepositional object pronouns

The forms of prepositional object pronouns

Prepositional object pronouns have the same forms as subject pronouns, except in the cases of **yo** and **tú**, for which the corresponding prepositional object pronouns are **mí** and **ti** respectively.

In addition to the forms listed in Table 8.1, special forms exist for the combination of **con** with **mí** and **ti**, namely **conmigo** and **contigo**.

8.3.1   *General uses of prepositional object pronouns*

These must generally be used when the pronoun is governed by a preposition and stands apart from the verb (hence they are strong pronouns):

Esto es para ustedes.	This is for you.
Estaban corriendo hacia vos. [LA]	They were running towards you.
Quería discutirlo contigo.	He wanted to discuss it with you.
Para ello necesito tu ayuda.	To do it I need your help.

Note: Some prepositions are used with *subject* pronouns, see 8.1.2.2.

8.3.2   *Uses of prepositional object pronouns after* a

8.3.2.1

The sequence **a** + prepositional object pronoun is often used *in addition to* a weak pronoun (direct or indirect object) for purposes of clarity, emphasis or contrast:

A mí no me han dicho nada.	No one has said anything to me.
¿A ti te apetece cenar fuera?	Do you fancy going out for a meal?
Lo han detenido a él, pero no a ella.	He has been arrested but not her.

8.3.2.2

When the preposition **a** indicates movement, direction or destination, usually only the prepositional object pronoun is used (*not* in addition to a weak pronoun):

Vino a mí corriendo.	She ran up to me.
Se dirigió a mí.	He addressed me.
Nos acercamos a ellas.	We approached them.

Note: When some verbs are used reflexively (e.g. **acercarse** 'to approach'), and particularly when they are used in the *3rd person*, they are found either with **a** + prepositional object pronoun, or with an indirect object pronoun. Compare **El chico se acercó a mí** with **El chico se me acercó**, both meaning 'The boy approached me'. A sentence using the 1st person plural, such as **Nos le acercamos** 'We approached him' would generally be considered colloquial or [LA].

8.3.2.3

The sequence **a** + prepositional object pronoun may occur in isolation as the response to a question:

– **¿A quién tengo que entregar los documentos?**	– Who do I have to give the documents to?
– **A mí.**	– 'To me'.
– **¿A quién quieren ver?**	– Who do they want to see?
– **A ustedes.**	– 'You'.

8.4   Reflexive pronouns

Reflexive pronouns are required when the pronoun refers back to the subject of the sentence, as in 'The cat was washing itself'. English reflexive pronouns end in '-self' or '-selves'. The Spanish forms are shown in Table 8.2.

A special form exists for the combination of **con** with **sí**, namely **consigo**.

The *weak* (i.e. non-prepositional) reflexive pronouns generally precede finite verb forms, but see 8.5:

Me corté.	I cut myself.

See Chapter 14 for more examples involving weak reflexive pronouns.

Table 8.2	Reflexive pronouns	
Person	Forms used with verbs	Prepositional forms
Singular		
1st	**me**	**mí**
2nd	**te** familiar (with **tú** and **vos** [LA])	**ti** (or **vos**)
	se polite (with **usted**)	**sí**
3rd	**se**	**sí**
Plural		
1st	**nos**	**nosotros/as**
2nd	**os** familiar [SP]	**vosotros/as** [SP]
	se polite (with **ustedes**) [SP] and [LA]	**sí** [SP] and [LA]
	se familiar (with **ustedes**) [LA]	**sí** [LA]
3rd	**se**	**sí**

The *prepositional* forms are used after a preposition, often in addition to a weak reflexive pronoun. An appropriate form of **mismo** 'myself', 'yourself' etc. can be added for extra emphasis:

Estaba enfadado consigo mismo.	He was angry with himself.
No cabía en sí de alegría.	She was beside herself with joy.
No nos fiamos de nosotras mismas.	We do not trust ourselves.
Te estás engañando a ti mismo.	You are deceiving yourself.

Notes:

1 English forms in '-self' can be used merely to emphasize the subject (rather than reflexively), as in 'She told me so herself'. This is not possible in Spanish: **Me lo dijo ella misma** (not ×**Me lo dijo sí misma**×).

2 Particularly after the preposition **entre** 'among', the prepositional reflexive pronoun **sí** is often replaced by the non-reflexive prepositional object pronouns **él, ella, ellos, ellas, usted,** or **ustedes**: **Lo comentaron entre ellos** 'They discussed it among themselves'.

8.5 The position and order of personal pronouns

The weak pronouns (i.e. direct and indirect object pronouns, together with non-prepositional reflexives) directly precede the verb *except* in the following cases: positive commands, infinitives and gerunds. For examples, see 8.2 above and Chapter 14 (for reflexives).

8.5.1 The position of personal pronouns in commands

Personal pronouns always *follow* and are joined to the verb in *positive* commands, but they always *precede* the verb in *negative* commands:

Ábrelo.	Open it.	**No lo abras.**	Don't open it.
Termínenlos.	Finish them.	**No los terminen.**	Do not finish them.
Acércate a mí.	Come towards me.	**No te acerques a mí.**	Do not approach me.

8.5.2 The position of personal pronouns with infinitives and gerunds

Weak personal pronouns frequently *follow* and are joined to infinitives and gerunds to form one word:

Acaba de llamarme.	She has just called me.
Ha estado consultándonos.	He has been consulting us.

However, personal pronouns may *precede* some verbs (especially auxiliary verbs) that govern an infinitive or gerund, rather than being attached to the latter:

Le quería dar una sorpresa.	She wanted to give him a surprise.
Le sigue escribiendo a pesar de todo.	She continues to write to him despite everything.
Me lo hizo traer.	He made me bring it.

This is common with the following verbs that govern an infinitive:

acabar de	to have just	**preferir**	to prefer
conseguir/lograr	to manage	**querer**	to want
deber	to have to	**soler**	to usually (do)

empezar a	to begin	**tener que**	to have to
hacer	to make	**terminar de**	to finish
ir a	to be going to	**tratar de/ intentar**	to try
necesitar	to need	**poder**	to be able
volver a	to (do) again		

and with the following verbs when they take a gerund (see 18.4):

andar	to go about	**estar**	to be
continuar/seguir	to continue	**venir**	to have been

This usage is *not* possible when the infinitive is governed by a reflexive verb.

Position of personal pronouns

1 If in doubt when positioning personal pronouns in constructions
   with dependent infinitives and gerunds, usually the safest option
   is to attach them to the end of these verb forms: **Se negó a
   comprármelo** 'She refused to buy it for me'.
2 But it is important to take care when adding personal pronouns
   to infinitives or gerunds, since in doing so it might be necessary
   also to add a written accent to the verb, as in the previous
   example, in order to preserve the correct stress pattern in its
   pronunciation. On written accents, see 1.3.2.3.

8.5.3 | *The order of personal pronouns*

In sentences where a verb has two weak pronouns, the indirect object
precedes the direct object, with the exception of reflexive **se**, which is
always in initial position:

No pienso dártelo.	I do not intend to give it to you.
Os [SP] lo han descrito detalladamente.	They have described it to you in detail.
Se nos presentó como un especialista.	He introduced himself to us as a specialist.

Whenever two pronouns of the 3rd person come together, the indirect object (**le** or **les**) is always replaced by **se** in initial position. In other words combinations of pronouns beginning with l-, such as **les** + **lo** or **le** + **las**, are *always* incorrect.

Depending on the context, it might be necessary for emphasis or clarity to indicate the exact person to whom **se** refers by adding a prepositional object pronoun preceded by **a**:

Ya se lo he mandado.	I've already sent it to him.
¿Por qué no se lo propones a ella?	Why don't you ask her?
Queremos ofrecérselo a usted.	We want to offer it to you.

8.6 Use of *le(s)* in place of *lo(s)* and *la(s)*

8.6.1 Le *instead of* lo

The majority of Spanish speakers today use **lo** as the direct object pronoun with the meaning of 'him'. This usage is the preferred choice of the Spanish Academy. However, especially in Madrid and parts of central and northern Spain, the preferred choice of individuals and the media is **le**, a usage which the Academy is obliged to accept:

Lo veremos mañana/Le [SP] veremos mañana.
We shall see him tomorrow.

The use of **le** in place of **lo** is referred to as **leísmo**. This term is also applied to the use of **les** for **los**, which is much less common (see 8.6.2.4).

8.6.2 *Other uses of* le *and* les

Students of Spanish will also encounter the following uses both in Spain and Latin America.

8.6.2.1

Le/Les as the polite 2nd person direct object pronoun for **usted/ustedes** (common in Spain and parts of Latin America):

No sé cómo esto le va a afectar a usted.
I do not know how this is going to affect you.

Encantado de conocerles.
Pleased to meet you.

Le(s) in place
of *lo(s)* and
La(s)

8.6.2.2

Le/Les is preferred with psychological verbs, especially when the subject is an inanimate noun or a clause (e.g. **molestar** 'to bother', **preocupar/in-quietar** 'to worry'; also **creer** 'to believe', **entender** 'to understand'). This is common throughout the Spanish-speaking world:

Le molesta la luz del sol.
The sunlight is bothering him.

Le preocupa que el niño pese tan poco.
She is worried because the boy weighs so little.

8.6.2.3

Le/Les is required after **se** used impersonally, when the object is human (obligatory in Spain, usual in Latin America):

Se le considera un autor importante.
He is considered to be an important author.

8.6.2.4

Les for **los** ('them', male persons) is used commonly in central and northern Spain:

Les llevaron a su casa. [SP]
They took them to their home.

Note: Especially in central and northern Spain, **la** may be encountered in place of **le** when the reference is to *female* human beings: **Dila que venga** 'Tell her to come'. This usage, known as **laísmo**, is not recognized by the Spanish Academy.

Chapter 9

Indefinite adjectives, pronouns and adverbs

These are used: (i) to quantify imprecisely persons, places or things ('some', 'a few', 'several', 'enough', 'many'), (ii) to distinguish one item from another ('a certain', 'such a', 'other'), or (iii) to relate one item to another ('both', 'each' and 'the rest').

Care needs to be taken to ensure that Spanish indefinite adjectives and pronouns are used in the correct variable (for number and gender) or invariable forms.

Indefinite pronouns with reference to persons

When used as pronouns, many of the indefinite forms discussed in this chapter are assumed to refer to persons unless some other item is specified: **Muchos lo han intentado pero pocos lo han conseguido** 'Many people have tried but few have actually done it', **Algunos/Otros piensan así** 'Some/Other people think that'.

Used in this way the plural forms of the indefinites are sometimes used with 1st or 2nd person plural verbs, to convey ideas such as 'many of us', 'all of you': **Muchos teníamos miedo** 'Many of us were frightened', **¿Todos estáis de acuerdo?** 'Do you all agree?'

An indefinite pronoun referring to a person requires the personal **a** if used as the direct object of a verb (see 21.1.1.2).

9.1 Algo

Algo (invariable) is used as a pronoun (referring only to things) and as an adverb.

As a pronoun it usually means 'something', or 'anything' in questions and after words such as **único** and **poco**:

Están tramando algo sospechoso.	They are plotting something suspicious.
¿Quieres algo?	Do you want anything?
Era la única que escribió algo.	She was the only one who wrote anything.

As an adverb, before adjectives or another adverb, it means 'rather', 'somewhat':

La sopa está algo fría.	The soup is rather cold.
Están corriendo algo despacio.	They are running rather slowly.

Algo de + uncountable noun can be used with the meaning of 'some', 'a little':

Necesita algo de sal.	It needs a little salt.

9.2 Alguien

Alguien (invariable) is a pronoun referring only to persons. It means 'someone', or sometimes, in questions, 'anyone':

Alguien ha dejado la ventana abierta.	Someone has left the window open.
¿Estás esperando a alguien?	Are you waiting for someone?
¿Ha llamado alguien?	Has anyone phoned?

9.3 Alguno

This can be used as an adjective or as a pronoun referring to persons, places or things. It varies in number and gender, and is shortened to **algún** before singular masculine nouns (see 6.3.1).

Alguno usually means 'some', 'a few' or, in questions, 'any'. As a pronoun it may also correspond to English 'one/some of them':

En algunas aldeas no hay tiendas.	In some villages there are no shops.
Conozco a algunos (de ellos).	I know some (of them).

85

Spanish does not use **alguno** to translate 'some' or 'any' before nouns which cannot be counted:

Vamos a comprar pan. We are going to buy some bread.

¿Quieres leche? Do you want any milk?

When **alguno** is placed after a noun in a negative sentence it carries the meaning of 'no' and is equivalent to **ninguno**:

No hay motivo alguno. There is no reason at all.

en modo alguno not in the slightest

Notes:

1 The phrase **alguno** (or **algún**) **que otro/alguna que otra** is used in the singular to mean 'a few', 'the occasional': **Alguna que otra cigüeña anida allí** 'An occasional stork nests there'.

2 **Alguna** is often shortened in speech (but usually not in writing) before a feminine noun beginning with a stressed **a** or **ha**: **algún arma** 'some weapon'.

9.4 *Uno*

In addition to its use as a numeral and indefinite article (see 23.1.1 and 3.3), **uno** in the plural is found with the meaning of 'some', 'a few'. It is often followed by **cuantos/as** or **pocos/as** in the plural:

Comimos unas enchiladas riquísimas.
We ate some delicious enchiladas.

Había unos cuantos libros en la estantería.
There were a number of books on the shelf.

Note: Uno and **alguno** are sometimes interchangeable but never before the preposition de. In the singular **uno/a + de** is the norm: **Salí con uno de mis amigos** 'I went out with one of my friends', but in the plural it is replaced by **algunos/as + de**: **Salí con algunos de mis amigos**.

Placed before a cardinal numeral, the plural forms **unos/unas** indicate approximation (see 23.1):

Tiene unos veinte años. He is about twenty years old.

In the singular **uno/a** is used to signify the indefinite 'one/you', sometimes with implied 1st person plural reference:

–A veces una se preocupa– dijo Teresa.
'One sometimes worries,' said Teresa.

Uno intenta ayudarles, pero no nos lo agradecen.
One tries to help them, but they do not thank us for it.

9.5 Mucho, poco

These can be used as adjectives and pronouns (variable in number and gender) or as adverbs (invariable).

9.5.1 Used as adjectives and pronouns

As an adjective or pronoun, **mucho/a/os/as** means 'much', 'many', 'great', 'a lot (of)'. **Poco/a/os/as** means 'few', 'little':

Tengo pocos libros.	I have few books.
Habla con mucha/poca emoción.	He speaks with great/little feeling.

Mucho and **poco** can also be used as invariable neuter pronouns:

Tengo mucho/poco que hacer.	I have a lot/little to do.

Not infrequently **mucho/a** and **poco/a** convey the sense of 'too much' and 'too little':

Esto es mucha/poca comida para él.
This is too much/too little food for him.

9.5.2 Used as adverbs

As an adverb **mucho** means 'much', 'a lot'. **Poco** means 'little', but can also be used to negate an adjective (sometimes corresponding to the English prefix 'un-'):

Lee mucho.	She reads a lot.
Esta tierra es poco fértil.	This land is not fertile.
poco interesante/probable	uninteresting/unlikely

Preceded by the indefinite article, **poco** means 'a little':

un poco raro	a bit strange
¿Quieres un poco de pan?	Do you want a little bread?

Notes:

1 **Una poca de,** used by some speakers with feminine nouns, is best avoided.

2 The forms **poquísimo** and **muchísimo** strengthen the original word, 'very little', 'very much'. **Poco** is also strengthened when preceded by **muy: Se ven muy pocos/ poquísimos Ferraris aquí** 'You see very few Ferraris here'.

9.6 Bastante, suficiente

As an adjective or pronoun each is invariable for gender but has a regular plural form:

¿Crees que hay bastantes sillas?   Do you think there are
                                          enough chairs?

No hay suficientes.   There aren't enough.

They can also be used as invariable neuter pronouns: **Esto es suficiente/ bastante para mí** 'This is enough for me'.

Bastante is also an invariable adverb (the corresponding invariable form for **suficiente** is **suficientemente**):

Los ganchos no son bastante grandes.
The hooks are not big enough.

No pensaron suficientemente en el resultado.
They did not think enough about the result.

Note: In speech **bastante** is commonly used to indicate moderately large quantity or extent: **Tiene bastante dinero** 'He has quite a lot of money', **Su casa es bastante grande** 'Their house is quite big'.

9.7 Varios

As an indefinite adjective and pronoun with the meaning of 'several', it is found only in the plural with a regular feminine form:

Varios invitados no comieron nada.
Several guests did not eat anything.

Las desventajas son varias.
There are several disadvantages.

Note: When placed after a noun, **vario** (normally in the plural) can mean 'varied', 'different': **carpetas de colores varios** 'folders of different colours'.

9.8　Demasiado

Demasiado is an adjective or pronoun that varies in number and gender. The meaning is 'too much', 'too many':

Tiene demasiado poder.
She wields too much power.

Había demasiada gente en la fiesta.
There were too many people at the party.

Antes no tenía trabajo, ahora tengo demasiado.
Before I didn't have any work; now I've got too much.

Demasiado can also be used as an adverb meaning 'too (much)' and as an invariable neuter pronoun:

Los colores son demasiado fuertes.
The colours are too bright.

Suelen exigir demasiado.
They usually demand too much.

Note: For **demasiado** with the meaning of 'very' (rather than 'too much') in Latin America, see 30.6.3.5.

9.9　Todo

As an adjective or pronoun **todo** varies in gender and number. As an adverb **todo** is invariable.

9.9.1　Todo *as an adjective*

9.9.1.1　Basic use

As an adjective, the basic meaning of **todo** is 'all (of)', 'the whole'. In this sense it can be used with a noun preceded by the definite article or a possessive or demonstrative adjective:

todo el edificio　　　　the whole building

todos nuestros colegas　all (of) our colleagues

It can also be used before a pronoun or place name:

todos ellos/ustedes　　all of them/you

todo París　　　　　　the whole of Paris

89

In the above examples **todo** appears before the item it modifies. However, it can be moved to other positions in the sentence, still agreeing with the associated noun:

Los alumnos son todos muy simpáticos.
The students are all very nice.

La habitación estaba toda pintada de azul.
The whole room was painted blue.

Used with nouns referring to periods of time, **todos/as** + definite article translates English 'every':

todos los meses   every month

todas las semanas   every week

9.9.1.2 | *Todo* + neuter article or demonstrative

Todo can be used as in 9.9.1.1 but with the neuter article or a neuter demonstrative:

todo lo demás   everything else

todo esto/eso/aquello   all this/that

9.9.1.3 | *Todo* + relative pronoun

Todos los que/todas las que 'all (those)/everyone who' and the neuter **todo lo que** 'all/everything that' are common relative constructions. **Los/las** and **lo** cannot be omitted:

Entrevistamos a todos los que asistieron.
We interviewed all those who attended.

Nos mostraron todo lo que habían encontrado.
They showed us everything that they had found.

Notes:
1 For the use of **cuanto** as an alternative to the above, see 25.8.

2 **Todos los que** is also occasionally replaced by **todo el que** with a singular verb: **Todo el que pasó la saludó** 'Everyone who passed waved to her'.

9.9.1.4 | *Todo* + indefinite article

This pattern is possible but it tends to have an emphatic rather than a literal meaning. Thus it usually means 'a real' rather than 'a whole':

Habéis [SP] tenido toda una aventura.
You've had a real adventure.

The safest way of translating English 'a whole/an entire' is by means of the adjective **entero** 'entire':

un día entero   a whole day

| 9.9.1.5 | *Todo* + noun |

Used in the singular, **todo/a** + noun generally specifies an entire class or type of person, place or thing. It means 'every/any'.

Toda buena persona sabe lo que se debe hacer.
Every good person knows what must be done.

This pattern of usage is not common, except in fixed phrases such as the following:

en todo caso	in any case	**a toda costa**	at all costs
en todo momento	at any time	**a toda prisa**	as quickly as possible
todo tipo de	all kinds of		

The pattern of **todo** + noun is even rarer in the plural, except in set phrases such as the following:

de todas clases	of all kinds	**a todas horas**	at all hours
por todos lados	on all sides	**de todas formas**	in any case
por todas partes	everywhere	**de todos modos**	in any case

See 9.10 **cualquiera** 'any', which is more common than **todo** in this sense.

| 9.9.2 | **Todo** *as a pronoun* |

| 9.9.2.1 | *Todos/Todas* |

Todos/as means 'all' or, if the reference is to persons in general, 'everyone'.

When used as the direct object of a verb, the object pronouns **los** or **las** are usually added:

desde el punto de vista de todos
from everyone's point of view

En cuanto a sus primos, los conozco a todos.
As for his cousins, I know all of them.

Eso se lo dice a todas.
That's what he says to all women.

Note: The phrase **todo el mundo** is equivalent to (and more common than) the
pronoun **todos** in the sense of 'everyone'.

9.9.2.2 | *Todo* as invariable neuter pronoun

Todo as an invariable neuter pronoun corresponds to 'all', 'everything'.
When used as the direct object of a verb the object pronoun **lo** is normally
used, as in English 'it all':

Me gustaría un poco de todo.	I would like a bit of everything.
Lo he comprado todo.	I've bought everything/it all.

9.9.3 | **Todo** *as an adverb*

As an invariable adverb **todo** appears between the verb **ser** and a noun. In
this use, it corresponds to English 'all', 'entirely', 'nothing but':

Esta carne es todo grasa.	This meat is all fat.
Su pelo era todo rizos.	Her hair was all curly.
Era todo sonrisas.	She was all smiles.

9.10 *Cualquiera*

Cualquiera translates English 'any', except in negative sentences (in which
ninguno should be used, see 24.2.4) and in some questions (where **alguno**
may be more appropriate).

It is invariable for gender. The plural form is only used in cases like **cau-
lesquiera que sean sus motivos** 'whatever his motives are'.

As an indefinite adjective it is commoner *before* nouns, and in this use it is
always shortened to **cualquier**. When used as a pronoun **cualquiera** is never
shortened:

Cualquier libro sirve.	Any book(s) will do.
Se puede comprar en cualquier tienda.	It can be bought in any shop.
El se lleva bien con cualquiera.	He gets on with anyone.

Note: Used as an adjective *after* a noun, **cualquiera** means 'any (at all)', 'any (old)': **un libro cualquiera** 'any old book'.

9.11 *Ambos/as*

Always in the plural, it is used especially in the written language as an adjective or pronoun, to refer to two persons, places or things.

In speech it is usually replaced by **los/las dos**:

Se discutieron ambas ofertas.	Both offers were discussed.
–¿Con cuál de las hermanas hablaste?	'Which of the sisters did you talk to?'
–Hablé con las dos.	'I talked to both of them.'

Misuse of *ambos*

English speakers should avoid the temptation to use **ambos** as a translation equivalent to 'both' in sequences such as 'both Carlos and María'. In this type of case, the word 'both' is for emphasis only and cannot be translated literally: **Hablé con Carlos y con María** 'I spoke to both Carlos and María'.

9.12 *Cada*

Cada is invariable and is used only as an adjective:

| **Cada número gana un premio.** | Each/every number wins a prize. |
| **cada cinco años** | every five years |

Notes:

1 **Cada vez más** and **cada vez menos** mean 'more and more', 'less and less': **Es cada vez menos tolerante** 'He is less and less tolerant'.

2 **Cada uno/a** (also, less commonly, **cada cual**) means 'each (one)': **Cada uno llevaba un banderín** 'Each one carried a pennant'.

9.13 Solo

As an adjective, **solo** is variable for number and gender, meaning: 'alone' and sometimes 'mere':

Andrea y Adela fueron solas a la fiesta.
Andrea and Adela went alone to the party.

La sola mención del asunto provocó una pelea.
The mere mention of the subject provoked a quarrel.

Solo and único

The adjective **solo** cannot be used to translate English 'only' if this means 'one and only', as in 'The only shop that sells it is Zara'. Instead **único** must be used: **La única tienda que lo vende es Zara.**

As an adverb **solo** is invariable (equivalent in meaning to **solamente** 'only'). Although many writers still use it, the written accent on the adverbial form **sólo** is now only considered necessary when there is a danger of confusion with **solo** meaning 'alone':

Solo me quedaban dos.   I only had two left.

Notes:

1 **Tan** is used for emphasis before the adverbial form **solo**: **Quedaban tan solo cinco ejemplares** 'There were only five copies left'.

2 **A solas** means 'alone': **¡Vamos a celebrarlo a solas!** 'Let's celebrate alone!'.

9.14 Demás

Preceded by the definite article with the meaning 'the rest', 'the other(s)', **demás** is invariable both as adjective and pronoun:

Las demás (joyas) no valen nada.
The rest (of the jewels) are not worth anything.

The invariable neuter **lo demás** means 'everything else':

Los niños están a salvo, lo demás no me importa.
The children are safe, the rest does not matter.

Note: The phrase **y demás** . . . is found without a definite article to close an enumeration: **franceses, españoles y demás naciones extranjeras** 'French, Spanish and other foreign nations'.

9.15 *Cierto*

This is normally an adjective (variable for number and gender) meaning '(a) certain'. Although once deprecated, the use of the indefinite article before **cierto** is now quite common in speech and writing:

Ciertas plantas son venenosas.
Certain plants are poisonous.

Ahora se nota (una) cierta fatiga en su comportamiento.
Now one notes a certain weariness in her behaviour.

Note: When placed after the noun, **cierto** means 'certain', 'reliable', 'definite': **No hay noticias ciertas de su paradero actual** 'There is no reliable news of his present whereabouts'.

9.16 *Tal, semejante*

These words vary in number only. **Tal** 'such (a/an)' can only come before a noun.

Semejante can come before or after a noun. When placed *before* the noun it emphatically means 'such', especially in negative phrases. It can have this sense when placed *after* the noun but more commonly it means 'similar' or 'alike'.

In general neither **semejante** nor **tal** is followed by the indefinite article, in contrast to similar English constructions:

en tal caso	in such a case
Nunca vi semejante chapucería.	I've never seen such poor workmanship.
Compraron dos sillones semejantes.	They purchased two similar armchairs.

Notes:

1 **Un/a tal** means 'a certain' and is found especially with personal names: **Una tal Magdalena te buscaba** 'A certain Magdalena was looking for you'.

2 **El/la tal** refers to who or what is under discussion, sometimes with a familiar, humorous or mocking tone: **El tal Martínez es un verdadero granuja** 'That Martínez is a real rascal'.

9.17 *Otro*

Otro (variable for gender and number) is used as an adjective with the meaning '(an)other' and as a pronoun meaning 'another one', 'others':

La otra máquina nunca funciona. The other machine never works.

¿No tienes otra cosa? Don't you have anything else?

¿Dónde están los otros? Where are the others?

Spanish *otro* and English 'other'

1 Unlike English 'other', Spanish **otro** is *never* used with the indefinite article: **otra mesa** 'another table'.

2 **Otro** is placed *before* cardinal numbers: **otros cuatro** 'four others', **otras cien libras** 'another hundred pounds', but *after* other indefinites: **alguna otra razón** 'some other reason'.

Chapter 10

Verb forms

Spanish verbs are organized into three main classes or *conjugations* depending on whether the infinitive form ends in -ar, -er or -ir. In the tables below, the verbs **hablar** 'speak', **beber** 'drink' and **subir** 'climb' are used to illustrate the regular patterns of verb formation in the three conjugations, while other verbs are used to illustrate irregularities. Each verb form can be divided into a *stem*, which often remains the same, and an *ending* which changes. Thus **hablamos** 'we speak' can be split into the stem **habl-** and the ending -**amos**. Changes to the ending express distinctions of tense (such as past, present, future), person (1st, 2nd or 3rd), number (singular or plural) and mood (indicative or subjunctive).

Our aim is not to list the correct forms for all Spanish verbs but to facilitate the understanding of Spanish verbs by discussing regular forms and explaining how and in what ways irregularities occur, wherever possible revealing underlying patterns common to some verbs. For the meanings and uses of tenses, see Chapter 11.

Verb forms – general features

1   Generally speaking, 2nd person singular verb forms end in -s, 2nd person plural forms end in -is/-ís, 1st person plural forms end in -mos, and 3rd person plural forms end in -n.
2   In the most common pattern of usage, distinctive verb forms exist for Latin American **vos** 'you' *only* in the present indicative and in the singular imperative. In the remaining tenses the verb forms that go with **vos** are the same as for **tú**. See also 30.2.1.

10.1 Present indicative and present subjunctive

The endings for the present subjunctive are generally predictable from the endings for the present indicative. The subjunctive forms are created from the indicative forms by changing the vowel in the verb ending: -ar verbs have e in the subjunctive ending, while -er and -ir verbs have a.

Present subjunctive forms

In contrast to the indicative, the 1st and 3rd person singular forms of the present subjunctive are identical: (yo) hable, (él) hable.

For the uses of the subjunctive see Chapter 12.

10.1.1 Regular present indicative and present subjunctive verb forms

The regular forms are illustrated in Tables 10.1 and 10.2.

Table 10.1 Regular present indicative

Person	**Hablar** 'speak'	**Beber** 'drink'	**Subir** 'go up'
Singular			
1 (yo)	hablo	bebo	subo
2 (tú)	hablas	bebes	subes
(vos)	hablás [LA]	bebés [LA]	subís [LA]
3 (él etc.)	habla	bebe	sube
Plural			
1 (nosotros)	hablamos	bebemos	subimos
2 (vosotros)	habláis [SP]	bebéis [SP]	subís [SP]
3 (ellos etc.)	hablan	beben	suben

Table 10.2 Regular present subjunctive

Person	**Hablar**	**Beber**	**Subir**
Singular			
1 (yo)	hable	beba	suba
2 (tú/vos)	hables	bebas	subas
3 (él etc.)	hable	beba	suba
Plural			
1 (nosotros)	hablemos	bebamos	subamos
2 (vosotros)	habléis [SP]	bebáis [SP]	subáis [SP]
3 (ellos etc.)	hablen	beban	suban

Present tense of -er and -ir verbs

In the present indicative and present subjunctive, the endings in the -er and -ir conjugations are identical, except in the 1st and 2nd persons plural present indicative and with **vos**.

10.1.2 Irregular present indicative and present subjunctive verb forms

In the present indicative and subjunctive, irregularities in the stem of the verb are not uncommon.

10.1.2.1 Radical changing verbs

In some cases there is a variation in the last vowel in a verb's stem, e.g. **recordamos** 'we remember' but **recuerdo** 'I remember'. Verbs whose stem vowel varies in this way are often called *radical changing verbs*, as the term 'radical' refers to the part of the stem that contains the vowel subject to variation.

The -ar and -er conjugations

Radical changing verbs in the **-ar** and **-er** conjugations undergo a change in their final stem vowel in the present indicative and present subjunctive, whenever the spoken stress falls on the stem rather than the ending.

In other words, the vowel is changed in the 1st, 2nd (excluding the vos form) and 3rd persons singular, and in the 3rd person plural. The vowels that are affected are e, which changes to ie, and o, which changes to ue. These two patterns of change are illustrated in Tables 10.3 and 10.4.

Table 10.3 -*ar* and -*er* radical changes (indicative)

Person	**Pensar** 'think'	**Volver** 'return'
Singular		
1 (yo)	pienso	vuelvo
2 (tú)	piensas	vuelves
(vos)	pensás [LA]	volvés [LA]
3 (él etc.)	piensa	vuelve
Plural		
1 (nosotros)	pensamos	volvemos
2 (vosotros)	pensáis [SP]	volvéis [SP]
3 (ellos etc.)	piensan	vuelven

Table 10.4 -*ar* and -*er* radical changes (subjunctive)

Person	**Pensar**	**Volver**
Singular		
1 (yo)	piense	vuelva
2 (tú/vos)	pienses	vuelvas
3 (él etc.)	piense	vuelva
Plural		
1 (nosotros)	pensemos	volvamos
2 (vosotros)	penséis [SP]	volváis [SP]
3 (ellos etc.)	piensen	vuelvan

Other common verbs that follow this pattern include:

acordarse de	remember	**mostrar**	show
acostarse	lie down	**negar**	deny
atravesar	cross	**oler**	smell
calentar	heat up	**perder**	lose
cerrar	close	**plegar**	fold
comenzar	begin	**poder**	be able to
confesar	confess	**probar**	prove/try
consolar	console	**recomendar**	recommend
contar	count	**recordar**	remember
costar	cost	**resolver**	resolve
defender	defend	**rogar**	ask
disolver	dissolve	**soler**	be accustomed to
doler	hurt	**soltar**	release
encontrar	find	**sonar**	sound
fregar	wipe	**soñar**	dream
morder	bite	**volar**	fly

Compounds of the above follow this pattern.

Apart from their 1st person forms **tengo** and **vengo**, the verbs **tener** 'have' and **venir** 'come' also follow this pattern in the present indicative, in the latter case with appropriate -**ir** endings.

Oler 'smell' adds an **h** whenever o > **ue**: **huelo, hueles** etc.

Notes:
1 If a noun that is derived from a verb contains stressed ie or ue, this usually indicates that the verb belongs to this group of radical changing verbs, e.g. **recuerdo** 'memory' (from **recordar**), **vuelta** 'return' (from **volver**), **cierre** 'closure' (from **cerrar**), **sueño** 'dream' (from **soñar**). The converse is not necessarily the case, however. For example, although **costar** is radical changing, the associated noun is **coste** or **costo**.

2 The verbs **jugar** 'play' and **adquirir** 'acquire' behave like the verbs illustrated in Tables 10.3 and 10.4, except that the vowel changes are from **u** > **ue** and from **i** > **ie**: e.g. **juego, juegas** etc. and **adquiero, adquieres** etc.

The -ir conjugation

There are two discernible patterns of conjugation:

Pattern I – In the present indicative and subjunctive, the occurrence of the changes from e > ie (and in the cases of **morir** 'die' and **dormir** 'sleep' from o > ue) is the same as for -ar and -er verbs (see Tables 10.3. and 10.4.).

In addition, in the present subjunctive there are changes in the 1st and 2nd persons plural from e > i as shown in Table 10.5, and in the cases of **morir** and **dormir** from o > u.

Table 10.5 -ir radical changes (pattern I)

Person	Sentir 'feel'	
	Indicative	Subjunctive
Singular		
1 (yo)	siento	sienta
2 (tú)	sientes	sientas
(vos)	sentís [LA]	sientas
3 (él etc.)	siente	sienta
Plural		
1 (nosotros)	sentimos	sintamos
2 (vosotros)	sentís [SP]	sintáis [SP]
3 (ellos etc.)	sienten	sientan

Other common verbs that follow this pattern include:

advertir	warn	**hervir**	boil
arrepentirse	regret	**mentir**	lie
consentir	consent	**preferir**	prefer
convertir	convert	**referir(se)**	refer
divertir(se)	amuse	**sugerir**	suggest
herir	wound		

Pattern II – In the present indicative some verbs have a change from **e** > **i** whenever the stress falls on the stem, and make the same change in all persons of the present subjunctive. See Table 10.6.

Table 10.6 -ir radical changes (pattern II)

Person	**Medir** 'measure'	
	Indicative	Subjunctive
Singular		
1 (yo)	mido	mida
2 (tú)	mides	midas
(vos)	medís [LA]	midas
3 (él etc.)	mide	mida
Plural		
1 (nosotros)	medimos	midamos
2 (vosotros)	medís [SP]	midáis [SP]
3 (ellos etc.)	miden	midan

Other common verbs that follow this pattern include:

competir	compete	**pedir**	ask for
concebir	conceive	**rendirse**	surrender
corregir	correct	**repetir**	repeat
derretir(se)	melt	**seguir**	follow
elegir	elect/choose	**servir**	serve
gemir	groan	**vestir(se)**	dress

Compounds of the above follow this pattern.

Verbs like **freír** 'fry' and **reír** 'laugh' are essentially the same, except that a written accent is required whenever i is stressed: **frío, fríes, (vos) freís, fríe, freímos, freís, fríen** (present indicative), **fría, frías, fría, friamos, friais, frían** (present subjunctive).

Radical changing verbs

No radical changing verbs in any conjugation show a vowel change in the 1st or 2nd persons plural of the present indicative.

10.1.2.2 Consonant changing verbs

An important category of stem irregularities comprises verbs in which a consonant is inserted or changed at the end of the stem, e.g. **pones** 'you put' but **pongo** 'I put', **dices** 'you say' but **digo** 'I say'.

Stem consonant irregularities

1   When the irregularity affects the 1st person singular of the present indicative, this also affects the present subjunctive which is usually based upon it: **salg-** (from **salgo** 'I go out') becomes **salga**, **salgas** etc.
2   Stem consonantal irregularities never occur in the 1st or 2nd persons plural of the present indicative.

Insertion of g or change to g

In a small but important group of -er and -ir verbs a **g** is inserted between the stem and the ending in the 1st person singular present indicative and throughout the present subjunctive. In other words, **g** is inserted whenever **o** or **a** follow the stem. This type of irregularity is illustrated in Table 10.7.

Other common verbs that follow this pattern include:

salir	go out	**tener**	have
venir	come	**valer**	be worth

Decir 'say' and **hacer** 'do' have a similar pattern, except that in their case **g** replaces another consonant, namely **c**: **digo**, **dices**, (**vos**) **decís**, **dice**, **decimos**, **decís**, **dicen** (present indicative), **diga**, **digas**, **diga**, **digamos**, **digáis**, **digan** (present subjunctive).

Caer 'fall', **traer** 'bring' and **oir** 'hear' also follow the **poner** pattern, but the **a** or **o** in the stem is changed to **ai** or **oi** whenever the **g** is inserted: **caigo**,

Table 10.7 Insertion of *g* in certain verbs

| Person | **Poner** 'put' | |
	Indicative	Subjunctive
Singular		
1 (yo)	pongo	ponga
2 (tú)	pones	pongas
(vos)	ponés [LA]	
3 (él etc.)	pone	ponga
Plural		
1 (nosotros)	ponemos	pongamos
2 (vosotros)	ponéis [SP]	pongáis [SP]
3 (ellos etc.)	ponen	pongan

caes, (vos) caés, cae, caemos, caéis, caen (present indicative), caiga, caigas, caiga, caigamos, caigáis, caigan (present subjunctive).

In addition, in **oír** y is inserted at the end of the stem in the 2nd and 3rd persons singular and in the 3rd person plural of the present indicative: **oigo, oyes, (vos) oís, oye, oímos, oís, oyen** (present indicative), **oiga, oigas, oiga, oigamos, oigáis, oigan** (present subjunctive).

Verbs ending in -ucir and -ecer

All verbs in **-ucir** and most verbs in **-ecer**, plus **conocer** 'know' and **nacer** 'be born', show a change from c to zc in the same circumstances in which g is inserted into verbs like **poner** (i.e. 1st person singular present indicative and throughout the present subjunctive). This pattern is illustrated in Table 10.8.

Other common verbs that follow this pattern include:

conocer	know	**lucir**	shine
deducir	deduce	**merecer**	merit
florecer	flower	**padecer**	suffer
introducir	introduce	**producir**	produce

Table 10.8 Change from c to zc in certain verbs

| Person | Conducir 'drive' | | | Aparecer 'appear' | |
	Indicative	Subjunctive		Indicative	Subjunctive
Singular					
1 (yo)	conduzco	conduzca		aparezco	aparezca
2 (tú)	conduces	conduzcas		apareces	aparezcas
(vos)	conducís [LA]	conduzcas		aparecés [LA]	aparezcas
3 (él etc.)	conduce	conduzca		aparece	aparezca
Plural					
1 (nosotros)	conducimos	conduzcamos		aparecemos	aparezcamos
2 (vosotros)	conducís [SP]	conduzcáis [SP]		aparecéis [SP]	aparezcáis [SP]
3 (ellos etc.)	conducen	conduzcan		aparecen	aparezcan

Verbs ending in -uir

Since Spanish does not permit an unstressed **i** between vowels, these verbs show insertion of **y** in all persons of the present indicative except 1st and 2nd persons plural, and throughout the present subjunctive. This pattern is illustrated in Table 10.9.

Table 10.9 Insertion of *y* in certain verbs

Person	**Huir** 'flee' Indicative	Subjunctive
Singular		
I (yo)	huyo	huya
2 (tú)	huyes	huyas
(vos)	huís [LA]	huyas
3 (él etc.)	huye	huya
Plural		
I (nosotros)	huimos	huyamos
2 (vosotros)	huís [SP]	huyáis [SP]
3 (ellos etc.)	huyen	huyan

Other verbs that follow this pattern include:

construir construct   **disminuir** diminish   **intuir** sense

The verb **argüir** 'contend/indicate' is like **huir** except that it requires the dieresis when **u** is followed by **i**: compare **arguyo, arguyes** with **argüimos** and **argüís**.

| 10.1.2.3 | Irregular stress

In quite a large group of verbs, the irregularity in the present indicative and subjunctive has to do with the placement of the stress, e.g. **continuar** 'continue' but **continúo** 'I continue'.

Verbs ending in -iar or -uar

A large number of -ar verbs have a stem that ends in **i** or **u**, e.g. **envi-ar** 'send' and **continu-ar** 'continue'. In some of these verbs this **i** or **u** is stressed throughout the present indicative and subjunctive, except in the 1st and 2nd persons plural (and in the **vos** indicative forms). This pattern is illustrated in Tables 10.10 and 10.11.

Table 10.10 Verbs in *-iar* and *-uar* (present indicative)

Person	**Enviar** 'send'	**Continuar** 'continue'
Singular		
1 (yo)	envío	continúo
2 (tú)	envías	continúas
(vos)	enviás [LA]	continuás [LA]
3 (él etc.)	envía	continúa
Plural		
1 (nosotros)	enviamos	continuamos
2 (vosotros)	enviáis [SP]	continuáis [SP]
3 (ellos etc.)	envían	continúan

Table 10.11 Verbs in *-iar* and *-uar* (present subjunctive)

Person	**Enviar**	**Continuar**
Singular		
1 (yo)	envíe	continúe
2 (tú/vos)	envíes	continúes
3 (él etc.)	envíe	continúe
Plural		
1 (nosotros)	enviemos	continuemos
2 (vosotros)	enviéis [SP]	continuéis [SP]
3 (ellos etc.)	envíen	continúen

Common verbs like **enviar** include the following:

confiar	trust	**fiarse**	trust
criar	bring up/raise	**guiar**	guide
desafiar	defy/challenge	**liar**	tie up
desviar	deflect/divert	**vaciar**	empty
enfriarse	go cold	**variar**	vary
espiar	spy		

However, the majority of verbs ending in -**iar** are regular: **cambio** 'I change', **cambias** 'you change' etc.

Most verbs ending in -**uar** follow the pattern of **continuar**. Examples are:

acentuar	stress	**graduarse**	graduate
actuar	act	**habituar**	accustom
atenuar	attenuate	**situar**	situate
efectuar	effect	**valuar** [LA]	value
evaluar	assess		

However, the small group of verbs ending in -**cuar** and -**guar** are regular: **averiguar** 'verify', **evacuar** 'evacuate'.

Two adjoining vowels in the stem

Some verbs have a diphthong in their stem, e.g. **aislar** 'isolate' and **reunir** 'join/gather'. In the case of a small number of verbs in this category, the diphthong is broken into two syllables. This occurs in the singular (excluding the **vos** indicative form) and in the 3rd person plural, in both the present indicative and the present subjunctive.

The **h** in verbs like **prohibir** 'prohibit' and **rehusar** 'refuse' is irrelevant to pronunciation and so these verbs also follow this pattern. See Tables 10.12 and 10.13.

Other verbs that follow this pattern are:

airar	anger	**europeizar**	Europeanize
aullar	yell	**enraizar**	take root

Table 10.12 Verbs with stem diphthong (present indicative)

Person	Aislar 'isolate'	Reunir 'gather'	Prohibir 'forbid'
Singular			
1 (yo)	aíslo	reúno	prohíbo
2 (tú)	aíslas	reúnes	prohíbes
(tú/vos)	aislás [LA]	reunís [LA]	prohibís [LA]
3 (él etc.)	aísla	reúne	prohíbe
Plural			
1 (nosotros)	aislamos	reunimos	prohibimos
2 (vosotros)	aisláis [SP]	reunís [SP]	prohibís [SP]
3 (ellos etc.)	aíslan	reúnen	prohíben

Table 10.13 Verbs with stem diphthong (present subjunctive)

Person	Aislar	Reunir	Prohibir
Singular			
1 (yo)	aísle	reúna	prohíba
2 (tú/vos)	aísles	reúnas	prohíbas
3 (él etc.)	aísle	reúna	prohíba
Plural			
1 (nosotros)	aislemos	reunamos	prohibamos
2 (vosotros)	aisléis [SP]	reunáis [SP]	prohibáis [SP]
3 (ellos etc.)	aíslen	reúnan	prohíban

Verbs with a diphthong in their stem that do *not* follow this pattern include:

arraigarse	take root	**peinar**	comb
causar	cause	**reinar**	reign

10.1.2.4 Orthography changing verbs

Given the general principles of Spanish orthography, a verb's stem may
require a spelling adjustment depending on the vowel that immediately fol-
lows it, e.g. **elige** 'he/she chooses' but **elijo** 'I choose' (**j** is required before **o**).
These adjustments are designed to preserve correct pronunciation and so they
do not constitute a genuine irregularity. Nevertheless, a proper understanding of such adjustments is crucial to the correct writing of Spanish. See 1.2.

-ar verbs

In the **-ar** conjugation, throughout the present subjunctive there are changes
from **g > gu, z > c** and **c > qu**, when the following vowel is **e**. See Table 10.14.

Table 10.14 Spelling changes in certain -ar verbs

Llegar 'arrive'		**Cazar** 'hunt'		**Sacar** 'take out'	
indicative	subjunctive	indicative	subjunctive	indicative	subjunctive
llego	llegue	cazo	cace	saco	saque
llegas	llegues	cazas	caces	sacas	saques
llegás [LA]	llegues	cazás [LA]	caces	sacás [LA]	saques
llega	llegue	caza	cace	saca	saque
llegamos	lleguemos	cazamos	cacemos	sacamos	saquemos
llegáis [SP]	lleguéis [SP]	cazáis [SP]	cacéis [SP]	sacáis [SP]	saquéis [SP]
llegan	lleguen	cazan	cacen	sacan	saquen

Note: In the verb **averiguar** 'verify', the **gu** is changed to **gü** throughout the present
subjunctive: **averigüe, averigües** etc. (compare the present indicative **averiguo,
averiguas** etc.).

-er and -ir verbs

In the **-er** and **-ir** conjugations, in the 1st person singular of the present
indicative and throughout the present subjunctive, the changes are **gu > g, g
> j** and **c > z** (when the following vowel is **a** or **o**). This pattern is illustrated
in Table 10.15.

Table 10.15 Spelling changes in certain *-er* and *-ir* verbs

Seguir 'follow'		Vencer 'defeat'		Recoger 'collect'	
indicative	subjunctive	indicative	subjunctive	indicative	subjunctive
sigo	siga	venzo	venza	recojo	recoja
sigues	sigas	vences	venzas	recoges	recojas
seguís [LA]	sigas	vencés [LA]	venzas	recogés [LA]	recojas
sigue	siga	vence	venza	recoge	recoja
seguimos	sigamos	vencemos	venzamos	recoge-mos	recojamos
seguís [SP]	sigáis [SP]	vencéis [SP]	venzáis [SP]	recogéis [SP]	recojáis [SP]
siguen	sigan	vencen	venzan	recogen	recojan

Note: The pattern shown in Table 10.15 does not apply to verbs like **aparecer** (see Table 10.8).

10.1.2.5 Miscellaneous irregularities

A small group of verbs exhibits idiosyncratic irregularities in the present indicative and/or subjunctive, and so are best learned separately. The most common verbs in this category are illustrated in Tables 10.16 and 10.17.

Caber 'fit' is like **saber,** except in the 1st person singular present indicative **guepo** (which also provides the stem of the present subjunctive), initial c > qu: **quepo, cabes, (vos) cabes, cabe, cabemos, cabéis, caben** (present indicative), **quepa, quepas, quepa, quepamos, quepáis, quepan** (present subjunctive).

10.2 Imperative

10.2.1 Regular imperative forms

The singular forms of the imperative, except among those Latin American speakers who use the pronoun **vos**, are usually identical to the 3rd person singular present indicative forms. The plural imperative forms are created by replacing the final **r** of the infinitive with **d** (see Table 10.18).

Table 10.16 Verbs with idiosyncratic irregularities (indicative forms)

Ser 'be'	Estar 'be'	Ir 'go'	Dar 'give'	Ver 'see'	Haber (aux.)	Saber 'know'
soy	estoy	voy	doy	veo	he	sé
eres	estás	vas	das	ves	has	sabes
es	está	va	da	ve	ha	sabe
somos	estamos	vamos	damos	vemos	hemos	sabemos
sois [SP]	estáis [SP]	vais [SP]	dais [SP]	veis [SP]	habéis [SP]	sabéis [SP]
son	están	van	dan	ven	han	saben

Note: Apart from ser (vos sos) and saber (vos sabés), these verbs do not have distinct vos forms.

Table 10.17 Verbs with idiosyncratic irregularities (subjunctive forms)

Ser 'be'	Estar 'be'	Ir 'go'	Dar 'give'	Ver 'see'	Haber (aux.)	Saber 'know'
sea	esté	vaya	dé	vea	haya	sepa
seas	estés	vayas	des	veas	hayas	sepas
sea	esté	vaya	dé	vea	haya	sepa
seamos	estemos	vayamos	demos	veamos	hayamos	sepamos
seáis [SP]	estéis [SP]	vayáis [SP]	deis [SP]	veáis [SP]	hayáis [SP]	sepáis [SP]
sean	estén	vayan	den	vean	hayan	sepan

Table 10.18 Regular imperative forms

	Hablar	**Beber**	**Subir**
Singular			
(tú)	habla	bebe	sube
(vos)	hablá [LA]	bebé [LA]	subí [LA]
Plural			
(vosotros)	hablad [SP]	bebed [SP]	subid [SP]

For more on imperatives, **vos** forms and commands, see Chapter 19.

10.3 Imperfect tense

For uses, see 11.1.3.

10.3.1 *Regular imperfect tense forms*

See Table 10.19.

Table 10.19 Imperfect tense (regular forms)

Person	**Hablar**	**Beber**	**Subir**
Singular			
1 (yo)	hablaba	bebía	subía
2 (tú/vos)	hablabas	bebías	subías
3 (él etc.)	hablaba	bebía	subía
Plural			
1 (nosotros)	hablábamos	bebíamos	subíamos
2 (vosotros)	hablabais [SP]	bebíais [SP]	subíais [SP]
3 (ellos etc.)	hablaban	bebían	subían

10.3.2 *Irregular imperfect tense forms*

Only the verbs **ser** 'be', **ir** 'go' and **ver** 'see' are irregular in the imperfect tense. Their forms are shown in Table 10.20.

Table 10.20 Imperfect tense (irregular forms)

Person	**Ser**	**Ir**	**Ver**
Singular			
I (yo)	era	iba	veía
2 (tú/vos)	eras	ibas	veías
3 (él etc.)	era	iba	veía
Plural			
I (nosotros)	éramos	íbamos	veíamos
2 (vosotros)	erais [SP]	ibais [SP]	veíais [SP]
3 (ellos etc.)	eran	iban	veían

The imperfect tense – general features

1 The 1st and 3rd person singular forms of the imperfect tense are always identical.
2 Except in the cases of **ser** and **ir**, the stress in the imperfect is always on the first vowel of the ending.

10.4 Preterite tense

For uses see 11.1.2.

10.4.1 *The regular preterite*

See Table 10.21. **Vos** [LA] usually takes the regular 2nd person singular endings.

Table 10.21 Preterite tense (regular forms)

Person	**Hablar**	**Beber**	**Subir**
Singular			
1 (yo)	hablé	bebí	subí
2 (tú/vos)	hablaste	bebiste	subiste
3 (él etc.)	habló	bebió	subió
Plural			
1 (nosotros)	hablamos	bebimos	subimos
2 (vosotros)	hablasteis [SP]	bebisteis [SP]	subisteis [SP]
3 (ellos etc.)	hablaron	bebieron	subieron

10.4.2 Irregular preterite forms

10.4.2.1 Radical changing verbs

Apart from **venir** 'come', which is dealt with in 10.4.2.2, all -**ir** radical changing verbs exhibit a stem vowel change in the 3rd person forms of the preterite. In almost every case the change in question is from **e** to **i**.

In the verbs **morir** 'die' and **dormir** 'sleep' the change is from **o** to **u**. The two patterns are illustrated in Table 10.22.

Table 10.22 Radical changes in preterite

Person	**Pedir** 'ask for'	**Dormir** 'sleep'
Singular		
1 (yo)	pedí	dormí
2 (tú/vos)	pediste	dormiste
3 (él etc.)	pidió	durmió
Plural		
1 (nosotros)	pedimos	dormimos
2 (vosotros)	pedisteis [SP]	dormisteis [SP]
3 (ellos etc.)	pidieron	durmieron

Notes:

1 For a list of other common -ir radical changing verbs see 10.1.2.1 above.

2 Note that in verbs like **freír** 'fry' and **reír** 'laugh', the i that results from the e >
i change in the 3rd person forms absorbs the i of the corresponding endings: **frió**
(not ×friió×), **frieron** (not ×friieron×).

10.4.2.2 Verbs with irregularities of stem and stress

Some common verbs are stressed on the *stem* in the 1st and 3rd persons
singular (e.g. **vine** 'I came', **vino** 'he/she came'), in contrast to the regular
forms of the preterite, in which the stress is pronounced on the ending.

All verbs in this group are also irregular in view of their unpredictable stems
(e.g. **tuve** 'I had', from **tener**).

There are three main patterns within this category, each of which is illustrated in Table 10.23. Note that no forms in this category carry a written
accent.

Person	**Tener** 'have'	**Venir** 'come'	**Decir** 'say'
Singular			
1 (yo)	tuve	vine	dije
2 (tú/vos)	tuviste	viniste	dijiste
3 (él etc.)	tuvo	vino	dijo
Plural			
1 (nosotros)	tuvimos	vinimos	dijimos
2 (vosotros)	tuvisteis [SP]	vinisteis [SP]	dijisteis [SP]
3 (ellos etc.)	tuvieron	vinieron	dijeron

Table 10.23 Irregular preterite forms (stress and stem
irregularities)

(a) Verbs similar to **tener**:

andar	**anduve**	walk		**poder**	**pude**	be able to
caber	**cupe**	fit		**poner**	**puse**	put
estar	**estuve**	be		**saber**	**supe**	know
haber	**hube**	(auxiliary/impersonal)				

(b) Verbs similar to **venir**:

querer	**quise**	want	**hacer**	**hice** (but **hizo** 3rd person singular)	do

(c) Verbs similar to **decir**:

traer	**traje**	bring	**producir**	**produje**	produce

Notes:

1 The 3rd person plural ending for verbs in this group is -**eron** rather than -**ieron**.

2 All verbs ending in -**ducir** follow the pattern of **producir**.

ver	**vi**	**vio**	see

The verbs **ir** 'go' and **ser** 'be' share the same preterite forms (with regular stress on the endings). These are: **fui, fuiste, fue, fuimos, fuisteis, fueron.**

Dar 'give' and **ver** 'see' have a stem reduced to a single consonant (i.e. **d** and **v**) and regular stress (on the endings): **di, dio,** etc.

| 10.4.2.3 | *I changed to y or deleted in 3rd person endings*

In -**er**/-**ir** verbs whose stem ends in a vowel, e.g. **le-er, ca-er, constru-ir**, the 3rd person endings will be -**yó** and -**yeron** rather than -**ió** and -**ieron**. As in the present tense and present subjunctive, the reason is that Spanish does not permit an unstressed **i** between vowels.

In verbs whose stem ends in one of the consonants **ll** or **ñ**, the 3rd person endings will be -**ó** and -**eron** rather than -**ió** and -**ieron**. These patterns are illustrated in Table 10.24.

Other common verbs like **leer** are **creer** 'believe' and **oír** 'hear'.

Verbs that pattern like **construir** are **huir** 'flee' and **disminuir** 'diminish'.

Like **gruñir** are **teñir** 'dye/tint' and **reñir** 'quarrel' (these two are also radical changing).

Examples of -**ll** verbs are: **bullir** 'seethe/boil' and **zambullirse** 'dive'.

Table 10.24 Irregular preterite forms (*i* > *y* or is deleted in 3rd
person endings)

Person	Leer 'read'	Construir 'build'	Gruñir 'grunt'
Singular			
I (yo)	leí	construí	gruñí
2 (tú/vos)	leíste	construiste	gruñiste
3 (él etc.)	leyó	construyó	gruñó
Plural			
I (nosotros)	leímos	construimos	gruñimos
2 (vosotros)	leísteis [SP]	construisteis [SP]	gruñisteis [SP]
3 (ellos etc.)	leyeron	construyeron	gruñeron

10.4.2.4 Orthographic changes in the preterite

Among -**ar** verbs the following spelling changes occur before **e** in the 1st
person singular: **c** > **qu**, **g** > **gu**, **z** > **c**, **gu** > **gü** (see Table 1.1).

These changes are illustrated in Table 10.25.

Table 10.25 Spelling changes in certain -*ar* verbs in the
preterite

Tocar 'touch'	Llegar 'arrive'	Cazar 'hunt'	Averiguar 'check'
toqué	llegué	cacé	averigüé
tocaste	llegaste	cazaste	averiguaste
tocó	llegó	cazó	averiguó
tocamos	llegamos	cazamos	averiguamos
tocasteis [SP]	llegasteis [SP]	cazasteis [SP]	averiguasteis [SP]
tocaron	llegaron	cazaron	averiguaron

10.5 Imperfect subjunctive

For uses see Chapter 12.

10.5.1 Regular imperfect subjunctive forms

The imperfect subjunctive has two sets of forms, one containing -ra and the other -se. Except in conditional sentences, where the -ra form is usual (see Chapter 13), and except when the imperfect subjunctive is used as an alternative to another tense (12.5), these sets are entirely interchangeable, although the -ra set is statistically the commoner of the two.

The forms are illustrated in Table 10.26.

Table 10.26 Imperfect subjunctive (regular forms)

Hablar		**Beber**		**Subir**	
-ra form	**-se** form	**-ra** form	**-se** form	**-ra** form	**-se** form
hablara	hablase	bebiera	bebiese	subiera	subiese
hablaras	hablases	bebieras	bebieses	subieras	subieses
hablara	hablase	bebiera	bebiese	subiera	subiese
hablára-mos	habláse-mos	bebiéra-mos	bebiése-mos	subiéra-mos	subiése-mos
hablarais [SP]	hablaseis [SP]	bebierais [SP]	bebieseis [SP]	subierais [SP]	subieseis [SP]
hablaran	hablasen	bebieran	bebiesen	subieran	subiesen

10.5.2 Irregular imperfect subjunctive forms

The stem of the imperfect subjunctive derives from the 3rd person plural of the *preterite* tense and is used for *all* persons.

The ending -ron is removed and replaced by the -ra or -se endings: e.g. **pidieron** > **pidie** + **ra** or **pidie** + **se**, **produjeron** > **produje** + **ra** or **produje** + **se**.

Other typical patterns so produced are: leyera/leyese, construyera/construyese, dijera/dijese, trajera/trajese, gruñera/gruñese and bullera/bullese.

10.6 Future and conditional tenses

In both of these tenses the stem is supplied by the infinitive.

The endings for the future are identical to the present indicative endings of the auxiliary verb **haber** (see Table 10.16), except that written accents are required on the final syllable in all persons other than 1st person plural.

The endings for the conditional are identical to the endings of -er/-ir verbs in the imperfect tense.

The forms for the two tenses are illustrated in Tables 10.27 and 10.28.

The following verbs have irregular stems in the future and conditional, although the endings are the same as those shown in Tables 10.27 and 10.28:

caber	**cabr-**	fit
decir	**dir-**	say
haber	**habr-**	(auxiliary/impersonal)
hacer	**har-**	do
poner	**pondr-**	put
querer	**querr-**	want
saber	**sabr-**	know
salir	**saldr-**	go out
tener	**tendr-**	have
valer	**valdr-**	be worth
venir	**vendr-**	come

10.7 Future subjunctive

For (very rare) uses, see 12.6.

The forms are identical to the -ra forms of the imperfect subjunctive except that final a is replaced by e: **hablare, bebiere, subiere** etc.

Table 10.27 Regular future tense

Person	**Hablar**	**Beber**	**Subir**
Singular			
I (yo)	hablaré	beberé	subiré
2 (tú/vos)	hablarás	beberás	subirás
3 (él etc.)	hablará	beberá	subirá
Plural			
I (nosotros)	hablaremos	beberemos	subiremos
2 (vosotros)	hablaréis [SP]	beberéis [SP]	subiréis [SP]
3 (ellos etc.)	hablarán	beberán	subirán

Table 10.28 Regular conditional tense

Person	**Hablar**	**Beber**	**Subir**
Singular			
I (yo)	hablaría	bebería	subiría
2 (tú/vos)	hablarías	beberías	subirías
3 (él etc.)	hablaría	bebería	subiría
Plural			
I (nosotros)	hablaríamos	beberíamos	subiríamos
2 (vosotros)	hablaríais [SP]	beberíais [SP]	subiríais [SP]
3 (ellos etc.)	hablarían	beberían	subirían

10.8 Non-finite forms

The non-finite forms in Spanish are the infinitive, the past participle and the gerund. They normally require another verb in order to be used in a sentence.

The regular forms of these are illustrated in Table 10.29. For the uses of the infinitive and the gerund, see Chapters 17 and 18.

Table 10.29 Non-finite forms (regular verbs)

	Hablar	Beber	Subir
Infinitive	hablar	beber	subir
Gerund	hablando	bebiendo	subiendo
Past participle	hablado	bebido	subido

10.8.1 Irregular gerunds

10.8.1.1

All -ir radical changing verbs exhibit a vowel change in the gerund. This is nearly always **e > i**:

pedir	**pidiendo**	ask
servir	**sirviendo**	serve
decir	**diciendo**	say
venir	**viniendo**	come

However, in **morir** 'die', **dormir** 'sleep' and **poder** 'be able' the change is **o > u**, as in **durmiendo**.

10.8.1.2

Most -**er** and -**ir** verbs whose stem ends in a vowel have a **y** to avoid an unstressed **i** between vowels:

leer	**leyendo**	read
huir	**huyendo**	flee
oír	**oyendo**	hear
traer	**trayendo**	bring

However, **reír** 'laugh' and **freír** 'fry' take the forms **riendo** and **friendo**. The verb **ir** 'go' takes the form **yendo**.

10.8.1.3

-er and -ir verbs whose stem ends in **ñ** or **ll** drop the **i** from the regular ending:

gruñir	**gruñendo**	grunt
bullir	**bullendo**	seethe/boil

10.8.2 *Irregular past participles*

The commonest are:

abrir	**abierto**	open
cubrir	**cubierto**	cover
decir	**dicho**	say
escribir	**escrito**	write
freír	**frito**	fry
hacer	**hecho**	do
morir	**muerto**	die
poner	**puesto**	put
resolver	**resuelto**	resolve
romper	**roto**	break
ver	**visto**	see
volver	**vuelto**	return

Absolver 'absolve/acquit' and **disolver** 'dissolve' follow the pattern of **resolver**.

10.9 Compound tenses

The perfect, pluperfect, future perfect and conditional perfect tenses are formed using either the present, imperfect, future or conditional of the auxiliary verb **haber** + a past participle.

Table 10.30 illustrates the pattern of formation.

Table 10.30 Compound tenses

Person	Tense		**Hablar**	**Beber**	**Subir**
Singular					
I	*Perfect*	he	hablado	bebido	subido
	Pluperfect	había			
	Future perfect	habré			
	Conditional perfect	habría			
2	*Perfect*	has			
	Pluperfect	habías			
	Future perfect	habrás			
	Conditional perfect	habrías			
3	*Perfect*	ha			
	Pluperfect	había			
	Future perfect	habrá			
	Conditional perfect	habría			
Plural					
I	*Perfect*	hemos			
	Pluperfect	habíamos			
	Future perfect	habremos			
	Conditional perfect	habríamos			
2	*Perfect*	habéis [SP]			
	Pluperfect	habíais [SP]			
	Future perfect	habréis [SP]			
	Conditional perfect	habríais [SP]			
3	*Perfect*	han			
	Pluperfect	habían			
	Future perfect	habrán			
	Conditional perfect	habrían			

Subjunctive counterparts to the perfect and pluperfect tenses illustrated in Table 10.30 are formed using the present and imperfect subjunctive forms of **haber** respectively: **haya hecho, hayas hecho** etc.; **hubiera/hubiese hecho, hubieras/hubieses hecho** etc.

The auxiliary verb **haber** can be used with a past participle to create what is often called a perfect infinitive, as in **después de haber hablado** 'after having spoken' or **por haber hecho eso** 'for having done that'.

When reading literature (but not in speech) students will encounter what is called the past anterior tense. It is formed from the preterite of **haber** + a past participle, e.g. **hube hablado, hubiste hablado** etc. See 11.2.5 on its use.

The future perfect subjunctive, which is all but extinct except in legal and ecclesiastical phraseology, is formed from the future subjunctive of **haber** plus the past participle of another verb, e.g. **hubiere hablado, hubieres hablado** etc.

10.10   Progressive or continuous tenses

The progressive tenses are formed by combining the gerund of the verb in question with an appropriate form of the verb **estar**. The main possibilities are as in Table 10.31.

The progressive auxiliary **estar** can be used in a compound tense to form compound progressive forms such as **he estado hablando** 'I have been talking', **había estado hablando** 'I had been talking' and **habré estado hablando** 'I will have been talking'.

For the use of the progressive tenses see 11.3.

Table 10.31 Progressive tenses

Person	Tense	Hablar	Beber	Subir
Singular				
I	*Present*	estoy	hablando bebiendo subiendo	
	Imperfect	estaba		
	Preterite	estuve		
	Future	estaré		
2	*Present*	estás		
	Imperfect	estabas		
	Preterite	estuviste		
	Future	estarás		
3	*Present*	está		
	Imperfect	estaba		
	Preterite	estuvo		
	Future	estará		
Plural				
I	*Present*	estamos		
	Imperfect	estábamos		
	Preterite	estuvimos		
	Future	estaremos		
2	*Present*	estáis [SP]		
	Imperfect	estabais [SP]		
	Preterite	estuvisteis [SP]		
	Future	estaréis [SP]		
3	*Present*	están		
	Imperfect	estaban		
	Preterite	estuvieron		
	Future	estarán		

Chapter 11

Uses of tenses

Leaving aside the subjunctive mood, which is considered in Chapter 12, the tenses in Spanish can be divided into three categories as follows:

Simple tenses	Present, preterite, imperfect, future, conditional
Compound tenses	Perfect, pluperfect, future perfect, conditional perfect, past anterior
Progressive/continuous tenses	Present progressive, imperfect progressive, preterite progressive, future progressive, progressives of compound tenses

The main uses of each of these tenses are discussed below.

11.1 Simple tenses

11.1.1 Present tense

The Spanish tense corresponds to English 'I run' etc., but does not exclusively denote present time.

11.1.1.1 In habitual sentences

The present tense is used to express an action that happens habitually or is generally considered to be true:

Andrés vende coches.	Andrés sells cars.
El sol se pone por el oeste.	The sun sets in the west.

11.1.1.2 In state sentences

The present tense describes a state or condition which exists at the present moment:

Luis quiere a Andrea.   Luis loves Andrea.

11.1.1.3 With reference to future time

The present tense is also commonly used to refer to imminent events or pre-arranged future intentions:

Venga, cenamos aquí.   OK, we'll have dinner here.

Le pago mañana.   I'll pay you tomorrow.

It is frequently used in conditional sentences that confirm an agreed arrangement, or in questions asking for advice or approval for some imminent action:

¿Qué hago si no está?   What shall I do if he isn't there?

¿Compro pan?   Shall I buy some bread?

11.1.1.4 With reference to past time

The present tense can also be used to refer to the past to make past events more vivid:

Luego llega el conserje y me dice que qué demonios hago allí.
Then the porter arrives and says what on earth am I doing there.

11.1.1.5 In place of the English perfect

Spanish uses the simple present in sentences that say 'this is the first time that . . .':

Esta es la primera vez que viajo en barco.
This is the first time I have travelled by boat.

11.1.2 The preterite tense

The Spanish tense corresponds to the simple past in English: 'I ran' etc.

The preterite talks about events that took place in the past and are now complete, or states of affairs that existed in the past but have now ended.

The two basic uses of the preterite are illustrated in 11.1.2.1 and 11.1.2.2. Certain other uses are best explained by means of a direct comparison between the preterite and the imperfect (see 11.1.4).

11.1.2.1 With completed actions or events

The preterite describes actions that singly or in sequence were completed in the past:

Me levanté, me lavé y salí.
I got up, washed and went out.

Construyeron la urbanización en cuatro meses.
They built the housing complex in four months.

Nicolás me llamó cinco veces anoche.
Nicolás called me five times last night.

11.1.2.2 With states that have come to an end

The preterite also refers to states of affairs that lasted during specified (possibly very long) time limits in the past and have now ended.

Often, but by no means always, the prepositions **durante** 'for' or **hasta** 'until' signal this usage:

Jugaron durante media hora.
They played for half an hour.

Felipe González fue presidente del gobierno desde 1982 hasta 1991.
Felipe González was president of the government (prime minister) from 1982 to 1991.

Lo negó desde el principio.
He denied it from the start.

11.1.3 *The imperfect tense*

Characteristically the imperfect tense deals with actions or states of affairs that were in progress in the past, or were habitual or customary in the past. The English phrases 'was happening' or 'used to happen' suggest the use of the imperfect tense in Spanish.

| 11.1.3.1 | To express actions in progress

The imperfect tense is used to talk about events or actions that *were* taking place at some time in the past. The beginning and end of these occurrences is unspecified.

A typical narrative strategy involves using the imperfect to describe the setting for an event that is narrated using the preterite:

Alberto y Juan se reían a carcajadas.
Alberto and Juan were roaring with laughter.

Me caí mientras bajaba la escalera.
I fell while I was going down the stairs.

Note: In this usage the imperfect has a similar meaning to the imperfect progressive. The latter may be preferred to emphasize being 'in the middle' of an activity: **No pude contestar al teléfono porque <u>estaba dando de comer</u> al bebé** 'I couldn't answer the telephone because I was feeding the baby'. See 11.3.2.

| 11.1.3.2 | To describe states and conditions

The imperfect tense describes states, conditions or characteristics in the past:

La responsable era María.	The person in charge was María.
No sabía su nombre.	I didn't know his name.
Carmen estaba enferma.	Carmen was ill.

| 11.1.3.3 | To describe habitual actions

The imperfect tense expresses actions or events that were repeated habitually, events to which the English phrase 'used to' may be applicable.

Habitual actions are sometimes signalled as such by phrases like **a menudo** 'frequently', **de vez en cuando** 'from time to time', **siempre** 'always', **cada día** 'every day', **todas las semanas** 'every week':

Antes Lole trabajaba en un hospital.
Lole used to work in a hospital.

Ibamos todos los jueves al cine.
We used to go to the cinema every Thursday.

Cenábamos fuera a menudo.
We frequently dined out.

The imperfect and habitual actions

Sometimes the Spanish imperfect corresponds to English 'would': **Por las mañanas iba a correr en el parque** 'In the morning I would (= 'used to') go for a run in the park'.

Care should be taken with the word **nunca** 'never'. This can be a frequency phrase [e.g. **Nunca íbamos al cine** 'We would never (= 'never used to') go to the cinema'] but it can also be used to deny that a particular action took place, in which case the preterite is required: **Yo nunca fui a su casa** 'I never went to his house'.

11.1.3.4 For intended or expected actions

The imperfect is used to talk about actions or events that were intended or expected to take place in the future:

Ese día llegaba Manolo.	Manolo was arriving that day.
Pensaba que venías mañana.	I thought you were coming tomorrow.

11.1.3.5 To express politeness

The imperfect is commonly used to make a request or question appear less direct:

Quería pedirle un favor.	I wanted to ask you a favour.

11.1.4 Comparison between preterite and imperfect

The correct selection of tense poses a challenge for English speakers of Spanish. This is due to the fact that Spanish can denote a different perspective by choosing one or other of the two tenses, whereas English uses a single verb form for both. For example, where Spanish has **no podía entrar** (often the first choice of English speakers) and **no pude entrar**, English has 'I could not enter'.

With certain verbs the distinction between the preterite and the imperfect is best illustrated by means of a direct comparison.

11.1.4.1 With *ser* and *estar*

With **ser** and **estar** the *preterite* is used to refer to states or conditions that have now ended, or to talk about distinct periods of time in the past.

The *imperfect* is used when the intention is merely to say that the state or condition existed at some time in the past.

Adriana <u>estuvo</u> enferma la semana pasada.
Adriana was ill last week (had a bout of illness).

Cuando fui a su casa Adriana <u>estaba</u> enferma.
When I went to her house Adriana was ill.

Sánchez <u>fue</u> presidente tres veces.
Sánchez was president three times (had three presidential terms).

Sánchez <u>era</u> presidente en aquella época.
Sánchez was president at the time.

11.1.4.2 The preterite indicates action, the imperfect indicates state

The preterite denotes an *action* in many constructions (e.g. in the pattern **ser** + adjective + infinitive).

The imperfect describes a *state*.

<u>Fue</u> fácil hacerlo.	It was easily done (and it was done).
<u>Era</u> fácil hacerlo	It was an easy thing to do.
<u>Tuve que</u> pagar la cena yo.	I had to pay for the dinner (and I did pay).
El niño <u>tenía que</u> acostarse a las ocho.	The boy's bedtime was eight o'clock.
<u>Costó mucho la casa.</u>	The house was expensive (a lot was paid).
<u>Costaba mucho la casa.</u>	The house was expensive.

For different translations of **querer** and **poder** with the imperfect and preterite tenses see 16.4 and 16.5.1(c).

11.1.4.3 Psychological verbs

With psychological verbs the preterite indicates an *act* (such as recognition, learning, understanding) while the imperfect indicates *a state of mind*.

With some verbs, notably **saber** and **conocer**, the English translation of the preterite and imperfect may be different:

Después de hablar con él <u>supe</u> hacerlo.
After speaking to him I understood how to do it.

<u>Sabía</u> cómo hacerlo antes de hablar con él.
I knew how to do it before talking to him.

<u>Conocí</u> a Susana en la fiesta.
I met Susana at the party.

Ya <u>conocía</u> a Ana antes de ir a la fiesta.
I knew Ana before going to the party.

11.1.5 The future tense

For the future tense in conditional sentences, see 13.2.

11.1.5.1 With reference to future time

The future tense is used to make predictions or statements about what is expected to happen. It can also be used in promises or undertakings:

Llegarán a las diez.	They will arrive at ten o'clock.
Lo haré mañana.	I'll do it tomorrow.

Note: The future tense is often replaced both in Spain and Latin America by the present tense of **ir + a + infinitive**: **Van a llegar a las diez** 'They're going to arrive at ten o'clock'. In Latin America **haber + de + infinitive** is sometimes used in this way.

11.1.5.2 To conjecture

The Spanish future tense is additionally used to suggest possibility or to make guesses and suppositions. In questions this use can express surprise:

Ahora mismo estará Alicia en Málaga.
Right now Alicia must be in Malaga.

¿Será Paco el que ha hecho esto?
Could it be Paco who did this?

11.1.6 *The conditional tense*

The conditional tense is used primarily in the main clause of a conditional sentence (see Chapter 13). For its use with **deber** 'to have to', **poder** 'to be able to' and **querer** 'to want', see Chapter 16.

In addition it has the following uses.

11.1.6.1 Reported speech

The conditional tense can be used to report what was originally expressed in the future tense:

Anunció que se jubilaría en julio.
He announced that he would retire in July.

Note: In this use the imperfect tense of **ir** + **a** + infinitive, e.g. **iba a jubilarse**, is more common.

11.1.6.2 Supposition

The conditional tense is also used to indicate possibility or supposition about *past* states:

Serían las diez cuando llegamos.
It must have been ten o'clock when we arrived.

However, in the media it commonly occurs with reference to the *present*, to express possibilities or rumours when the precise facts are not known:

El huracán se localizaría ahora en el sur del golfo.
The hurricane now appears to be in the southern gulf.

El objetivo sería eliminar las dudas.
The aim seems to be to remove the doubts.

11.2 Compound tenses

As in English 'I have run', the compound tenses in Spanish consist of an auxiliary verb (**haber**) + past participle.

The four compound tenses are discussed individually below. However, the following generalizations apply to all of them.

(a) A past participle *never* agrees with the subject or object of the auxiliary verb **haber**, e.g. **María y Andrea se han ido** 'María and Andrea have gone', **No la he visto nunca** 'I have never seen her'.

(b) With one exception, no words may be inserted between **haber** and a past participle, e.g. **Lo he dicho siempre** 'I have always said so'. The exception is the addition of an object pronoun to **haber** when it occurs as an infinitive or a gerund, e.g. **después de haberlo dicho** 'after having said it', **habiéndoles escrito** 'having written to them'.

(c) English 'have/had just done' is expressed in Spanish using the present, imperfect, future or conditional tense of the verb **acabar** 'to finish': **Alberto acaba/acababa/acabará/acabaría de llegar** 'Alberto has/had/will have/would have just arrived'.

(d) With transitive verbs, the auxiliary **haber** is replaced on some occasions by **tener** in order to emphasize the result of the past action. This can only happen when the verb has a direct object, with which the past participle must agree, e.g. **Tengo corregidos los ensayos** 'I've got the essays marked'.

11.2.1 Perfect tense

Considerable variation surrounds the use of the perfect tense. The picture given below reproduces Peninsular usage, excluding Asturias and Galicia which in this respect are more like Latin America, where the preterite is more common (see 30.4.2).

The perfect and preterite tenses compared

The *preterite tense* relates to a period of time that began and was completed in the past: **Mi padre estuvo enfermo la semana pasada** 'My father was ill last week'.

The *perfect tense* relates to a period of time that began in the past and carries over into the present: **Desde entonces mi padre ha estado contento** 'Since then my father has been happy'.

11.2.1.1 When time is unspecified

The perfect tense is used when the time of a past event or state is unspecified, especially when the consequences are still relevant:

Ha vuelto Juan.	Juan has returned.
Nunca he comido pulpo.	I've never eaten octopus.

11.2.1.2 With unfinished periods of time

The perfect tense is used for events that have occurred in a designated period of time that has not ended. Typically it is accompanied by terms like **hoy** 'today', **ahora** 'now', **todavía/aún no** 'still not' or time phrases formed using **este** 'this':

Lo he hecho hoy.	I did it today.
Este verano hemos ido a Portugal.	This summer we went to Portugal.

11.2.1.3 For very recent events

The perfect tense is used for very recent events (usually occurring during the present day), even in cases where the simple past tense would be used in English:

¿Qué has dicho?	What did you say?
Hemos perdido el tren de las dos.	We missed the two o'clock train.
¿Quién ha llamado?	Who called?

11.2.2 The pluperfect tense

The pluperfect denotes what *had* happened, or a state of affairs that *had* existed, before some particular time in the past:

A las dos todavía no habían llegado.	They still hadn't arrived at 2 o'clock.
No sabía si me habían visto.	I didn't know whether they had seen me.

Note: For the replacement of the pluperfect tense by the -ra form of the imperfect subjunctive, see 12.5.

11.2.3 The future perfect tense

This is used to refer to what *will have* happened at some point in the future. Additionally, it can be used to makes guesses and suppositions:

| **Para entonces habré terminado.** | By then I'll have finished. |
| **¿Lo habrá hecho Miguel?** | Could it be Miguel who did it? |

11.2.4 The conditional perfect

The conditional perfect is used to refer to what *would have* happened or existed:

Adela nunca habría elegido una película tan violenta.
Adela would never have chosen such a violent film.

Especially in media contexts, like the conditional but in this case with reference to *past* events, the conditional perfect is used to suggest that the precise facts are in doubt:

Chávez habría nacido en Arequipa en 1930.
Chávez appears to have been born in Arequipa in 1930.

For its use in conditional sentences see Chapter 13.

11.2.5 The past anterior

This is now confined to literature and extremely rare in speech. When used, it is with reference to an action that *had* occurred before another in the past. It is found primarily after temporal conjunctions such as **después (de) que** 'after', **cuando** 'when', **luego que** 'as soon as', **apenas** 'scarcely', in sentences where the main verb is in the preterite:

Después de que hubo salido, empezaron a criticarlo.
When he had left, they began to criticize him.

Apenas la hube visto, se fue.
Scarcely had I seen her when she left.

In modern Spanish the past anterior is replaced by the *preterite* or, less commonly, the pluperfect:

En cuanto vino, comenzó la reunión.
As soon as she had arrived, the meeting began.

11.3 Progressive or continuous tenses

Like their English counterparts the Spanish progressive tenses are used primarily with action verbs to indicate, for example in the present, that an action *is taking place*.

Spanish progressive tenses contrasted with English usage

1 Unlike in English, Spanish progressive tenses are *not* available to refer to future time: **El sábado llega Angela** (not: ×**está llegando**×) 'Angela is coming on Saturday'. This restriction excludes the future progressive tense – see 11.3.4.

2 The Spanish progressive tenses are *not* used with the verb **ir** 'to go' (except to refer to recurrent events), **llevar** 'to wear', or with verbs stating physical posture: **¿Adónde va Luis?** (not ×**está yendo**×) 'Where is Luis going?', **Ana llevaba puesta una camisa muy bonita** (not ×**estaba llevando**×) 'Ana was wearing a very nice shirt', **Estaban sentados en el sofá** (not ×**estaban sentando**×) 'They were sitting on the sofa'.

11.3.1 *The present progressive*

11.3.1.1 For actions in progress

The present progressive is normally used for actions that are taking place at the present moment:

No puedo hacerlo ahora porque estoy vistiendo a los niños.
I can't do it now because I'm dressing the children.

No podemos ir al parque, está lloviendo.
We can't go to the park, it's raining.

11.3.1.2 For recurrent events

To a lesser extent, the present progressive can be used in sentences that describe recurrent actions:

Estás teniendo mucha suerte este mes.
You're having a lot of luck this month.

Están comprando casas y remodelándolas.
They are buying up houses and doing them up.

11.3.2 The imperfect progressive

This is used in similar ways to the present progressive, but with reference to past time:

Cuando llegué estaban cenando.
When I got there they were having supper.

Se estaban viendo demasiado.
They were seeing too much of each other.

11.3.3 The preterite progressive

This is used primarily when the action is set within a specific time frame (typically indicated by words such as **durante** 'for' and **hasta** 'until'):

La estuve esperando hasta las dos.
I was waiting for her until two o'clock.

11.3.4 The future progressive

This is used to describe an action that *will be* in progress at a certain time in the future or to express supposition about the present:

A estas horas estarán acostando a los niños.
At this time they'll be putting the children to bed.

Note: The conditional progressive can also be used to express supposition, but with reference to the past: **Estarían cenando** 'They must have been having supper'.

11.3.5 The progressive forms of the compound tenses

The perfect and pluperfect progressive tenses are used for actions that *have* or *had* been in progress recently:

(Este mes) he estado haciendo cuentas.
(This month) I've been looking at the finances.

Habían estado buscando casa.
They had been looking for a house.

The future perfect progressive occurs primarily in conjectures:

¿Habrá estado intentando llamar?
Do you think she's been trying to call us?

11.4 Expressions of time with *hacer, desde* and *llevar*

Spanish differs substantially from English in terms of the structures that are employed to say how long *ago* an event took place or how long a situation *has* (or *had*) *been* continuing.

11.4.1 Constructions involving **hacer**

11.4.1.1 Translating 'ago'

Hace (or **hacía** when the main verb is in the pluperfect) + a time phrase, corresponds to English 'ago':

La vi hace tres meses.
I saw her three months ago.

Se habían conocido hacía un par de años.
They had met a couple of years before.

11.4.1.2 *Hace/hacía + que + verb*

This sequence has two meanings. First, it can be used to indicate how much time *has* or *had* elapsed since a past event:

Hace solamente una hora que salió.
It's only an hour since she left.

Hacía solamente dos semanas que se casaron.
It was only two weeks since they got married.

Less commonly **hacer** is found in the future:

El jueves hará un año que nació la niña.
On Thursday it will be a year since the girl was born.

Second, this sequence can be used to refer to something which began in the past and is (or was) still continuing. This is often expressed in English as 'have/has been doing' or 'had been doing'.

141

In this usage Spanish has the *present* tense where English has the perfect, and it has the *imperfect* where English has the pluperfect:

¿Cuánto tiempo hace que la visitas?
How long have you been visiting her?

Hace mucho tiempo que no vienen.
They haven't been coming for a long time.

Hacía dos meses que no lo veían.
They hadn't seen him for two months.

11.4.2 Desde + hace/hacía

Desde combines with **hace/hacía** to refer to something which began in the past and is/was still continuing. Therefore, it offers an alternative to **hace/hacía + que** above:

Trabaja para nosotros desde hace dos años.
He has worked for us for two years.

Estaba aprendiendo español desde hacía un mes.
I had been learning Spanish for a month.

For **que desde** see 12.2.2.1 and for **desde** as a preposition see 21.8.

11.4.3 *Constructions involving* llevar

Routinely in speech, the verb **llevar** is used to indicate how long a situation *has* been continuing (with **llevar** in the present tense) or *had* been continuing (with **llevar** in the imperfect tense).

Llevar is followed by a location phrase, a past participle or a phrase introduced by **como** 'as':

¿Cuánto tiempo llevas aquí?
How long have you been here?

La puerta lleva rota un mes.
The door has been broken a month.

Adriana llevaba dos años como directora del colegio.
Adriana had been the principal of the school for two years.

Llevar also commonly occurs with a *gerund*, but since this cannot be used negatively it is replaced by **sin** + infinitive or one of the patterns in 11.4.1.2 or 11.4.2.

Llevaba dos años viviendo en esta casa.
He had been living in this house for two years.

Llevo muchos años sin jugar al rugby.
I have not played rugby for many years.

Note: An alternative construction in Latin America uses **tener**: **Tengo/Tenía dos años en Panamá** [LA] 'I have/had been in Panama for two years'.

11.5 Verbs like *gustar*

There are a number of verbs whose basic meaning in Spanish may be conveyed in a rather different form in English. For example, **gustar** which is probably the most common of them basically means 'to please', 'to be pleasing' but is used to translate 'to like':

Me gusta caminar.
I like walking.

A mí me gusta, pero tal vez a ti no.
I like it, but maybe you don't.

What is common to all these verbs is that the English subject is represented in Spanish as the indirect object, whereas the English direct object becomes the Spanish subject.

In Spanish the subject may be a noun, an infinitive, a clause or merely 'it' conveyed by the 3rd person of the verb:

Me gustan tus zapatos.
I like your shoes (your shoes are pleasing to me).

Nos gusta cenar temprano.
We like having supper early (having supper early pleases us).

No me gusta que vuelvas tan tarde.
I don't like you coming back so late (the fact that you come back so late doesn't please me).

Nos gusta.
We like it (it pleases us).

Verbs like **gustar** include the following:

(a) Verbs of emotional reaction:

A Sara le encanta tu peinado nuevo.
Sara loves your new hairstyle.

Nos preocupa que no haya venido.
We are worried because he has not come.

Le apasionan los aeromodelos.
He's mad about model planes.

Me molesta que fume.
I don't like him smoking.

(b) Verbs of needing, lacking, remaining:

Nos hace falta consultar el mapa.
We need to look at the map.

Me faltan dos etiquetas.
I am short of two labels.

Me quedan dos.
I have two left.

Nos sobra comida.
We have more than enough food/We have food left over.

(c) Verbs of interest, appreciation and reflection:

Me apetece/provoca [LA] una copa de cava.
I fancy a glass of cava.

¿Qué te parece Carlota?
What do you think of Carlota?

A number of other verbs are similar, in that the main participant appears as the indirect object, but they correspond to impersonal sentences in English where the subject is 'it':

Me tocó pagar.
It was my turn to pay.

No te conviene hacer eso.
It isn't in your interests to do that.

Chapter 12

The subjunctive mood

In modern Spanish, the subjunctive mood is far more alive and less avoidable than in English or even some other Romance languages. Contexts do occur in which the option sometimes exists of choosing between the indicative and the subjunctive in Spanish, but this choice almost always implies a change of meaning.

Whilst there are exceptions to general guidelines, it is possible to establish some key characteristics of the subjunctive mood in Spanish. First, as its name suggests, it occurs most frequently in *sub*ordinate clauses that are *joined* (or at least linked) to a main clause in the indicative mood. Second, whereas the indicative mood affirms actions or states that are already facts, the subjunctive is commonly required in contexts which express hypotheses, future possibilities, uncertainty, doubts, and desires for the future, although this distinction is by no means absolute.

In modern Spanish there are only four tenses of the subjunctive in common use: present, perfect, imperfect and pluperfect (for the forms see Chapter 10).

12.1 Subjunctive in subordinate *que* clauses

The subjunctive occurs most frequently in subordinate clauses, which are typically introduced by **que**. Some item in the main clause (often a verb) will require the verb in the subordinate clause to be in the subjunctive.

This does not of course mean that all subordinate clauses will be in the subjunctive mood. For example, compare **Dudo que vengan** (subjunctive) 'I doubt they will come' with **Sé que vendrán** (indicative) 'I know they will come'.

The subjunctive – key characteristics

1   When the verb in the main clause requires the subjunctive in the subordinate clause, the subjunctive is generally only used if the subject of the main verb is different from that of the subordinate verb:

Quiere que yo venga.
He wants me to come.

When the subjects are the same, typically the infinitive is used:

Quiere venir.
He wants to come.

2   English speakers should note that a very common pattern of use converts an English infinitive construction such as 'I asked him to go yesterday' into a main clause linked to a following subordinate clause by **que**:

Le pedí que se fuera ayer.
(literally: 'I asked that he should go yesterday.')

Similarly **que** + subjunctive may correspond to a gerund construction in English:

Insisto en que lo haga Antonio.
I insist on Antonio doing it.

12.1.1   *Subjunctive after verbs which exert influence upon other persons or things*

This widespread use includes verbs which *request, command* or *order, want* or *desire, propose* or *suggest, permit, allow* or *approve, encourage*, and *cause*.

The influence may also be a negative one through verbs which *avoid, prohibit, prevent* or *forbid*:

Ordenó que la flota zarpara.	He ordered the fleet to set sail.
Quería que lloviera.	I wanted it to rain.
Propongo que se anule el contrato.	I propose that the contract be annulled.

No se puede permitir que termine.	It cannot be permitted to end.
Hay que hacer que cambien de opinión.	We must make them change their mind.
No podemos impedir que ella se vaya.	We can't prevent her from going.

Sometimes the influence may be expressed in Spanish not by a verb but by a phrase such as **el deseo de que** 'the desire that', **la orden de que** 'the order that':

su deseo de que se separaran	her wish that they should separate

For the use of the infinitive in place of **que** + subjunctive, after a small number of verbs (such as **mandar, impedir, permitir**), even though the subject in the main clause is different from that in the subordinate clause, see 17.1.2.

The infinitive is also a common alternative with verbs that exert influence and require the preposition **a** before a following infinitive, such as: **animar a** 'encourage', **ayudar a** 'help', **forzar a** 'force', **obligar a** 'oblige', **invitar a** 'invite', **persuadir a** 'persuade'. The infinitive replaces a clause introduced by **a que** + subjunctive:

Me obligaron a pagarlo. or **Me obligaron a que lo pagara.**	They forced me to pay it.
Les he invitado a venir. or **Les he invitado a que vengan.**	I have invited them to come.

12.1.2 Subjunctive after verbs and phrases expressing doubt, denial or uncertainty

This usage occurs following verbs which specifically mean 'to doubt' or 'to deny':

Dudo que venga el fontanero/plomero [LA].
I doubt whether the plumber will come.

Negó que hubiera ocurrido un error.
He denied that an error had occurred.

However, when **negar** and **dudar** are used negatively they lose their expression of doubt or uncertainty and so are followed by the indicative:

No negó que hubo un error.
He didn't deny there had been a mistake.

Conversely, other verbs and expressions only come to express doubt or uncertainty when used negatively and only then require the subjunctive:

Él no dice que estés equivocado.
He does not say that you are wrong.

No creo que vaya a quedarse contenta.
I don't think she will be pleased.

No es que hayan aceptado la propuesta.
It is not that they have accepted the proposal.

No me parece que sea importante.
It does not seem important to me.

Other phrases that are similar in this respect include:

no está claro que	it is not clear that
no es verdad que	it is not true that
no es seguro que	it is not certain that
no significa que	it does not mean that

Particularly in Latin America, the subjunctive can also be found after phrases which place an alternative limitation on the level of certainty, such as **lo más cierto es que** 'the most likely outcome is that', **casi es seguro que** 'it is almost certain that':

Casi es seguro que renuncie [LA].
It is almost certain that he will give up.

12.1.3 Subjunctive after verbs or phrases which express a feeling or personal opinion

This use of the subjunctive is triggered by phrases with meaning such as 'to be sorry that', 'to be pleased that', 'it is terrific that' or 'it is important that'. There are four basic patterns in Spanish.

(a) The subjunctive is used after **ser/estar** + adjective + **que** (this corresponds to the case in which the main subject in English is impersonal 'it'):

Es aburrido que pongan tanto fútbol en la tele.
It's boring that they have so much football on TV.

Era importante que lo leyeran con cuidado.
It was important that they read it carefully.

This category also includes items such as:

es mejor que	it is better that
está bien/mal que	it is good/bad that
es una pena que	it is a pity that
es una vergüenza que	it is scandalous that
es imprescindible que	it is essential that
es posible/probable que	it is possible/probable that
es curioso/normal/lógico que	it is strange/natural/logical that

Also, impersonal phrases such as:

puede ser que	it may be that
más vale que	it would be better that
hace falta que	it is necessary that

Note that the subjunctive *is not used* after phrases that are factual and do not express a feeling, emotion or opinion:

Está claro/Es obvio que está mintiendo.   It's clear that he's lying.

Compare the negative use of these and similar phrases in 12.1.2.

(b) In the second pattern, **que** + subjunctive follows a verb indicating an emotional response. In this case, the subject in the English main clause is normally expressed in Spanish as an indirect object (see 11.5):

Me gustaría que lo arreglara ahora.   I would like you to fix it now.

Me sorprende que lo hagan tan mal.   I am surprised that they are so bad at doing it.

Other verbs in this category include:

alegrar	to make happy	**enfadar**	to anger
asustar	to frighten	**molestar**	to bother
encantar	to delight		

149

(c) In the third pattern, the subjunctive is used after verbs such as: **esperar** 'to hope', **odiar** 'to hate', **preferir** 'to prefer', **sentir** 'to regret/be sorry', and **temer** 'to fear'. In this case, the subject in the English main clause is also the subject in Spanish:

Espero que apruebe el examen.   I hope he passes the exam.

Siento que haya estado enferma.   I am sorry she has been ill.

(d) In the final pattern, the subjunctive clause follows **de que** rather than just **que**. This occurs after certain verbs used reflexively, such as **alegrarse** 'to be happy' and **sorprenderse** 'to be surprised', as well as **tener miedo** 'to be frightened':

Se sorprendió de que hubiera tanta gente.
He was surprised that there were so many people.

Tendrá miedo de que me haya perdido.
She will be afraid that I have got lost.

12.1.4 Subjunctive after a relative pronoun referring to a negative or unknown antecedent

The subjunctive is used when the relative pronoun introducing a subordinate clause refers back to someone or something in the main clause that does not exist or is not known. In English this occurs in sentences such as 'There is *no one* who knows me as she does' (negative antecedent) and 'Is there *anyone* who knows me as she does?' (unknown antecedent). The antecedent may be a person, thing, idea or place.

12.1.4.1 Negative antecedent

The identification of a negative antecedent is not usually a problem for English-speaking students of Spanish:

No tienen ningún vestido que me guste.
They don't have any dresses that I like.

No conozco a nadie que pueda hacerlo.
I don't know anyone who can do it.

12.1.4.2 Indefinite antecedent

The identification of an unknown antecedent requires speakers of English to make a distinction which is not explicitly indicated in their own language. In the sentence below, for example, both subjunctive **mida** and indicative **mide** (from **medir** 'to measure') are possible, but they have very different implications, although the English translation remains the same:

Lucas quiere subir una montaña que mida/mide más de 3000 metros.
Lucas wants to climb a mountain that is more than 3000 metres high.

The version with subjunctive **mida** states merely that Lucas has an objective, namely to climb a mountain (any mountain) that exceeds 3000 metres in altitude. In other words, the antecedent of the relative pronoun **que** is something that is unknown and this is why the subjunctive is used in the relative clause.

The version with indicative **mide** states that Lucas is intending to climb a particular mountain, which happens to be more than 3000 metres high. In this case, then, the antecedent is known and this is why the indicative is used in the relative clause.

Other examples are:

¿Conoces a algún vecino que me ayude?
Do you know a local who can help me?

Los libros que no tengan cubierta han de ser retirados.
Books which have no cover are to be withdrawn.

Necesito a alguien que limpie la casa.
I need someone to clean the house.

Although the subordinate clause is frequently introduced by the relative pronoun **que**, in this usage it may be introduced by other relatives: **cuyo** 'whose', **como** 'how(ever)', **cuando** 'when(ever)', **cuanto** 'all that', **donde** 'where(ever)', **quien** 'who(ever)', **lo que** 'what(ever)', and **el/la/los/las que** 'which(ever)':

Colócalos como te parezca mejor.
Arrange them as you see fit.

Ven cuando quieras.
Come whenever you want.

Debes buscar un país donde el clima sea templado.
You must find a country where the climate is mild.

Escribe lo que te dé la gana.
Write whatever you want.

Compra el que más te guste.
Buy whichever one you like best.

Relative clauses after *cualquiera, dondequiera, quienquiera*

Spanish has a set of indefinite expressions ending in **-quiera,** of which only **cualquiera** 'whatever/whichever', **dondequiera** 'wherever' and **quienquiera** 'whoever' have any currency outside literary contexts.

The remaining forms **comoquiera** 'however' and **cuandoquiera** 'whenever' are now replaced by **como** and **cuando** (see 12.1.4.2).

Relative clauses following **cualquiera** (used as a pronoun) and **quienquiera** are invariably in the subjunctive.

Relative clauses following **dondequiera** will be in the *indicative* if the reference is to past or habitual occurrences, and in the *subjunctive* if the reference is to unknown or future occurrences and locations:

> **quienquiera que sea responsable**
> whoever is/may be to blame

> **cualquiera que sea su decisión**
> whatever his decision is/may be

> **dondequiera que usted se encuentre**
> wherever you are/may be

> **dondequiera que ella iba**
> wherever she went

Relative clauses after *por (muy)* and *por mucho*

The phrases **por (muy)** + adjective or adverb and **por** + **mucho/a/os/as** (or **más**) + noun or verb can be used with a relative clause to convey the idea expressed in English by 'however (much/many)' + clause, e.g. 'However much I asked him'.

In Spanish this construction generally takes the *subjunctive* if the reference is to present or future situations and the *indicative* if the reference is to habitual or past events:

por (muy) caro que sea	however expensive it is
por mucho que grites	however much you shout
por mucho que estudió	however hard he studied
por muchos trofeos que ganen	however many cups they win

12.2 Subjunctive required by certain subordinating conjunctions

The *subjunctive* is required by some subordinating conjunctions, when an action or state has not yet occurred or is denied in some way. Conversely, if the action or state is presented as something that has already occurred or that is factual, the *indicative* mood is likely to be used.

Some types of conjunction always require the subjunctive in a following clause. With others, both the subjunctive and the indicative are possible, although the use of one mood rather than the other may change the meaning of the conjunction.

12.2.1 Conjunctions always followed by the subjunctive

12.2.1.1 Conjunctions expressing purpose

The most common conjunction of this type is **para que** 'so that', but **a fin de que**, **con el objeto de que** and **con el propósito de que** (all meaning 'in order that') will also be encountered:

Lo pondré aquí para que nadie lo robe.
I will put it here so that no will steal it.

12.2.1.2 Conjunctions indicating proviso

The two most common are **con tal (de) que** 'provided that' and **a condición de que** 'on condition that':

Lo explicaré de nuevo con tal (de) que todos se callen.
I shall explain it again provided that everyone keeps quiet.

Note: The conjunction **siempre que** requires the subjunctive when it means 'provided that': **siempre que no llueva** 'provided it doesn't rain'. However, with the indicative it means 'whenever', see 12.2.2.1.

12.2.1.3 Conjunctions meaning 'unless'

The main ones are **a no ser que** and **a menos que**:

No vamos a poder moverlo a no ser que alguien nos ayude.
We aren't going to be able to move it unless someone helps us.

Notes: **Excepto que** and **salvo que** can also mean 'unless', in which case they take the subjunctive: **salvo que él insista** 'unless he insists'. However, when they mean 'except for the fact that' they take the indicative: **Es un buen muchacho salvo que miente** 'He is a good lad except that he tells lies'.

12.2.1.4 *Sin que* 'without'

Tienes que entrar sin que nadie te vea.
You have to go in without anyone seeing you.

Note: In negative sentences **sin que** means 'unless': **¡No lo mande sin que se firme!** 'Do not send it unless someone signs it!'.

12.2.1.5 Conjunctions expressing supposition

The most common of these is **en caso de que** 'in case', athough (**en el**) **supuesto que** 'supposing that' may also be encountered in literary or formal contexts:

Sal temprano en caso de que haya un atasco.
Leave early in case there is a traffic jam.

Note: **Suponiendo que** expresses supposition, with a *subjunctive* when stating a hypothesis: **suponiendo que lleguen a tiempo** 'assuming they arrive in time', and with an *indicative* when accepting something as fact: **suponiendo que ha sido él** 'assuming it was him'.

12.2.1.6 *Antes (de) que* 'before'

This is the only common temporal conjunction that is *always* followed by the subjunctive, whatever the tense in the main clause:

Pagó el impuesto mucho antes (de) que fuese necesario.
He paid the tax long before it was necessary.

12.2.2 *Conjunctions that are followed by the subjunctive or the indicative*

12.2.2.1 Temporal conjunctions

Examples of common temporal conjunctions are:

a medida que	as	**en cuanto**	as soon as
cuando	when	**hasta que**	until

desde que	since	**siempre que**	whenever
después (de) que	after	**una vez (que)**	once

With the exception of **antes (de) que** (see 12.2.1.6), the subjunctive is only used when the subordinate verb refers to future time:

Siguieron luchando hasta que se rindieron los enemigos.
They continued to fight until their enemies surrendered.

Debemos seguir luchando hasta que nuestros enemigos se rindan.
We must continue fighting until our enemies surrender.

Cuando sale el equipo les dan una calurosa bienvenida.
Whenever the team comes out they give them a warm welcome.

Cuando salga el equipo les darán una calurosa bienvenida.
When the team comes out they will give them a warm welcome.

No me ha hablado desde que llegó.
He has not spoken to me since he arrived.

Una vez que llegue, vamos a discutirlo.
Once he arrives we will discuss it.

Notes:
1 The conjunction **mientras** 'while/as long as' represents an exception to the general rule concerning temporal conjunctions. It is routinely used with the indicative even when the subordinate verb refers to future time, especially when it cannot be translated by 'as long as': **Voy a estudiar mientras duermes al niño** 'I'm going to study while you get the baby off to sleep'. On the other hand, **mientras** does call for the subjunctive when 'while' and 'as long as' are alternative translations: **Mientras viva no va a abdicar la corona** 'As long as she lives she will not give up the crown'. When it refers to past events **mientras** is, of course, followed by an indicative tense.

2 After **esperar** and **aguardar** 'to wait', **a que** is commonly used instead of **hasta que** when the subjunctive is required: **¡Espere a que se abra el banco!** 'Wait until the bank opens!'

 12.2.2.2 Concessive conjunctions

Concessive conjunctions are those that mean 'although/even if'. By far the most common concessive conjunction is **aunque**. This usually takes the *indicative* if the clause that follows is factually true (when English uses 'although') and it takes the *subjunctive* when the clause that follows is hypothetical (when English uses 'even if').

Le pagan poco, aunque él nunca se queja.
They don't pay him very much, although he never complains.

Vamos a nadar aunque llueva.
We are going to swim even if it rains.

No iría a su fiesta aunque él me invitara personalmente.
I wouldn't go to his party even if he invited me personally.

However, like English 'even if', **aunque** + subjunctive can also be factual in cases when something is expressed as being contrary to expectation:

Tiene que pensar en ello aunque sea todavía muy joven.
He has to start to think about it, even if he is still very young.

Notes:
1 **A pesar de que** 'despite the fact that' can be used in a concessive sense, in which case it takes the subjunctive with the meaning 'even if': **No aceptaría la resolución a pesar de que la mayoría la adoptara** 'He would not accept the resolution even if the majority adopted it'.

2 There are several other concessive conjunctions in Spanish, namely **aun cuando, si bien** and the literary **así** and **siquiera**, which generally follow the usage of **aunque**.

| 12.2.2.3 | Conjunctions indicating purpose and result |

Items like **de manera/modo/forma que** 'in order that', 'with the result that' indicate result when used with the *indicative* and they express purpose (like **para que** in 12.2.1.1) when they are followed by the *subjunctive*:

¡Escóndelo en el cajón de modo que nadie lo descubra!
Hide it in the drawer in order that/so that no one will find it!

Lo escondió en el cajón de modo que nadie lo descubrió.
He hid it in the drawer with the result that no one found it.

| 12.2.2.4 | Conditional conjunctions |

The most common conditional conjunction is **si** 'if', which is discussed in Chapter 13.

However **como**, which means 'as' when followed by the indicative, is conditional when followed by the subjunctive:

Como no salgamos en los próximos cinco minutos vamos a perder el avión.
If we don't leave in the next five minutes we're going to miss the flight.

|12.2.2.5| Conjunctions indicating cause

The most common of these is **porque** 'because'. This takes the indicative unless it is negated:

Se quejó porque la habitación estaba sucia.
He complained because the room was dirty.

No se quejó porque la habitación estuviera sucia, sino porque no había agua caliente en la ducha.
He didn't complain because the room was dirty, but because there was no hot water in the shower.

Note: **Porque** can follow a negated clause without being negated itself. In this case **porque** takes the indicative, in accordance with the general rule: **No me cae bien porque es muy cínico** 'I don't like him because he is very cynical'.

12.3 Subjunctive in main clauses

As explained above, the subjunctive mainly occurs in subordinate clauses, with the following exceptions.

For the subjunctive to express commands, see 19.2, 19.3.3.

|12.3.1| *Subjunctive after words meaning 'perhaps'*

In present and past time, after **tal vez** (**talvez** [LA]), **quizá(s)** and **posiblemente**, the choice of the subjunctive rather than the indicative is made to express what is considered to be a less likely possibility.

With regard to future time, the present subjunctive is the most common choice, although the future indicative (never the present) is also found:

Tal vez no ha/haya pensado en ir.
Maybe he has not thought of going.

Quizás al final se pongan/se pondrán de acuerdo.
Perhaps in the end they will agree.

A lo mejor 'perhaps' is very common in speech and is followed by the *indicative*.

Acaso is more formal in use, rare in speech and usually followed by the *subjunctive*.

Subjunctive used to exclaim a wish

With the meaning of 'if only' or 'I wish', the subjunctive is used after **ojalá**
(**que**). Use of the imperfect subjunctive implies the wish is less likely to be
fulfilled:

¡Ojalá que encuentres a tu amiga!	I hope you find your friend.
¡Ojalá viniera!	If only he would come!

The phrase **quién** + imperfect subjunctive can be used to express envy:

¡Quién tuviera su suerte!	I wish I had their luck!

Subjunctive used in set phrases

Some common phrases are formed with the subjunctive, such as:

o sea que	in other words
que yo sepa/recuerde	as far as I know/remember

There are also a number of constructions in which the verb is repeated:

sea lo que sea	whatever it may be
venga lo que venga	come what may
diga lo que diga	whatever he/she says
pase lo que pase	whatever happens
cueste lo cueste	whatever it costs
quieras o no (quieras)	whether you are willing or not

12.4 **The sequence of tenses – which subjunctive tense to use**

Since there are fewer subjunctive tenses than indicatives, it is useful to
establish the most common distribution of these fewer tenses with their
indicative counterparts. At best, this is a statement of common patterns in
the sequence of tenses rather than a declaration of fixed rules that must
always be followed.

Additional
uses of the
-*ra* form of
the imperfect
subjunctive

Verb in main clause	Subjunctive in subordinate clause
present, future, perfect indicative	present, perfect
imperfect, preterite, conditional, pluperfect indicative	imperfect, pluperfect
any form of command	present

Me sorprende que haya cancelado.
I am surprised that he has cancelled.

No voy a sugerir que sea así.
I will not suggest that it may be so.

Le dije que no me molestara más.
I told her to stop bothering me.

¡Pídele que salga!
Ask him to leave!

Obviously, the above patterns are not fixed, since contexts occur in which, for example, a present tense must by followed by a past tense and vice versa, in order to convey the correct meaning.

Es una pena que estuvieras enfermo.
It is a pity that you were ill.

¿Qué hizo para que digas eso?
What did he do that makes you say that?

12.5 Additional uses of the -*ra* form of the imperfect subjunctive

For the use of the -**ra** form as an alternative to the conditional tense in the case of the verbs **querer** 'to want', **deber** 'to have to' and **poder** 'to be able to', see Chapter 16.

For the use of **hubiera** + past participle in place of the conditional perfect tense, see 13.1.2.2 (note 2).

Imperfect subjunctive for preterite or pluperfect indicative

The -ra form of the imperfect subjunctive is sometimes used in place of a past indicative tense. This occurs primarily in the press and in literary contexts in Spain, but more widely in Latin America.

Two notable instances are (i) in relative clauses and (ii) after temporal conjunctions, especially **después (de) que** 'after', **luego que** 'as soon as' and **desde que** 'since':

La iniciativa vino en una carta que dirigiera al presidente.
The initiative came in a letter he had sent to the president.

Volvió a la que fuera su casa antes del temblor.
She returned to what had been her house before the earthquake.

Realizó cambios fundamentales desde que fuera elegido. [LA]
He carried out fundamental changes after his election.

12.6 The future subjunctive

In marked contrast with modern Portuguese, the future subjunctive in Spanish is virtually obsolete and unlikely ever to be used by foreign speakers.

It might be encountered in the occasional outmoded phrase such as **sea lo que fuere** 'whatever it might be' and **venga lo que viniere** 'come what may'.

It is found in legal, ecclesiastical or other forms of official written language, and possibly even in journalistic style in some parts of Latin America.

Chapter 13

Conditional clauses

A conditional clause is one that refers to an event (often hypothetical) on which something else depends. For example, in the sentence 'If Jones arrives on time we will go to the theatre', the conditional clause 'if Jones arrives on time' refers to a hypothetical event on which another possible event, namely going to the theatre (in the main clause), is dependent.

Typically, but not always, conditional clauses are introduced by a word meaning 'if', which in Spanish is **si**.

In Spanish, a conditional clause introduced by **si** may or may not require the subjunctive mood. In general, if the event referred to in the si-clause is contrary to fact or unlikely (what is called a 'closed condition'), then the subjunctive is used. If on the other hand the statement in the si-clause is an open possibility ('an open condition'), then the mood is indicative.

13.1 Use of the subjunctive after *si*

13.1.1 Clauses requiring the pluperfect subjunctive

This is used in the conditional clause when the condition has *not* been fulfilled in the past, e.g. '*If I had been rich* (but I wasn't) I would have given you the money'. In the main clause either the conditional tense or the conditional perfect tense is used:

Si no hubieras dejado la ventana abierta la habitación no estaría llena de mosquitos.
If you hadn't left the window open the room wouldn't be full of mosquitoes.

Si nos hubiera consultado, habría sido posible discutirlo con él.
If he had consulted us, it would have been possible to discuss it with him.

13.1.2 Clauses requiring the imperfect subjunctive

13.1.2.1

This is used when the condition is not fulfilled in present time, e.g. 'If I had money (but I haven't) I would buy it'. The conditional tense is used in the main clause:

Estaría más a gusto si hiciera mejor tiempo.
I would be happier if the weather was better.

Si la casa fuera más grande podríamos tener invitados.
If the house were bigger we could have friends to stay.

13.1.2.2

The imperfect subjunctive is also used in conditional clauses that, without actually being contrary to fact, refer to future events considered unlikely or improbable:

¿Qué harías si te ofrecieran el puesto?
What would you do if they offered you the job?

Notes:

1 On occasions the English conditional does not contain the word 'if', whereas the Spanish equivalent usually would: **Si se hubiera comportado de la manera apropiada, se le habría admitido** 'Had he behaved properly (i.e. if he had behaved properly), he would have been admitted'.

2 It is possible to use the -ra form (but not the -se form) of the pluperfect subjunctive in the main clause of conditional sentences: **Si hubieran tenido más cuidado no hubiera pasado lo que pasó** 'If they had been more careful what did happen wouldn't have happened'.

3 In speech the conditional tense in a main clause is often replaced by the imperfect tense: **Pues yo me iba (si pudiera)** 'Well I would go (if I could)'.

Conditional clauses – points to remember

1 The *only* tenses of the subjunctive which can be used in the si-clause are the imperfect and the pluperfect.

2 The -ra form of the imperfect subjunctive is nowadays commoner than the -se form.

3 A present or perfect subjunctive after si is almost certain to be incorrect. The one rare exception is in formal style, primarily in

Latin America, after **no saber: No sé si sea cierto** [LA] for **No sé
si es cierto** 'I do not know if it is true'.

4   **Como si** 'as if' is always followed by the imperfect or pluperfect
subjunctive: **Gasta dinero como si fuera millonario** 'He spends
money as though he were a millionaire'.

5   If the words 'were to' occur in an English sentence (or can be
inserted), as in 'If they offered more/were to offer more, would
you sell?', this is an indication that it is a closed condition
requiring an imperfect subjunctive: **Si ofrecieran más, ¿venderías?**

13.2   Indicative tenses after *si*

In conditional clauses other than those discussed in 13.1, indicative tenses
are used:

Si hablo mucho, me canso.	If I speak a lot, I get tired.
Si llegas temprano, iremos juntos.	If you arrive early, we shall go together.
Si se reían, no estaban enfadados.	If they were laughing, they weren't angry.

This includes conditional clauses that appear in reported speech referring
to the past, where the original words expressed an open condition, e.g. 'He
stated that he would help me if it was possible'. The original words were,
'I will help you if it is possible' (i.e. **Te ayudaré si es posible**) and so the
report of that statement is translated using the indicative: **Me afirmó que
me ayudaría si era posible.** Other examples:

Prometió que lo devolvería si todavía lo tenía.
He promised he would return it if he still had it.

Dijo que limpiaría la cocina si yo pasaba la aspiradora.
He said he would clean the kitchen if I vacuumed the floor.

Future and conditional tenses after *si*

Generally these only occur after **si** when it can be translated as
'whether' in English: **No sé si iré al trabajo** 'I don't know if/whether
I'll go to work', **No sabía si ella vendría** 'I didn't know if/whether
she would come'.

13.3 **Conditional sentences without *si***

Conditional sentences in Spanish can be constructed without the use of **si**.

For the use of **de** + infinitive in a conditional sense, see 17.2.5.2. For **como** + the subjunctive in a conditional sense, see 12.2.2.4.

Chapter 14

Reflexive verbs

A reflexive verb is one that is used with an object pronoun which refers back to the verb's subject. In English, the object pronoun of a reflexive verb has the suffix '-self' or '-selves', e.g. 'I cut myself', 'they cut themselves'.

For reflexive verbs with passive meaning, see 15.2.

14.1 Formation of reflexive verbs

In Spanish, reflexive verbs are formed by using the appropriate reflexive pronouns (see 8.4), which change according to the subject of the verb as in the following example of the present tense of **lavarse** 'to wash':

me lavo	I wash myself	**nos lavamos**	we wash ourselves
te lavas	you wash yourself	**os laváis** [SP]	you wash yourselves
(vos) te lavás [LA]	you wash yourself	**se lavan**	they wash themselves
se lava	he/she/it washes him/her/itself	**(ustedes) se lavan**	you wash yourselves
(usted) se lava	you wash yourself		

The above pattern is followed for all tenses of the verb but, like other weak pronouns, reflexive pronouns follow and are attached to infinitives, gerunds and positive commands (see 8.5).

Note: In contrast with English, which permits the omission of the pronoun, e.g. 'I washed before dinner', the pronoun cannot be omitted in Spanish: **Me lavé antes de cenar.**

14.2 Reflexive verbs with a reflexive meaning

In some cases, though by no means always, the action of a reflexive verb reflects back on to its subject. This genuinely 'reflexive' usage arises in the following instances.

(a) The reflexive pronoun as the direct object of the reflexive verb:

Usted tendrá que cuidarse.	You will have to look after yourself.
Podía verse en el espejo.	She could see herself in the mirror.

(b) The reflexive pronoun as the indirect object of the reflexive verb:

Typically the indirect object pronoun identifies the person interested in or affected by the action of the verb (as in 'I bought *myself* several books' or 'I bought several books *for myself*'):

Ayer nos compramos un perrito.	Yesterday we bought ourselves a puppy.
Se ha conseguido un empleo.	He has found himself a job.

In addition, the reflexive pronoun as an indirect object is commonly found in constructions where English has a possessive adjective, especially when referring to parts of the body or to clothing (see also 5.5):

Andrea se ha torcido el tobillo.	Andrea has twisted her ankle.

14.3 Reflexive verbs with a reciprocal meaning

This refers to persons acting upon one another and corresponds to English 'each other' or 'one another'. It necessarily only occurs with verbs used in the plural:

Las dos profesoras se odian.	The two teachers hate each other.
Nos saludamos al salir de la iglesia.	We greeted one another as we came out of the church.

Since the true reflexive and the reciprocal forms are identical in Spanish, ambiguity may occur in some contexts, e.g. **Se felicitaron** could mean 'They congratulated themselves' or 'They congratulated one another'. To avoid confusion, any of the following phrases or words may be added to a reflexive verb: **el uno al otro** (literally: 'one to the other'), **(los) unos a (los) otros** (literally: 'some to others') or **mutuamente** 'mutually':

> **Nos presentamos el uno al otro.**
> We introduced ourselves to each other.

> **Los jugadores se felicitaron unos a otros.**
> The players congratulated one another.

14.4 Reflexives with an indirect object pronoun

A number of common verbs are frequently used reflexively in the *3rd person* together with an indirect object. This creates the pattern se + an indirect object that corresponds to the English subject. It is often used for unplanned or unexpected actions:

> **Se le cayeron las botellas que llevaba.**
> He dropped the bottles he was carrying.

> **Se nos ha agotado el aceite.**
> We've run out of oil.

> **Se me han perdido los guantes.**
> I've lost my gloves.

Other verbs that can be used in this way include:

ocurrirse	to occur to	**olvidarse**	to forget
romperse	to break		

The indirect object in this construction can also be used to refer to someone who is an interested party in an event, without actually being the English subject:

> **Se le llenaron los ojos de lágrimas.**
> Her eyes filled with tears.

> **Se te ha subido la temperatura.**
> Your temperature has risen.

Note: This construction can be an alternative to the usual reflexive construction for parts of the body discussed in 14.2(b). For example, 'I have twisted my ankle' could be translated by either **Me he torcido el tobillo**, in which **yo** (not explicitly mentioned) is the subject of the verb, or **Se me ha torcido el tobillo**, in which case the subject of the verb is **el tobillo**.

14.5 Se as an indefinite subject

The reflexive pronoun **se** can be used as an indefinite or impersonal subject equivalent to English 'one', 'we', 'they', 'you', 'people'. The Spanish verb is always *3rd person singular* (see also 15.2.3):

Se cena muy tarde en España.	People have dinner late in Spain.
Se cierra los lunes.	We close on Mondays.
¿Se puede pasar?	Can we come in?

Note: If the Spanish verb is already reflexive, the indefinite subject must be introduced as **uno/a**: **Uno se aburre de leer libros largos** 'One gets tired of reading long books'.

14.6 Reflexive verbs 'to get/have something done'

With a few verbs the reflexive can be used to express the idea of getting something done:

Quiero cortarme el pelo.	I want to get my hair cut.
Tuvo que ir a Francia para operarse.	He had to go to France to have an operation.

14.7 Verbs reflexive in form but not in meaning

Some of the most common are:

abstenerse de hacer	to abstain from doing
arrepentirse de hacer algo	to regret doing
atreverse a hacer	to dare to do
(com)portarse	to behave
constiparse	to catch a cold [SP], to become constipated [LA]
enfermarse [LA]	to fall ill
fugarse	to escape/run away
jactarse de	to boast about
quejarse de	to complain about
Me abstuve de votar.	I abstained from voting.
Se quejaron del mal servicio.	They complained about the bad service.

Transitive
verbs used
reflexively
with
intransitive
meaning

14.8 Transitive verbs used reflexively with intransitive meaning

Verbs commonly used transitively (i.e. with a direct object) are also often found in reflexive form without an object (i.e. are used intransitively). Some of the most frequently used such verbs are discussed below, grouped according to their meaning.

14.8.1 Change-of-state verbs

In their reflexive form, these verbs convey the idea of a change of state (often corresponding to English 'to become', 'to get', 'to go'):

Se asustan con el ruido de los animales.
They get frightened by the sound of animals.

En Canadá los lagos se hielan en invierno.
In Canada the lakes become frozen in winter.

La ropa todavía no se ha secado.
The clothes still haven't dried.

See similar verbs in Table 14.1.

14.8.2 Reflexive verbs describing what happens to the subject

Particularly when the subject is inanimate, a reflexive verb formed from a transitive verb states what happens to the subject. English can express this as 'get . . .' or 'got . . .':

Se hundieron las ruedas en el barro.
The wheels sank into/got stuck in the mud.

La comida se está quemando.
The food is burning/getting burned.

Al sacarlo, el vaso se rompió.
As it was taken out, the glass broke/got broken.

Las luces se apagan a medianoche.
The lights are/get switched off at midnight.

Table 14.1 Common reflexive change-of-state verbs

Transitive verb	Reflexive/Intransitive verb
aburrir to bore	**aburrirse** to get bored
admirar to admire	**admirarse** to be surprised
alegrar to make happy	**alegrarse** to become happy
asombrar to amaze	**asombrarse** to be amazed
asustar to frighten	**asustarse** to get frightened
casar to marry (off)	**casarse** to get married
dormir to put to sleep	**dormirse** to go to sleep
enfadar/enojar to anger	**enfadarse/enojarse** to get angry
entristecer to sadden	**entristecerse** to be saddened
fundir to melt	**fundirse** become thawed
helar to freeze	**helarse** to freeze (up)/(over)
mojar to make wet	**mojarse** to get wet
molestar to upset	**molestarse** to get upset
ofender to offend	**ofenderse** to take offence
preocupar to worry	**preocuparse** to be(come) worried
secar to dry	**secarse** to dry/become dry
tranquilizar to calm/quieten	**tranquilizarse** to calm down

14.8.3 | *Reflexive verbs of movement*

Some common transitive verbs, most expressing movement or motion, have reflexive forms which are used intransitively:

Al oírlo se retiró.   When he heard it he backed off.

See similar verbs in Table 14.2.

Note: **Volverse** 'to turn round' is similar to the verbs in Table 14.2, except that the non-reflexive form is already intransitive, with the meaning 'to return'. Parts of Latin America use **regresarse** or **devolverse** 'to return'.

Table 14.2 Some reflexive verbs of movement

Transitive verb	Reflexive/Intransitive verb
acercar to bring closer	**acercarse** to approach
alejar to move away	**alejarse** to go away
meter to put	**meterse** to meddle in
mover to move (something)	**moverse** to move
parar to (bring to a) stop	**pararse** to stop, to stand up [LA]
retirar to withdraw (something)	**retirarse** to back away, withdraw, retire
sentar to seat	**sentarse** to sit down

14.8.4 *Reflexive verbs for daily routines*

The reflexive forms of a number of otherwise transitive verbs are used for key daily routines:

acostarse	to go to bed	**levantarse**	to get up
afeitarse	to shave	**vestirse**	to get dressed
despertarse	to wake up		

¡Venga, vístete!   Come on, get dressed!

14.9   Verbs of becoming

The main verbs of becoming are all reflexive.

Convertirse 'to turn into' is used with nouns only. **Hacerse** 'to become' implies deliberate effort on the part of the subject. **Ponerse** 'to get' is used with adjectives describing temporary states. **Quedarse** 'to go' is common with certain disability adjectives and also some past participles, while **volverse** 'to become' is used principally with psychological adjectives:

Se está convirtiendo en una pesadilla.   It's turning into a nightmare.

Se ha hecho millonaria.   She's become a millionaire.

ponerse enfadado/gordo/ nublado	to get angry/fat/cloudy
quedarse ciego/sordo/dormido	to go blind/deaf, to fall asleep
Andrés se ha vuelto muy antipático.	Andrés has become very unfriendly.

14.10 Emphatic reflexive verbs

14.10.1

In some cases, making a verb reflexive produces a subtle difference in meaning that can be fully understood only after experience and careful study. The reflexive form tends to stress the suddenness or unexpectedness of the action, implies greater deliberateness on the part of the subject, or simply is more emphatic.

Reflexive verbs in this category may be transitive or intransitive:

Caer 'to fall'

Caerse 'to fall down/off', 'fall over'

La lluvia cayó todo el día.	The rain fell all day.
Al oírlo se cayó de la silla.	When he heard it he fell off his chair.

Bajar 'to go down'

Bajarse 'to get down/off', 'bend down'

Bajaba la escalera.	He was going downstairs.
(Me) bajo en la próxima esquina.	I'm getting off at the next corner.
Tienes que bajarte para verlo.	You must bend down to see it.

Dejar 'to leave/put'

Dejarse 'to leave (behind)'

¡Déjalo aquí!	Leave it here!
Me dejé el libro en el metro.	I left the book on the metro.

Despedir 'to see off', 'dismiss'

Despedirse (de) 'to say goodbye (to)'

Despidió a su hija en la estación.

She saw her daughter off at the station.

Nunca llegué a despedirme de ella.

I never got to say goodbye to her.

Estar 'to be'

Estarse 'to be' (in commands)

Estoy en Granada.

I am in Granada.

¡Estate quieto!

Be still!

Imaginar 'to imagine', 'envisage'

Imaginarse 'to imagine', 'suppose'

Imagínala con suelos de madera.

Imagine it with wooden floors.

Me imagino que sí.

I suppose so.

Ir 'to go'

Irse 'to go away'

También fueron Ana y Nicolás a la fiesta.

Ana and Nicholas also went to the party.

Ya se habían ido los muchachos.

The boys had already gone.

Llevar 'to take/carry'

Llevarse 'to take away'

Han llevado el perro al veterinario.

They have taken the dog to the vet.

Tras el ataque se llevaron un botín enorme.

After the attack they carried off an enormous booty.

Marchar 'to march'

Marcharse 'to leave/go away'

El regimiento marcha a paso lento.

The regiment marches at a slow pace.

Nos marchamos.

We are leaving.

Morir 'to die' (often accidental)

Morirse 'to die' (figurative or more emphatic)

Murieron debido a una serie de errores.	They died due to a series of errors.
Me muero si lo ven.	I'll die if they see it.
¡No me digas que se ha muerto!	Don't tell me that he has died!

Negar 'to deny'

Negarse (a) 'to refuse (to)'

Valle lo niega todo.	Valle denies everything.
Se niegan a quedar con nosotros.	They refuse to meet us.

Parecer 'to seem/appear'

Parecerse a 'to look like'

Parece estar vivo.	He seems/appears to be alive.
Martín se parece a Antonio.	Martín looks like Antonio.

Quedar 'to remain' (see also 11.5(b))

Quedarse 'to stay (on)' (see also 14.9)

Esto no puede quedar así.	This can't remain like this.
Decidió quedarse otro mes.	She decided to stay on another month.

Saber 'to know'

Saberse 'to know', 'be able to recall'

No sé quien lo ha roto.	I don't know who broke it.
Se sabe los nombres de todos los jugadores.	She knows the names of all the players.

Salir 'to leave/go out', 'come out'

Salirse 'to come out/off', 'leak'

Acaba de salir la segunda edición.	The second edition has just come out.

El avión se salió de la pista.	The plane came off the runway.	Emphatic reflexive verbs
Si abres el grifo, ¿sale agua?	If you turn on the tap/faucet, does any water come out? (normal)	
Se sale el agua de la cisterna.	Water is leaking from the tank. (unexpected)	

Subir 'to go up', 'rise'

Subirse 'to get in/on', 'climb on to'

Hay que subir a pie.	You have to go up on foot.
(Nos) subimos al tren en Córdoba.	We got on to the train in Córdoba.
Ignacio se subió al tejado.	Ignacio went on to the roof.

In the case of **callarse** 'to be quiet' and **reírse** 'to laugh' the non-reflexive form is used primarily as an infinitive following another verb:

¡No me mandes callar!	Don't tell me to be quiet!
¡Cállate!	Be quiet!
No me hagas reír.	Don't make me laugh.
Miguel se ríe de todos.	Miguel laughs at everyone.

14.10.2

This emphatic use of the reflexive pronoun is especially common with verbs of consumption (eating and drinking). The effect in this case is to stress quantity or speed:

| Se lo bebió de un trago. | He drank it in one gulp. |
| ¡Te has zampado el paquete entero! | You've guzzled the entire packet! |

Chapter 15

Passive constructions

In general, a passive construction is created when the object of an active construction becomes the subject of the passive verb. What was the subject of the active verb (if mentioned) is now linked to the passive verb by a preposition (commonly 'by' in English and **por** in Spanish):

Active			Passive		
Subject	Verb	Object	Subject	Verb	'by'
Mary	wrote	the book	The book	was written	by Mary
Everyone	loves	John	John	is loved	by everyone
(no subject)	posted	the letters	The letters	have been posted	(no 'by' phrase)

Although passive constructions such as those above can readily be transposed into Spanish, in practice Spanish frequently replaces passives with alternatives, see 15.2.

15.1 Ser and *estar* with the past participle

In order to understand the passive in Spanish, it is essential to be able to distinguish between the use of **estar** and **ser** with the past participle.

15.1.1 Estar *with a past participle*

Estar with a past participle indicates a *state* or a *condition*, often the end result or consequence of something that has taken place:

Cuando llegamos la puerta estaba abierta.
When we arrived the door was open.

Las entradas ya estaban vendidas.
The seats were already sold.

15.1.2 Ser *with a past participle*

Ser with a past participle focuses on an *action*, and refers to something being done. It forms the true passive construction, comparable with English 'is/was done (by)'. This construction should be used when the sentence reports the agent or 'doer' by whom something is done:

Cuando llegamos la puerta fue abierta por una criada.
When we arrived the door was opened by a maid.

Las entradas fueron vendidas antes de que llegáramos.
The seats were sold before we arrived.

Note: In English it is possible to create a passive construction in which the subject corresponds to an indirect object in the corresponding active sentence, e.g. 'Mary was awarded a scholarship' (compare active 'They awarded a scholarship to Mary'). A true passive construction in Spanish using **ser** is not possible in this instance. See 15.2.2 and 15.2.3.

15.2 Alternatives to passive constructions

Although passive constructions with **ser** are common in formal written and spoken Spanish, and in newspapers, they are sometimes over-used by English students who neglect a number of equivalent constructions more commonly employed by native speakers in certain contexts.

Typically, these are: (i) cases where a specific agent or 'doer' of an action is not expressed, (ii) in less formal written language, and (iii) in everyday speech.

The use of *ser* and *estar* with the past participle

1   For further clarification, compare the following examples of
    passive actions and states:

Passive action	State
Fui detenido.	**Estaba detenido.**
I was detained (i.e. placed under arrest).	I was detained (i.e. under arrest).
El informe fue preparado por mí.	**El informe está preparado.**
The report was prepared by me.	The report is prepared (i.e. is ready).

2   In common with other past participles, **sido** and **estado** are
    invariable when dependent on any form of **haber**. However, past
    participles *always* agree in number and gender when dependent
    upon **ser** or **estar**. This results in patterns such as the following.
    Agreements are underlined:

La lección había sido explicad͟a bien.	The lesson had been well explained.
Los textos han sido discutid͟os.	The texts have been discussed.

3   All tenses of **ser** are possible in passive constructions, although
    the present and imperfect tenses are rare except for sustained
    and repeated actions: **Las cuentas son pagadas diariamente** 'The
    accounts are paid every day'. This use is, however, growing for
    comments and photo captions in newspapers, e.g. **La capa (de
    petróleo) es avistada desde el avión** 'The (oil) slick is sighted
    from the plane'.

4   The agent or 'doer' of the passive voice (i.e. the person or thing
    'by whom' or 'by which' something is done) is nowadays usually
    introduced by **por**. However, **de** is found after certain past
    participles, particularly when they have an adjectival function:
    rodeado de 'surrounded by', **seguido de** 'followed by',
    acompañado de 'accompanied by', **cubierto de** 'covered with',
    forrado de 'lined with', **adornado de** 'adorned with': **Enviar el
    artículo acompañado de su CV** 'Send the article with your CV'.

15.2.1 Passive sentences whose subject is not a person

Particularly when the subject is not a person, the Spanish verb is used reflexively with se, and agrees with its subject:

Se construyó la casa en diez meses.
The house was built in ten months.

Se podan las rosas en primavera.
Roses are pruned in spring.

Note: Although it is sometimes found, it is considered incorrect to use the above construction with **por** to introduce an agent or 'doer', e.g. ×La casa se compró por los Martínez×. Instead, use a true passive construction as in 15.1.2: **La casa fue comprada por los Martínez** 'The house was bought by the Martínezes'.

15.2.2 Passive sentences involving an indirect object

In cases where an indirect object is involved, Spanish uses a reflexive construction. As in 15.2.1, the Spanish verb is used reflexively in the 3rd person with se, and agrees with its subject:

Se le concedió a María una beca.
María was awarded a scholarship.

Se le devolverán las muestras.
The samples will be returned to him.

15.2.3 Passive sentences whose subject is a person

A special use of the reflexive pronoun se is often found in cases where the subject of the sentence in English is a person. The reason is that the use of se as in 15.2.1, but with a personal subject, can be interpreted as having a true reflexive or reciprocal meaning (see 14.2 and 14.3), rather than an intended passive sense, e.g. **se miran** 'they look at themselves' or 'one another'.

To avoid this, the verb is still used with se but in the *3rd person singular* only. Persons being acted upon are introduced as the verb's direct object, which *must be* preceded by the personal **a**:

Se registra a todos los que entren.
All who come in are searched.

Se vio a las chicas en la calle.
The girls were seen in the street.

Se consultó a los autores del artículo.
The authors of the article were consulted.

When the object is a pronoun rather than a noun it is placed in the normal manner (see 8.5.3). However, it is usual to use **le** or **les** as the masculine direct object pronoun (rather than **lo** or **los**):

Se nos acusó.   We were accused.

Se le/les acusó.   He was accused./They were accused.

Understanding *se*

For practical purposes, it may be helpful to understand that **se** in the above construction functions as if it were an indefinite or unspecific subject of a singular active verb, e.g. **Se le interrogó** 'Someone questioned him'.

Note: Where there is no danger of ambiguity from using a reflexive verb with a personal subject, for example in notices or advertisements, a straightforward reflexive construction is used as for inanimate subjects: **Se busca niñera** 'Nanny wanted', **Se necesitan cocineros** 'Cooks needed'.

15.2.4 *Converting a passive construction into an active one*

Overuse of passive constructions in Spanish can be avoided, particularly in informal speech, by converting an English passive construction into an active one in Spanish:

Un colega me entregó los archivos.
I was handed the files by a colleague.

Sus amigas no la invitaron.
She was not invited by her friends.

15.2.5 Using an indeterminate 3rd person plural active verb

Where no agent or 'doer' is expressed it may be possible, if the context permits it, to use an active verb whose subject is an indeterminate 3rd person plural ('they', 'people'):

Lo nombraron director.
He was appointed director.

15.2.6 Replacing a passive construction when using an already reflexive verb

When using a reflexive verb such as **darse cuenta** 'to realize', it is not possible to add a second reflexive pronoun **se** to create a passive construction. It is possible, however, to convert the sentence to an active construction using **uno** 'one' or **la gente** 'people':

Uno no se da cuenta de su importancia.
Its importance is not realized.

La gente se olvida pronto de cantantes como él.
Singers like him are soon forgotten.

Chapter 16

Modal auxiliary verbs

Modal verbs are auxiliaries used to express attitudes or feelings generally in relation to an infinitive. They correspond in English to phrases such as 'you *can* go', 'you *must* go', 'you *want* to go', and 'you *have* to go'.

The most common Spanish verbs are several stating differing shades of obligation: **deber, tener que, haber**. Others are **poder, querer, saber** and **soler**.

16.1 Deber

16.1.1 Deber *and* deber de

Deber on its own expresses obligation: 'must', 'has/have to', 'should', 'ought to':

Debe traerlo mañana.	She must bring it tomorrow.
Ustedes deben exigir un reembolso.	You should demand a refund.

Deber de expresses supposition or inference:

Deben de haber viajado ayer.	They must have travelled yesterday.

In practice, in contemporary usage native speakers do not always make this clear distinction, sometimes using **deber** on its own to convey supposition: **El río no debe ser muy profundo** 'The river can't be very deep'.

However, **deber de** should not be used to express obligation.

16.1.2 *Tenses of* deber

Tenses other than the present of **deber** sometimes pose problems for English-speaking students.

The conditional may be safely used to translate 'ought':

Deberías vestirte de etiqueta. You ought to dress formally.

In formal Spanish in the Peninsula but more generally in Latin America, the **-ra** form of the imperfect subjunctive can be used in the same way:

Debieran confesar su error. They ought to own up to their mistake.

These tenses may also be used to refer to the past when followed by a perfect infinitive:

Deberíamos/Debiéramos haberle negado el permiso de residencia.
We ought to have refused him his residence permit.

Alternatively to refer to the past, the choice of the preterite or imperfect of **deber** with the meaning of 'must have', 'should have' or 'ought to have', is based on the tense that would have been used if **deber** had not been needed:

<u>**Debía**</u> **(de) tener tres hijos.**	He must have had three children.
(based on <u>**tenía**</u> **tres hijos**)	(based on 'he had three children')
<u>**Debí**</u> **eligir la otra opción.**	I should have chosen the other option.
(based on <u>**eligí**</u> **la otra opción**)	(based on 'I chose the other option')
<u>**Debía**</u> **(de) ser medianoche cuando volvieron.**	It must have been midnight when they returned.
(based on <u>**era**</u> **medianoche**)	(based on 'it was midnight')

16.2 *Tener que*

Interchangeable in most contexts with **deber, tener que** states a strong obligation viewed as a necessity, comparable to English 'have to'. When used in the preterite tense, the meaning is 'had to' and did:

Tendrás que cambiar de avión en París.	You will have to change planes in Paris.
Tuvo que presentar la tesis de nuevo.	He had to present the thesis again.

Note: **Tener . . . que** is also used to state that you have something 'to do' without the sense of obligation: **Tengo mucho que leer** 'I have a lot to read'.

16.3 *Haber*

This is of course the auxiliary verb used to form compound tenses (see 10.9).

In addition, in the forms **hay que** (present tense), **había que** (imperfect tense) and **habrá que** (future tense), it is used impersonally to express a generally applicable obligation or necessity. In the preterite it states what was necessary and done, i.e. a completed action.

Hay que lavar las sábanas.	The sheets need washing.
Había que hacer cola para entrar.	You had to queue to get in.
Habrá que prestar atención.	We'll have to pay attention.
Hubo que romper la ventana para entrar.	It was necessary to break the window to get in.

Nowadays less common than the above verbs, **haber de** is used (with a personal subject) to express milder obligation. In some cases this is no more than a statement of what *will* happen or *is expected* to happen:

¿Qué hemos de hacer?	What are we to do?
Juan ha de partir después de la cena.	Juan will leave after dinner.

Note: In place of **deber (de)**, **haber de** is also found to express supposition, especially in parts of Latin America: **Han de ser las seis** 'It must be six o'clock'.

16.4 *Querer*

As a modal verb before an infinitive this essentially means 'to want':

¿Quieres consultar el índice?	Do you want to consult the index?

Polite requests can be conveyed by using the **-ra** form of the imperfect subjunctive or the conditional tense:

Quisiera/querría ver el último modelo.	I should like to see the latest model.

Whereas the imperfect of **querer** merely states 'wanted to', the positive preterite generally suggests 'tried to':

Siempre queríamos ir a España.	We always wanted to go to Spain.
Quise pedirle un autógrafo pero no lo permitieron.	I wanted (and tried) to ask her for an autograph, but they did not allow it.

The negative preterite of **querer** carries the implication of 'refused to':

No quiso entrar en detalles.	He refused to give details.

16.5 Poder

16.5.1 Ability and permission

(a) In several tenses **poder** corresponds to English 'can', 'may', 'be able to':

No sé si pueden salvarlos.	I don't know if they can rescue them.
No ha podido encontrar a su mamá.	He has not been able to find his mother.
Usted puede pagar mañana.	You may pay tomorrow.
¿Se puede (entrar)?	Can I come in?

(b) Used in the *conditional*, **poder** corresponds to English 'could' (except when this refers to past time, see (c)) or '*would be* able':

¿Podríamos dormir aquí?	Could we sleep here?
Podrían hacerlo si quisieran.	They could do it if they wanted.

(c) The *imperfect* form of **poder** indicates 'could' or '*was* able to' in the past, without any indication of whether an attempt was made, i.e. a state or condition:

No podía desmentir la noticia.	He could not contradict the news.

The *preterite* has the sense of 'managed to' (in positive sentences) and of 'failed to' (in negative sentences):

Pudimos atravesar el río nadando.

We were able to swim across the river.

No pudimos abrir la puerta.

We could not open the door.

Translating English 'could'

English 'could' corresponds not just to preterite **pudo** and imperfect **podía**, but also to conditional **podría**. Care should be taken not to use the latter in place of either of the former.

For example, the conditional is correct with reference to *future* time in **Podría ir mañana** 'I could go tomorrow' (= 'I *would* be able to go tomorrow'), but it cannot replace imperfect **podía** to refer to *past* time in **Estaba tan borracho que no podía mantenerse de pie** 'He was so drunk he couldn't stay on his feet' (= 'He was so drunk he *was* unable stay on his feet').

Notes:

1 **Poder con** corresponds to 'manage', 'cope with': **¿Puedes con todos esos libros?** 'Can you manage all those books?'. Note also **No puedo más** 'I can't stand any more'.

2 In formal Spanish **no poder menos que** corresponds to 'cannot fail to' or 'have no choice but': **No pude menos que sentirme profundamente agradecido** 'I could not fail to be profoundly grateful'.

16.5.2 Possibility and supposition

16.5.2.1

The conditional form of **poder** can also indicate possibility, with the meaning 'might', 'could':

No hagas eso, podrías caer.   Don't do that, you might fall.

In this sense, both the conditional and the preterite of **poder** + **haber** + past participle can be used to speculate on what could have happened but did not:

¡Qué susto! Nos podríamos haber salido de la carretera.
What a fright! We could have come off the road.

Pudiste haberte desviado del sendero.
You could have strayed from the path.

16.5.2.2

The phrase **puede ser que** 'it is possible that' is only used impersonally (and the following clause is in the subjunctive mood):

Puede ser que hayan estado intentando llamarnos.
They may have been trying to call us.

The word **ser** is sometimes omitted from this construction, although not if **puede** is negated:

Puede que vengan mañana.　　They may come tomorrow.

16.6　Saber

When used as an auxiliary verb, **saber** corresponds to 'can' and 'could' but only with reference to an ability that has been learned. Therefore, it often translates 'to know how to':

¿Sabes jugar al ajedrez?　　Can you play chess?

Mario no sabía nadar.　　Mario couldn't swim.

16.7　Soler

Followed by an infinitive, **soler** means 'usually', 'to be accustomed to'. It is normally found only in the present and imperfect tenses:

Suelen alojarse en la Pensión　They usually stay in the
Angelita.　　　　　　　　　　Pensión Angelita.

Solía dar un paseo antes de　I normally went for a stroll
cenar.　　　　　　　　　　　before dinner.

Chapter 17

Infinitive constructions

Infinitive forms in Spanish consist of a single, invariable word ending in **-ar**, **-er** or **-ir**. In principle they correspond to English 'to + verb', but in addition they often translate forms ending in '-ing'.

The Spanish infinitive is often used after a preposition or a verb:

después de cenar	after having supper
Quiero hablar.	I want to speak.

It can also function as the subject of a finite verb (see 17.4) and as a verbal noun (see 17.6).

For the infinitive used as an imperative, see 19.3.2.

On the placement of object pronouns with infinitives see 8.5.2.

17.1 Finite verb + infinitive

17.1.1 Verbs with the same subject

When one verb follows another, the second verb almost always takes the infinitive form if the subject of the first verb is the same as that of the second.

This pattern is typical of the modal verbs (see Chapter 16) but is also common with most psychological verbs and also with verbs indicating concepts such as necessity and accomplishment:

Prefiero hablar con él.	I'd prefer to talk to him.
Recuerdo haberlo conocido en Jerez.	I remember having met him in Jerez.

Necesitamos comprar gasolina.	We need to buy petrol.
¿Lograste hacerlo?	Did you manage to do it?

17.1.2 Verbs with different subjects

A small number of verbs can take a direct infinitive when the subjects of the finite verb and the infinitive are not the same.

The main verbs that allow this construction are **hacer** 'to make', **mandar/ordenar** 'to order', **dejar** 'to allow', **permitir** 'to permit', **impedir** 'to prevent', **persuadir** 'to persuade', **prohibir** 'to forbid', as well as perception verbs such as **oír** 'to hear', **escuchar** 'to listen', **mirar** 'to watch', **sentir** 'to feel':

Nos hicieron traducir un texto medieval.	They made us translate a medieval text.
No permiten fumar a los pasajeros.	They don't allow the passengers to smoke.
Le prohibieron poner la tele.	They forbade him to put on the TV.
Lola mandó callar a su hermano.	Lola told her brother to be quiet.
Te oí entrar anoche.	I heard you come in last night.

Note: For alternative constructions based on the subjunctive, see 12.1.1.

The infinitive verb has a passive or impersonal sense after the above verbs if no subject is specified for it:

Hice llamar a la policía.	I had the police called.
Oí cantar una rumba.	I heard someone singing a rumba.
Mandó llenar los bidones.	He ordered the drums/cans to be filled.

17.2 Prepositions + infinitive

17.2.1 Preposition required by preceding verb

Often the choice of preposition depends on the preceding verb:

soñar <u>con</u> hacer	to dream about doing
dejar <u>de</u> hacer	to stop doing

Prepositions govern infinitives not gerunds

Except in one or two archaic constructions, the infinitive is the *only* verb form that can occur after a preposition in Spanish. Compare 'after speaking' **después de hablar** (never ×después de hablando×).

Which prepositions follow which verbs has to be learned on a case-by-case basis. It is possible, however, to set out some general (though not always reliable) guidelines:

(a) **A** + infinitive

Typically this pattern is used to express progress towards an action, after verbs that (i) state its beginning, (ii) express preparation or readiness to perform an action, (iii) express physical movement towards an action, or (iv) indicate obligation, influence or persuasion:

Empezó/Se puso a llorar.	He began to cry.
Se comprometen a devolver lo pagado.	They undertake to return what has been paid.
Han venido a pintar la casa.	They've come to paint the house.
Me obligaron a pagar la multa.	They obliged me to pay the fine.

Note: The preposition **a** is required when the verbs **ir** 'to go' and **volver** 'to return' are used figuratively, with the meanings 'to be going to do' and 'to do again' respectively: **No volveré a hacerlo** 'I won't do it again'.

(b) **De** + infinitive

Used after verbs expressing movement away from, such as refraining and dissuading from, corresponding to English 'from' + gerund:

Me abstuve de reír.	I refrained from laughing.

With verbs of cessation, it corresponds to a direct gerund in English:

¿Han terminado de hablar?	Have they finished speaking?

Similar verbs are:

cesar/dejar/parar de	to cease/stop
disuadir de	to dissuade from

Note: The preposition **de** is required when the verb **acabar** 'to finish' is used with the meaning 'to have just': **Acaban de llegar** 'They have just arrived'.

In other contexts an infinitive introduced by **de** relates to the cause or source of the action indicated by the finite verb:

Me alegro de haber ido.	I'm pleased I went.
Nos acusaron de ser espías.	They accused us of being spies.

Similar verbs are:

arrepentirse de	to regret
cansarse de	to tire of

In some cases, however, it is not easy to account for the use of **de**, thereby strengthening the general recommendation to learn verbs with their prepositions:

Acuérdate de apagar las luces.	Remember to turn off the lights.
Alicia trató de convencerlos.	Alicia tried to convince them.

(c) **Por** + infinitive

This pattern is characteristic of verbs expressing a powerful longing or struggle 'for':

Guillermo está luchando por triunfar.	Guillermo is fighting to succeed.
Se muere por poder hablar contigo.	She's dying to be able to talk to you.

Similar verbs are:

esforzarse por	to make an effort to
rabiar por	to be itching/dying to

Por is found also with verbs stating to begin/end 'by' or to opt 'for':

Siempre acaba por aceptarlo.	He always ends up by accepting it.
Al final optó por estudiar informática.	In the end she opted for studying computing.

(d) **En** + infinitive

Frequently this pattern matches English verb + 'in/on' + gerund:

Luis insistió en venir con nosotros.	Luis insisted on coming with us.

Quedamos en reunirnos a las dos.	We agreed on meeting at two o'clock.
Persisten en llamarnos.	They persist in calling us.

But note also **pensar en** 'to think of/about'.

(e) **Con** + infinitive

This occurs with a few common verbs:

Le han amenazado con quitarle el permiso de conducir.
They have threatened him with taking away his driving licence.

Me conformo con dormir en el sofá.
I'm happy to sleep on the sofa.

María sueña con vivir al lado del mar.
María dreams of living by the sea.

17.2.2 Preposition required by preceding noun

Sometimes what demands a specific preposition is not a preceding verb but a noun. If this noun is derived from a verb, it usually takes the same preposition as the corresponding verb:

su empeño <u>en</u> llamarme de usted
his insistence on addressing me as *usted*

In other cases, **de** is very common, although other prepositions are possible:

Tiene la suerte de vivir en Madrid.	He's lucky enough to live in Madrid.
la idea de veranear con ellos	the idea of going on holiday with them
el derecho a votar	the right to vote
cierta tendencia a criticar	a certain tendency to be critical

17.2.3 Translating 'the first/last to'

After the adjectives **último** 'last', **único** 'only', and **primero** 'first' etc., an infinitive is preceded by **en**:

Fue el tercero y último en terminar.	He was the third and last to finish.

17.2.4 | Preposition independent of a preceding item

Some prepositions are used independently, in that they are not specifically associated with a preceding verb or noun. The commonest prepositions used in this way are **para** 'in order to', **sin** 'without', **por** (when in it means 'because of'), and temporal prepositions such as **después de** 'after' and **antes de** 'before':

Jorge se acostó sin cenar.	Jorge went to bed without having supper.
Huélelo antes de beberlo.	Smell it before drinking it.

For examples with **por** and **para** see 22.1(b), 22.2(c).

17.2.5 | Special cases of prepositions + infinitives

Certain combinations of preposition and infinitive have an unexpected meaning and so are best learned on their own.

17.2.5.1 | Infinitives with a passive sense after *a, sin, a medio*

The sequences **sin** + infinitive and **a medio** + infinitive are equivalent in meaning to English 'un-' and 'half' + past participle respectively:

una camisa sin planchar	an unironed shirt
una casa a medio construir	a half-built house

The sequence **a** + infinitive means 'to be' + past participle:

una deuda a liquidar	a debt to be settled

For similar constructions with **por**, see 22.1(k).

17.2.5.2 | Special meanings of *de* + infinitive

The sequence **de** + infinitive has a variety of special meanings. It can indicate cause:

Estoy ronco de tanto hablar.	I'm hoarse from speaking so much.

Ser + **de** + infinitive means 'to be' + past participle:

Es de esperar que dimita.	It is to be hoped that he'll resign.
Su honestidad era de admirar.	His honesty was to be admired.

Finally, **de** + infinitive can have the effect of a conditional clause introduced by **si**:

De saberlo no habría pagado. If I had known I wouldn't have
paid.

|17.2.5.3| *Al* + infinitive

The sequence **al** + infinitive occurs with an equivalent sense to English 'on' + '-ing' or to mean 'when':

Al ver lo que había pasado se puso a llorar.
On seeing/When he saw what had happened he started crying.

17.3 Infinitives in impersonal constructions

Infinitives often occur in impersonal constructions, i.e. constructions in which no individual person or thing is the subject of the main verb. Possibly the most common construction of this sort is formed from **haber** + **que** + infinitive, for which see 16.3.

An infinitive may also be used after **ser** when followed by an obligation word like **preciso** 'necessary', **obligatorio** 'compulsory', **necesario** 'necessary':

Fue preciso llamar a un médico.	It was necessary to call a doctor.
Es obligatorio reservar una plaza.	It is compulsory to reserve a place.

An infinitive can also be used after the formulas **se ruega** and **se prohíbe**:

Se ruega no tocar las mercancías.	Customers are asked not to touch the merchandise.
Se prohíbe fumar.	Smoking is forbidden.

17.4 An infinitive as the subject of a verb

An infinitive (together with its object, if any) can function as the subject of a finite verb, although it may be placed after it:

Cenar con ellos fue una pesadilla.	Having dinner with them was a nightmare.

| En aquella universidad enseñar era un suplicio. | At that university teaching was a terrible ordeal. |
| No me conviene vivir tan lejos. | Living so far away is not convenient for me. |

Use of *ser* + adjective + *de* + infinitive

Students of French in particular should note that **de** is only used in sentences such as the following, when the subject of the finite verb is a noun or pronoun:

| Esa puerta es difícil de abrir. | That door is difficult to open. |
| Eso es imposible de averiguar. | That is impossible to verify. |

In cases where the infinitive itself is the subject of the finite verb, then **de** is not used:

| Es imprescindible tenerlo. Tenerlo es imprescindible. | It is essential to have it. |
| No era posible cruzar el río. Cruzar el río no era posible. | Crossing the river was not possible. |

17.5 An infinitive with an explicit subject

Unlike in English, the infinitive in Spanish may appear with its own subject in the form of a noun or pronoun. Such explicit subjects must follow the infinitive:

Por llegar tú tarde, a mí me echaron una bronca.
Because you arrived late, I got told off.

Al llegar Pedro se fue María.
When Pedro arrived María left.

Note: More usual than the above is the pattern of conjunction followed by a verb:
Me echaron una bronca porque tú llegaste tarde 'I was told off because you arrived late'.

17.6 The infinitive as a verbal noun

The Spanish infinitive can assume the role of verbal noun, which in English is fulfilled by the gerund. In particular, like the English gerund, the Spanish infinitive can be used with the definite or indefinite article (masculine) or by a demonstrative or possessive adjective.

It should be noted, however, that this usage is characteristic of literary Spanish rather than everyday conversation.

Se oye el gemir de muchos heridos.
The groaning of many wounded can be heard.

Oímos un chirriar de ruedas dentro de la máquina.
We heard a screeching of wheels inside the machine.

When used as a noun in this way, the infinitive can be modified by an adjective:

Ese continuo pelear no se puede tolerar.
That continuous fighting is intolerable.

el lento descargar de los buques
the slow unloading of the ships

As a result of their frequent use, some infinitives have established themselves as true masculine nouns with plural forms, e.g. **parecer** 'opinion', **amanecer** 'daybreak', **atardecer** 'dusk', **anochecer** 'nightfall', **acontecer** 'happening', 'sequence of events', **pesar** 'sorrow', 'grief', **saber** 'knowledge', **ser** 'being', **hablar** 'speech'. In a few other cases, the singular and plural forms have evolved with different meanings:

andar walk/gait	**andares** travels, adventures
deber duty	**deberes** homework/assignment
decir figure of speech/saying	**decires** sayings/rumours
haber credit	**haberes** assets, income, earnings

Chapter 18

Uses of the gerund

Spanish gerunds are invariable and always end in -ndo (for full details of forms, see 10.8). Broadly speaking the Spanish gerund conveys the idea of 'in doing', 'while doing' or 'by doing'. Students should note that English nouns and adjectives ending in '-ing' normally are *not* translated by a Spanish gerund (see 18.5).

The gerund is also used in combination with **estar** to form the progressive tenses (see 10.10).

18.1 Basic use of the gerund

The basic effect of the gerund is to indicate that the action it refers to occurs at the same time (more or less) as the action described by the main verb:

Antonio contestó sonriendo.	Antonio smiled as he replied.
Lo esperé leyendo el periódico.	While I waited for him I read the paper.

As an extension of this usage, the gerund can indicate method, cause or purpose. It may correspond to 'by' + gerund, 'as/since' + clause, or 'to' + infinitive:

Ganaron haciendo trampas.	They won by cheating.
Llamándola por teléfono la vas a espantar.	You'll frighten her off by phoning her.
Estando en Granada tienes que visitar la Alhambra.	As you are in Granada you have to visit the Alhambra.
Me gritaron pidiendo ayuda.	They shouted to ask for help.

Note: If the word **como** is inserted before the gerund, the simultaneous action becomes imaginary rather than real, similar to **como si** 'as if' + subjunctive: **Movió la cabeza como diciendo no** 'He shook his head as if saying no'.

18.2 Gerund and main verb with different subjects

In the examples above, the subject of the gerund is also the subject of the main verb. For example, **Antonio** in **Antonio contestó sonriendo** is the subject of both **contestar** and **sonreír**.

However, the gerund and the main verb can have different subjects. This is particularly common with perception verbs and verbs of depicting, visualizing or encountering.

In this case, the subject of the gerund is also the direct object of the main verb:

La vi bailando con Paco.	I saw her dancing with Paco.
Lo recuerdo jugando al fútbol.	I remember him playing football.
Sorprendimos a Pilar fumando.	We caught Pilar smoking.

Similarly used are:

describir	to describe	**imaginar**	to imagine
fotografiar	to photograph	**mostrar**	to show
mirar	to look at/watch	**pintar**	to paint

Notes:

1 If necessary the gerund's subject can be explicitly mentioned. This pattern often corresponds to an English phrase introduced by 'with': **Es difícil quedar, viviendo ellos tan lejos** 'It's difficult to meet up, with them living so far away'.

2 An infinitive is commonly used after the preterite of **ver** 'to see' to indicate that a past action is complete: compare **Lo vi tirar unas piedras** 'I saw him throw some stones' and **Lo vi tirando piedras** 'I saw him throwing stones'.

3 **Venir** 'to come' and **ir** 'to go' are generally used in the infinitive rather than the gerund: **Lo miramos venir hacia nosotros** 'We watched him come towards us'.

18.3 Gerund in place of a relative clause

The gerund is increasingly accepted in informal speech and writing to modify or qualify a noun, in place of a relative clause. The latter, however, remains the most widely accepted and the safer option for foreign learners:

Un coche circulando a la izquierda sería parado casi inmediatamente.

A car being driven on the left-hand side would be stopped almost immediately.

This use of the gerund is only available in the case of action verbs. With other verbs, a relative clause must be used:

un libro que describe su viaje a través de la selva (not ×**un libro describiendo su viaje a través de la selva**×)
a book describing his journey through the jungle

Notes:
1 This usage is common in official language: **Publicaron un comunicado pidiendo la paz** 'They published a communiqué asking for peace'.

2 It is also found in captions to images in the press: **el primer ministro besando a un bebé** 'the Prime Minister kissing a baby'.

18.4 Gerund with certain verbs

With a small number of verbs the gerund construction has an unpredictable meaning. These cases are best learned separately.

18.4.1 Ir and andar + gerund

In this construction both **ir** 'to go' and **andar** 'to walk' can have a literal sense, in which case they convey the idea of 'going about' performing some action. **Andar** + gerund may sound dismissive, disparaging or critical:

Iba cantando por las calles.	He went singing through the streets.
Ese chico anda diciendo tonterías.	That boy goes around talking nonsense.

However, **ir** in this construction frequently loses its usual meaning as a verb of motion and instead stresses gradual and sometimes slow progression or repetition:

Ve echando monedas.	Keep putting coins in.
La población del pueblo fue reduciéndose.	The village's population declined.

18.4.2 Venir + gerund

This combination commonly expresses what someone 'has/had been doing' or what 'has/had been happening':

Viene quejándose de su mala salud.	He's been complaining about his ill health.
Vienen diciendo eso desde hace años.	They've been saying that for years.

18.4.3 Pasar + *gerund*

With the verb **pasar** the gerund is used to indicate how time is spent:

Pasó la tarde durmiendo.	He spent the afternoon sleeping.

18.4.4 Seguir *and* continuar + *gerund*

Only the gerund can be used with these verbs to express 'to continue to do' or 'to carry on doing':

Seguimos/Continuamos hablando.	We carried on talking.

18.4.5 Acabar *and* terminar + *gerund*

These combinations express the idea of 'ending up doing':

Siempre acaban peleándose.	They always end up quarrelling.
Terminarás rompiéndolo.	You'll end up breaking it.

18.4.6 Salir + *gerund*

Depending on the verb that adopts the gerund form, this sequence has a variety of meanings:

Fue Ignacio quien salió perdiendo.	It was Ignacio who came off worst.
Salieron volando.	They were off like a shot.

18.5 Cases where the gerund is not used

There are a number of common situations in which English uses words ending in '-ing' that *cannot* be translated by a Spanish gerund.

18.5.1 After prepositions

Except in one or two archaic constructions, the *infinitive* must be used. See
17.2.

18.5.2 As a verbal noun

It is the *infinitive* rather than the gerund that forms a verbal noun:

No le gusta nadar.   He does not like swimming.

18.5.3 As an adjective

If the '-ing' form in English has acquired an adjective-like function (e.g. 'an
interesting book'), the Spanish gerund usually cannot be used to translate
it. This can be resolved in a number of ways:

(a) By the use of an appropriate adjective, sometimes ending in -**ante**
(derived from -**ar** verbs), or -**iente** or -**ente** (from -**er** and -**ir** verbs):

un objeto volador no   an unidentified flying object
identificado

un tipo de cambio flotante   a floating exchange rate

la Bella Durmiente   Sleeping Beauty

(b) By a prepositional phrase (e.g. **de** + a related noun or infinitive):

una clase de natación   a swimming lesson

botas de montar   riding boots

(c) By some other solution:

humedad de paredes   rising damp

Note: The only common exceptions are **ardiendo** 'burning' and **hirviendo** 'boiling'
which remain invariable and are placed after the noun: **aceite hirviendo** 'boiling oil',
una casa ardiendo 'a burning house'.

18.5.4 To describe a position or condition

In Spanish it is the *past participle* and not the gerund which describes a
position: 'kneeling' **arrodillado**, 'sitting' **sentado**.

Similarly, the past participle indicates a condition when alternative adjectives are not available: 'boring' **pesado**, 'amusing' **divertido**.

Chapter 19

Commands

Commands in Spanish can be expressed by the imperative forms of the verb and by the present subjunctive.

In English, commands generally take the pattern of 'Do that!' (a positive command), 'Don't do that!' (a negative command) or 'Let's do that!' (a 1st person plural command).

In addition, users of Spanish have to take account of (i) whether the command is addressed to one or more persons in familiar speech (**tú** or **vosotros/as** [SP], or **vos** [LA] or **ustedes** [LA]) and (ii) whether it is used in polite speech (**usted, ustedes**) – see 8.1.1.

For the position of object pronouns in commands, see 8.5.1.

19.1   Forms of the imperative

19.1.1 *Imperative forms with tú and vosotros [SP]*

Imperative forms of the verb exist only for *2nd person familiar* use in the singular and plural, and even then can only be used when the command is *positive* or *affirmative* (not negative).

The singular form used with **tú** is generally identical with the 3rd person of the present indicative, whether that is regular or not. The plural form, used only in Spain with **vosotros**, is generally obtained by replacing the final -r of the infinitive with -d. However, with the exception of **irse > idos**, this -d is omitted from reflexive verbs of all conjugations before the pronoun **os**.

Verb	*Tú* form	*Vosotros* form	
avanzar	avanza	avanzad [SP]	advance
pensar	piensa	pensad [SP]	think
enviar	envía	enviad [SP]	send
continuar	continúa	continuad [SP]	continue
leer	lee	leed [SP]	read
volver	vuelve	volved [SP]	go back
subir	sube	subid [SP]	go up
dormir	duerme	dormid [SP]	sleep
seguir	sigue	seguid [SP]	follow
reunir	reúne	reunid [SP]	meet
huir	huye	huid [SP]	flee
acostarse	acuéstate	acostaos [SP]	go to bed
tenderse	tiéndete	tendeos [SP]	stretch out
divertirse	diviértete	divertíos [SP]	amuse yourself/ ves

Note: For the written accents on some singular forms, and on the plural form of
-ir reflexive verbs, see 1.3.2 and 1.3.3.

If the above suggestions for the formation of imperatives are observed,
there are only eight irregular verbs which, have a shortened form in the
singular, whilst retaining the normal plural form:

Verb	*Tú* form	*Vosotros* form	
decir	di	decid [SP]	tell
hacer	haz	haced [SP]	do
ir	ve	id [SP]	go
poner	pon	poned [SP]	put
salir	sal	salid [SP]	leave
ser	sé	sed [SP]	be
tener	ten	tened [SP]	have
venir	ven	venid [SP]	come

Notes:

1 The irregular forms in the singular are also adopted by verbs which are compounds of the above, such as **detener** (**detén**), **deshacer** (**deshaz**), **proponer** (**propón**). Note the accent required on those forms ending in -n in order to preserve the correct stress, see 1.3.2.

2 The accent on **sé** distinguishes it from the pronoun **se** (though not from **sé**, 1st person singular of the present tense of **saber**).

3 The singular form of **estar** is frequently rendered by reflexive **estate**, e.g. ¡**estate tranquilo**! 'Be quiet'.

4 Occasionally the singular form of **valer** 'to be worth' is shortened to **val**.

Juan, cierra la puerta.	Juan, close the door.
Tenme preparada la cena.	Have dinner ready for me.
Colecciónalos.	Collect them.
Tomad lo que queráis. [SP]	Take whatever you want.
Limpiaos los zapatos. [SP]	Wipe your shoes.
Obtén tu email.	Get your email.
Satisfazlos pronto.	Satisfy them at once.

19.1.2 Imperative forms with vos [LA]

In regions of Latin America where the use of **vos** is common, especially in Argentina, foreign users of Spanish will note a singular, familiar imperative that is usually obtained by dropping the final -d from the **vosotros** form. This includes the verbs listed above which adopt the shortened form in the singular in Peninsular Spanish.

When forming the imperative with **vos**, a *written accent* is placed over the final vowel, except in the case of the monosyllables ¡**da**! 'give' and ¡**ve**! 'see'. This is frequently retained even when a pronoun is added.

Verb	**Vos** [LA]	Corresponding **tú** form
buscar	**buscá**	**busca**
probar	**probá**	**prueba**
vender	**vendé**	**vende**
volver	**volvé**	**vuelve**

vivir	viví	vive
dormir	dormí	duerme
seguir	seguí	sigue
tener	tené	ten
decir	decí	di
acostarse	acostáte	acuéstate

María, vení lo más pronto posible. [LA]	María, come as soon as you can.
Convertíte en estrella. [LA]	Turn yourself into a star.
Casáte con él. [LA]	Marry him.
Hacé click sobre el ícono. [LA]	Click on the icon.
Ingresá tu usuario y clave. [LA]	Enter your username and password.
Sentáte y calláte. [LA]	Sit down and be quiet.

19.2 Commands which use the present subjunctive

The appropriate singular and plural forms of the present subjunctive are required for *all* commands addressed to **usted** and **ustedes**, for all *negative* commands, and for *3rd person* commands after **que**. The *1st person plural* of the present subjunctive is used to convey commands that in English take the form 'let's do'.

19.2.1 Commands addressed to usted and ustedes

The 3rd person of the present subjunctive is required in the polite mode of speech using **usted** and **ustedes**, and in Latin America where **ustedes** replaces **vosotros** [SP] in familiar speech.

In these constructions the subject pronoun may be added after the verb for emphasis:

Dígame lo que quiere hacer. Tell me what you want to do.

Suban ustedes al próximo
autobús.

Get on the next bus.

Mis amigos, déjenlo aquí. [LA]

My friends, leave it here.

19.2.2 Negative commands

The 2nd or 3rd person of the present subjunctive, as appropriate, is used to express all negative commands, whether familiar or polite. Object pronouns precede the verb in negative commands:

No critiques a los que no
están.

Don't criticize those who are
not here.

No penséis [SP] **jamás que**
fue así.

Never think it was like that.

No lo confiese ahora.

Don't confess it now.

No salgan antes de que llegue.

Do not leave before I arrive.

Negative commands – verb forms and position of pronouns

1   Compare: (i) **Hazlo** but **No lo hagas**, and **Hágalo** but **No lo haga**; (ii) **Hacedlo** [SP] but **No lo hagáis** [SP], and **Háganlo** but **No lo hagan**. All of these mean 'Do it' or 'Don't do it'.

2   In regions of Latin America where the use of **vos** is common, students should use the standard 2nd person singular forms of the present subjunctive for negative commands, e.g. **No me toques (vos)** 'Don't touch me'.

19.2.3 1st person plural commands

The 1st person plural of the present subjunctive is used to express English 'let's' or 'let us'.

With verbs used reflexively, the final -s is always omitted before **nos**, so sentemos + nos > sentémonos 'let's sit down'.

Bailemos.

Let's dance.

Corramos.

Let's run.

Despidámonos ahora.

Let's take our leave now.

However, especially in informal speech this construction is replaced by **ir a** + infinitive:

Vamos a cenar en otro sitio.	Let's have dinner somewhere else.

Note: For 1st person plural commands, **ir** 'to go' and **irse** 'to go away' adopt present tense forms of the verb, **vamos** and **vámonos** 'let's go' (rather than **vayamos** and **vayámonos**).

19.2.4 Commands introduced by que

3rd person commands are expressed in Spanish through the use of **que** + the singular or plural of the present subjunctive. The English equivalent commonly begins with 'let':

Que nadie hable durante el examen.	There should be no talking during the examination.
Que discutan el proyecto mañana.	Let them discuss the plan tomorrow.

2nd person commands may also be conveyed in a similar fashion:

Que tengáis una feliz Navidad. [SP]	Have a happy Christmas.
Que te diviertas.	Have a good time.

19.3 Alternative ways of expressing commands

19.3.1 Softened commands

Native speakers of Spanish use direct commands more readily than native speakers of English, even in polite speech. However, in Spanish too there are formulas which can be used to soften the impact of commands. Alternatively they can be expressed as questions:

¡Háganme el favor de sentarse!	Please sit down.
¡Firme aquí, por favor!	Sign here, please!
¿Podría apagar la tele?	Would you switch off the TV?
¿Me da un poquito de pan?	Would you give me some bread?

19.3.2 The infinitive and the present and future tenses

The infinitive is increasingly common to express commands in the form of notices and instructions, especially when they are negative. In Spain, it also occurs commonly in speech to replace the plural imperative ending in -d used with **vosotros** [SP]:

No escupir.	No spitting.
Tachar la respuesta que no corresponda.	Cross out the incorrect answer.
Limpiaros [SP] **los dientes antes de acostaros.**	Clean your teeth before going to bed.

When preceded by **a**, the infinitive can sometimes fulfil the function of a 1st person plural command:

Y ahora muchachos, a trabajar. Now lads, let's get to work.

The present tense is found to express somewhat curt commands which some might find angry or rude (although they are common among friends):

Vas allá [LA] **y les dices que no.** You go there and tell them no.

Lo comes ahora, o te lo quito. Eat it now or I'll take it away from you.

The future tense is occasionally found to formulate authoritative and dogmatic commands:

¡No lo abrirás hasta que no te lo diga! You won't open it until I say so!

Note: For the above use of **no** after **hasta que**, see 24.3.1(d).

19.3.3 Impersonal commands

The 3rd person singular or plural of the subjunctive, with the reflexive pronoun **se**, is a common means of writing formal instructions or directions:

Después de abrir la lata, guárdese en la nevera.
After opening the tin, keep in the fridge.

Pónganse las almendras en la [SP] **sartén y déjense dorar.**
Place the almonds in the frying pan and let them brown.

Chapter 20

Ser *and* estar

There are two verbs in Spanish equivalent to English 'to be', namely **ser** and **estar**. Unfortunately for the learner of Spanish, they are not randomly interchangeable. However the distinction between the two verbs is in principle fairly clear.

Ser is used to categorize its subject (e.g. **Juan es médico** 'Juan is a doctor', **El suelo es de madera** 'The floor is a wooden one') while **estar** is used to assign acquired properties (e.g. **El suelo está sucio** 'The floor is dirty') or to locate persons and things in space (e.g. **Manolo está en el jardín** 'Manolo is in the garden').

As a start to understanding their use, it is possible to identify those situations which generally demand one or other of the verbs.

20.1 Situations which demand *ser*

20.1.1 When the verb 'to be' links the subject to a noun, pronoun or infinitive

(El) Perú es una república.	Peru is a republic.
Soy el nuevo jefe.	I am the new boss.
Este es el mío.	This is mine.
Su sueño es jugar para el Real Madrid.	His dream is to play for Real Madrid.

20.1.2 Ser *to indicate the origin of persons or things*

Mi madre es de Brasil.	My mother is from Brazil.
Juan es andaluz.	Juan is Andalusian.
Es de una familia pobre.	She is from a poor family.

20.1.3 Ser *to indicate ownership or possession*

Los libros son de la universidad.	The books belong to the university.

20.1.4 Ser *to indicate what something is made of*

El jersey es de lana.	The jersey is made of wool.

20.1.5 Ser *in mathematical calculations*

Dos y tres son cinco.	Two plus three makes five.

20.1.6 Ser *to refer to the time of day, date or seasons*

Es la una.	It is one o'clock.
Fue el 18 de mayo.	It was the 18th of May.
Es invierno.	It's winter.

20.1.7 Ser *to state where something happens or the location of events*

La clase será en el aula grande.	The class will be in the large classroom.
Aquí es donde se cayó.	This is where she fell.

20.2 Situations which demand *estar*

20.2.1 To express location or position (whether temporary or permanent)

Sus papeles estaban sobre la mesa.	His papers were on the table.
Lima está en (el) Perú.	Lima is in Peru.

Compare with 20.1.7.

20.2.2 To form the progressive (or continuous) tenses

See 10.10.

20.3 *Ser* and *estar* with adjectives

It is possible to use either **ser** or **estar** with adjectives, but not indiscriminately. If the following distinctions are borne in mind, the context of use should indicate which is the correct verb to choose.

20.3.1 Ser + adjective

Ser + adjective in general indicates an inherent or essential characteristic, with no idea of change. It implies that you are putting someone or something into a particular class or type. It is 'to be' by nature:

Ana es pálida.	Ana is pale (normally of pale complexion).
Estas peras son agrias.	These pears are sour (of a sour variety).
Mi hermano es alegre.	My brother is happy (of cheerful disposition).

| 20.3.2 | **Estar + *adjective*** |

Estar + an adjective frequently denotes an accidental or temporary state. It is 'to be' by condition:

Ana está pálida.	Ana is pale (has turned pale).
Estas peras están agrias.	These pears are sour (because they are unripe).
Mi hermano está alegre.	My brother is happy (in a happy state of mind).

It is important to realize that this construction indicates a condition that is not only susceptible or likely to change, but also the result of a change:

Está vivo.	He is alive.	**Está muerto.**	He is dead.
Está calvo.	He is bald.		

The use of *ser* and *estar* with adjectives

1   As a guide, if in doubt it is helpful to test for **ser** or **estar**. If it is possible to insert into an English sentence, the phrase 'in a . . . state/condition', this would indicate that **estar** is the correct choice. Likewise, if it is possible to insert the words 'person', 'type', 'variety' or 'sort', as appropriate, this could indicate that **ser** is the correct verb. For example, if 'The lady is elegant' means that she is 'an elegant person', use **ser**. If it means that she is 'in an elegant state', use **estar**.

2   Similarly, it is also possible on occasions to substitute the English verb 'to be' with 'to seem', 'to feel', 'to become' or 'to look'. This would also suggest that **estar** is the appropriate choice, e.g. **Estuve orgulloso al recibir el premio** 'I was proud on receiving the prize', i.e. 'I felt proud', **¡Qué alta está la niña!** 'How tall the girl is!' i.e. 'How tall she has become' or 'looks'.

3   In other cases the combination of a noun + adjective necessarily demands one or other of the two verbs, because the sentence states either an inherent characteristic or a state:

Inherent characteristics	*States*
La puerta es roja.	**La puerta está sucia.**
The door is red.	The door is dirty.

Luis es muy mentiroso.	**Luis está muy triste.**	
Luis is a liar.	Luis is very sad.	
Esta marca de salsa es picante.	**¡Qué picante está la sopa!**	
This brand of sauce is spicy.	The soup is really spicy!	

20.3.3 Adjectives which change their meaning with ser or estar

	Ser	Estar
cansado	tiresome, tiring	tired
listo	clever	ready
malo	bad	ill
bueno	good	well, tasty (food)
vivo	lively, clever	alive
aburrido	boring	bored
divertido	amusing	amused
fresco	cheeky	cool (e.g. a drink)
consciente	aware	conscious [SP]
rico	rich	tasty [SP]

The above is not intended to be a complete list, but serves to reinforce the general distinctions made between ser and estar.

20.3.4 Common adjectives predominantly with either ser or estar

1 Ser viejo and ser joven to say someone 'is old' or 'is young'.

Note: Estar with these words would suggest a change of state or condition, or at least one's perception of it: Estoy muy viejo para estos trotes 'I'm getting too old for all this rushing about'. Estar joven would similarly suggest that someone 'looks young', for example for their age.

2 Ser fácil/difícil 'to be easy', ser posible/probable 'to be possible/probable', ser evidente 'to be evident', ser necesario 'to be necessary', ser importante 'to be important', ser conveniente 'to be appropriate', ser

increíble 'to be incredible' and, perhaps more surprisingly, ser feliz 'to be happy' and ser desgraciado 'to be unlucky/unhappy' even though these appear to indicate states.

Note: Está claro que [SP] 'It's clear that'.

3 Estar lleno 'to be full', estar vacío 'to be empty', estar intacto 'to be intact'.

20.4 Ser and *estar* with past participles

Ser with a past participle forms the passive voice. Estar with a past participle describes a state. See 15.1 for these constructions.

20.5 Special uses of *estar*

20.5.1 Estar de

The phrase estar de (but never just estar) is used with a noun to indicate that a person is acting in a particular capacity, or occupying a position:

Está de cónsul en Newcastle.	He is acting as consul in Newcastle.
Estoy de jefe hasta que vuelva Juan.	I am the boss until Juan returns.

Note: Estar de is used in fixed prepositional phrases such as estar de vacaciones 'on holiday', estar de buen/mal humor 'in a good/bad mood', estar de viaje 'travelling'.

20.5.2 Colloquial expressions using estar

Notwithstanding the general principle that ser rather than estar is used when a noun follows, estar very occasionally combines with a noun to form a colloquial expression: Estoy pez en matemáticas 'I'm clueless about maths', Está fenómeno 'It's fantastic'.

Chapter 21

Prepositions

Like the English words 'to', 'from', 'after', 'with', Spanish prepositions are used to link words and express a relationship between them, e.g. **libro** and **mesa** in **El libro está <u>sobre</u> la mesa** 'The book is on the table'.

When a preposition is followed by a verb, in contrast to English which uses the gerund ending in '-ing', Spanish prepositions *must always* be followed by the infinitive, e.g. **antes de bailar** 'before dancing'. For the use of prepositions required after some verbs before an infinitive, e.g. **Trató de hacerlo** 'He tried to do it', see 17.2.

Verbs, nouns, adjectives and past participles which are used with prepositions before a following noun need to be learned with the appropriate preposition: e.g. **abundar en** 'to be rich in', **contar con** 'to count on', **amor a** 'love of', **interés en** 'interest in', **aficionado a** 'keen on', **convencido de** 'convinced of'.

Uses of some common Spanish prepositions are discussed below.

21.1   *A*

This occurs in a wide range of contexts.

21.1.1   *The personal* a

21.1.1.1

It is so named since it is required when the direct object of the verb is a noun referring to a specific, known person:

No conozco a Yolanda.	I don't know Yolanda.
Solo nominaron al director.	They only nominated the director.

When the person is not known or is unspecific, the personal **a** can be omitted:

Necesito jardinero.	I need a gardener.
Ese autobús lleva treinta personas.	That bus is carrying thirty people.

Note: The personal **a** is not used when referring to something inanimate indicated by a person's name: **No conoce todo Vargas Llosa** 'He does not know all (i.e. all the works of) Vargas Llosa'.

21.1.1.2

The personal **a** is also used before a noun which indicates a group of people, and before pronouns referring to persons (specific or not), such as **alguien, nadie, ninguno, usted, otro, todos**:

Leyendo ese libro conocí al pueblo chileno.	By reading that book I came to know the Chilean people.
Censuraron al concejo municipal.	They criticized the town council.
No vimos a nadie.	We didn't see anyone.
Recomendaron a otro para el puesto.	They recommended another (man) for the job.

21.1.1.3

Despite its name, the personal **a** is commonly used to refer to animals for which one feels affection or sympathy, especially pets:

Rescataron al pobre zorro.	They saved the poor fox.

Note: The personal **a** is not used in contexts such as the following: **Prepararon pollo para la cena** 'They prepared chicken for dinner', **Odia las arañas** 'He hates spiders'.

Similarly, the personal **a** is sometimes found before an inanimate object, particularly after verbs that express ideas like precedence and superiority, such as **obedecer** 'to obey', **preceder** 'to precede', **suceder** 'to come after', **seguir** 'to follow', **superar** 'to overcome', **sustituir** 'to substitute', **vencer** 'to defeat':

Cusqueña supera a sus competidores en esta categoría.
Cusqueña (beer) is better than its competitors in this category.

Nuestro equipo venció a Argentina.
Our team beat Argentina.

In addition, the personal **a** is sometimes felt to be necessary to identify unambiguously the object of a verb, even if it is not a person. This may be found for example, in relative clauses to reinforce the link between verb and object, and after verbs such as **llamar** which can have two following nouns:

Es enorme la distancia que separa al río del bosque.
The distance that separates the river from the wood is enormous.

Llamaban Banda Oriental a la zona que quedaba al este del río Uruguay.
They called the land to the east of the River Uruguay the *Banda Oriental*.

21.1.2 **A used to introduce an indirect object**

In this use **a** is equivalent to English 'to':

Van a dar un premio al mejor estudiante.
They are going to give a prize to the best student.

Note: Possible confusion can be caused when a sentence contains both a specific person as direct object and a personal indirect object, since both in theory should be preceded by **a**. To avoid this, the personal **a** is usually omitted: **Envió el jugador al director** 'He sent the player to the director'.

21.1.3 **A indicating movement**

Used after verbs of motion, this is generally equivalent to English 'to', but may also translate 'at', 'in', 'into', and 'onto':

Llegamos a Lima hoy.	We arrive in Lima today.
Los espectadores tiraron botellas al campo.	They spectators threw bottles on to the pitch.
Se sentaron a la mesa para almorzar.	They sat at the table to have lunch.
Tiraron las drogas al mar.	They threw the drugs into the sea.

Note: Unlike French and Italian, *static* position or location 'in' or 'at' is translated in Spanish by **en**, except with set phrases such as **al lado de** 'next to' (see 21.1.8(c) for others). Compare: **Estaremos en la frontera mañana** 'We shall be at the frontier tomorrow', but **Fuimos a verlo a Barcelona** 'We went to see him in Barcelona' (i.e. travelled 'to Barcelona to see him').

A with expressions of time and age

A usually translates 'at' and 'on':

> **Vino a las once y se fue al mediodía.**
> He came at 11 o'clock and went at midday.

> **A los quince años ya era futbolista.**
> At fifteen he was already a footballer.

> **A la mañana siguiente ya había pasado la tormenta.**
> The following morning the storm had passed.

It is also sometimes found to express 'after':

> **A los seis meses de regresar, se enfermó.**
> Six months after returning, she fell ill.

This meaning is also apparent in phrases such as the following:

a principios de   at the beginning of

a mediados de   in the middle of

a finales de   at the end of

a la llegada de   on the arrival of

21.1.5 **A indicating price, speed and rate**

> **¿A cuánto están las berenjenas?**
> How much are aubergines?

> **La ven una vez al año/al mes.**
> They see her once a year/month.

> **Viajaba a 100 kilómetros por hora.**
> She was travelling at 100 kilometres an hour.

21.1.6 **A after verbs of smell, taste and sound**

After verbs such as **oler** 'to smell', **saber** 'to taste', and **sonar** 'to sound', and after associated nouns such as **olor** 'smell', and **sabor** 'taste', a often corresponds to 'of' and 'like':

El vino sabe a vinagre.	The wine tastes like vinegar.
Dejó atrás un fuerte olor a colonia.	He left behind a strong smell of aftershave.
El auditorio suena a hueco.	The auditorium sounds hollow.

21.1.7 A with the meaning of 'from'

This is a common usage after some verbs which imply 'depriving', 'taking away' or 'purchasing from', especially **quitar** 'to take away', **cortar** 'to cut', **robar** 'to steal', **comprar** 'to buy':

| La policía le quitó la ropa al sospechoso. | The police took away the suspect's clothes. |
| Se lo compré a Carlos. | I bought it from Carlos. |

See also 8.2.2.4 for the use of the indirect object pronoun with this meaning.

21.1.8 Expressions constructed with a

(a) A is used to form phrases expressing manner such as the following:

a caballo	on horseback	**a mano**	by hand
a ciegas	blindly	**a la parilla/plancha**	grilled
a lápiz	in pencil	**a pie**	on foot

This includes methods of fuelling and powering:

| **una lámpara a querosén/ querosene** [LA] | a kerosene/paraffin lamp |
| **una olla a presión** | a pressure cooker |

Note: Means of mechanical transport are introduced by **en**: **Vine en avión/tren/carro** [LA] 'I came by plane/train/car'.

(b) **Al, a lo** and **a la** express a manner that is especially a style:

| **huevos a la flamenca** | i.e. baked eggs with sausage, ham and tomatoes |
| **el pelo a lo Beckham** | Beckham-style hair |

219

(c) **A** is used with many expressions that state location, for example:

al aire libre	in the open air	**al sol**	in the sun
a la derecha/ izquierda	on the right/left	**a la entrada**	at the entrance
a la orilla/ orillas de	on the bank(s) of	**a lo lejos**	in the distance

(d) **A** also links repeated words, such as: **cara a cara** 'face to face', **gota a gota** 'drop by drop', **poco a poco** 'little by little/gradually', **uno a uno** 'one by one'.

21.2 Antes de, ante, delante de

Antes de means 'before' with reference to time:

Se fueron antes de las seis. They went before six o'clock.

Ante usually translates 'before' with the meaning of 'in the presence of' (rather than literally 'in front of'). It also commonly expresses the notion of 'faced with', or 'as a result of':

Deben comparecer ante la comisión.	They must appear before the tribunal.
Ante las revelaciones el ministro dimitió.	Faced with the revelations the minister resigned.

Delante de signifies 'before' with reference to specific location 'in front of' or 'ahead of':

Nos veremos delante de la biblioteca.	We'll meet in front of the library.

Note: Some writers use **ante** with this meaning of location: **unos manifestantes ante la estatua de Pizarro** 'some protestors in front of the statue of Pizarro'.

21.3 Bajo, debajo de

Both words translate 'under(neath)', and 'beneath'.

Debajo de indicates position in a literal sense. **Abajo de** is a common alternative in Latin America:

Puso su bolso debajo/abajo [LA] de la silla.
She put her handbag underneath the chair.

Bajo can also be used literally of location, especially in a less restricted sense (e.g. 'under the sun'), and also figuratively when physical location is not intended (e.g. 'under the command of'):

bajo el sol/la lluvia/el cielo   under the sun/rain/sky

bajo el pretexto de estar   under the pretext of being ill
enfermo

21.4   Con

The basic function of **con** is to express the equivalent of English 'with'. This embraces uses such as 'accompanied by', **con** + the instrument 'with' which, or the means 'by' which, something is done, and **con** + noun to form adverbial phrases:

Maribel sale con Paco.   Maribel is going out with Paco.

Lograron taparlo con un   They managed to cover it with a
parche.   patch.

Lo saludaron con   They greeted him
entusiasmo.   enthusiastically.

However, **con** is found in a number of other contexts such as: (i) after verbs which express an encounter, collision or struggle (e.g. **tropezar con** 'to bump into to', **enfrentarse/encararse con** 'to face (up to)'), (ii) to indicate cause, and (iii) to express feelings or attitudes 'towards' someone or something:

Al pasar por la curva la moto chocó con un farol.
As it rounded the bend the motorcycle crashed into a lamp post.

Con pintar las paredes la casa ya parece otra.
Just by painting the walls the house already seems transformed.

Es simpático con todo el mundo.
He is friendly towards everyone.

Con also occurs with the meanings of 'in spite of', 'despite':

Con todo el dinero que tiene nunca invita.
In spite of all his money he never buys you a drink.

21.5 *Contra, en contra de*

Contra serves for most literal and figurative translations of 'against', and for firing weapons 'at'.

En contra de is sometimes preferred to express an opinion or a feeling:

Coloca la escalera contra el muro.	Place the ladder against the wall.
Dirigen sus misiles contra la ciudad.	They are aiming their missiles at the city.
Está en contra de los toros.	He is against bullfighting.

21.6 *De*

Another of the most common prepositions, **de** frequently indicates origin or source. It also expresses 'of' with regard to ownership and relationship, and in the sense of 'made of'.

There are, however, many meanings which cannot be compared directly with English usage.

21.6.1 **De to indicate origin and point of departure**

This may correspond not only to English 'from' but also 'in', especially in superlative phrases:

La palabra viene del latín.	The word comes from Latin.
Han llegado de Lisboa.	They have arrived from Lisbon.
el mejor hotel de Río de Janeiro	the best hotel in Rio de Janeiro

21.6.2 **De to indicate ownership, relationship and association**

This usage often corresponds to the apostrophe 's' in English:

los primos de José	José's cousins
la superficie de la luna	the surface of the moon

Note: De + personal name or noun is a disdainful or mocking means of reference: **el idiota de Juan** 'that idiot Juan'.

21.6.3 De *in geographical names*

la isla de **Aruba**	the island of Aruba
el camino de **Machu Picchu**	the track to Machu Picchu

21.6.4 De *to state what something is made of or contains*

una caja de madera	a wooden box

21.6.5 De *to refer to what is written or spoken 'about'*

Están hablando de su visita a México.	They are talking about their visit to Mexico.

Note: A formal and more exhaustive treatment of a subject is often conveyed by the use of **sobre**. See 21.10.4.

21.6.6 De *to indicate cause*

Falleció de cólera.	He died of cholera.
loco de alegría	wildly happy

21.6.7 De *to translate 'as' or 'like'*

This usage refers to a person's actual occupation, an assumed role, or their stage in life.

It can also indicate the use to which something is put:

Lole trabaja de azafata.	Lole works as an air hostess/flight attendant.
Se vistieron de payasos.	They dressed as clowns.
De niño vivía en otro país.	As a boy I lived in another country.
Este palo puede servir de bastón.	This stick could serve as a walking stick.

There are also several verbs that take **de** + adjective, to indicate a condition or characteristic:

Las dos presumían de guapas.
They both thought they were pretty.

21.6.8 De to form adjectival phrases

These may be purely descriptive but can also express intended use:

una niña de ojos azules	a girl with blue eyes
un edificio de techo plano	a flat-roofed building
un molinillo de café	a coffee grinder

21.6.9 De to form adverbial phrases

Examples from the many include:

de buena/ mala gana	willingly/ reluctantly	**de nuevo**	again
de golpe/repente	suddenly	**de paso**	in passing
de vez en cuando	from time to time	**de pie**	standing

21.6.10 Other uses of de

Other uses of **de** are discussed in the relevant sections as follows:

(a) In comparisons: see 26.4.
(b) With time of day and dates: see 23.1.5.1/2.
(c) Before infinitives: see 17.2.1(b), 17.2.5.2, 17.4.
(d) To introduce an agent after a past participle: see p. 178n4
(e) To form compound nouns: see 29.3.2.

21.7 Dentro de, fuera de

Dentro de expresses '(with)in' and 'inside' with regard to physical location, and '(with)in' with reference to time in the future:

La ciudad antigua está dentro de las murallas.
The ancient city is within the walls.

El avión llega dentro de media hora.
The plane arrives in half an hour.

Some Latin Americans use **adentro de** to indicate location, a form not generally accepted in Spain: **Papá está adentro de la casa** [LA] 'Daddy is in the house'.

Fuera de or **afuera de** [LA] means 'outside'.

21.8 Desde

Desde translates 'from', especially to emphasize distance and range (e.g. in prices), or to avoid any possible confusion between 'from' and 'of' that **de** might cause.

It also translates time 'from' or 'since', and in the phrase **desde . . . hasta** with somewhat greater emphasis than **de . . . a**:

Viajó desde Roma hasta Barcelona para verla.
He travelled (all the way) from Rome to Barcelona to see her.

camisas desde diez hasta cien dólares
shirts from ten to a hundred dollars

Estamos buscando casa desde febrero.
We have been looking for a house since February.

La conoce desde niña.
He has known her since childhood.

Note: See 11.4.2 for the use of **desde + hace/hacía** in sentences that state what began in the past and still continues.

21.9 Detrás de, tras

Detrás de means 'after' or 'behind' with reference to position. **Atrás de** is found in Latin America.

In more literary and sometimes journalistic style **tras** is found, especially with the implication 'hidden behind':

¿Qué hay detrás de la casa?   What's behind the house?

| **Alguien esperaba tras la cortina.** | Someone was waiting behind the curtain. |

Tras is regularly found to express 'after' in the form of temporal succession, and following verbs of motion (e.g. 'to run after'):

día tras día	day after day
Tras las lluvias vienen las inundaciones.	After the rains come the floods.
Isabel echó a andar tras él.	Isabel went off after him.

Notes:
1 In Latin America, expressions repeating the same word are often formed with a, día a día 'day after day'.
2 Después de is the usual alternative for a succession of events not expressed by the repetition of one noun: **Las señoras llegaron después de la cena** 'The ladies arrived after dinner'.

21.10 *En, encima de, sobre*

21.10.1 *'In', 'inside', 'into' and 'at'*

Of the above, *only* en indicates 'in(side)' or 'at' of place and time, both literally and figuratively:

Siempre lo lleva en el bolsillo.	He always carries it in(side) his pocket.
Estamos en el aeropuerto.	We are at the airport.
En aquel momento estaba en casa.	At that moment I was at home.
En una semana volvió a escribirlo.	In a week he wrote it again.
Es doctora en informática.	She is a doctor in computing science.

En also states action or movement 'into':

| **Mete el coche/carro [LA] en el garaje.** | Put the car in the garage. |
| **Van a convertirlo en teatro.** | They are going to convert it into a theatre. |

Note: In Latin America **en** after verbs such as **entrar, ingresar, penetrar** is often replaced by **a**: **Entró al cine** [LA] 'She went into the cinema'.

21.10.2 *'On', 'upon', and 'on top of'*

En, sobre and **encima de** are equivalent to '(up)on'. The correct choice to some extent is a matter of common sense and experience. **Arriba de** is used in Latin America.

Sobre and **encima de** are clearly preferable in contexts where **en** could be ambiguous (e.g. **en el armario** 'in' or 'on the cupboard'). In other cases **en** may be used without reservation (e.g. **en mi hombro** 'on my shoulder').

En el suelo hay una alfombrilla persa.	On the floor there is a Persian rug.
Puedes sentarte sobre la cama.	You can sit on the bed.

Although they are often interchangeable, **encima de** may be preferred to **sobre** for reference to greater or unexpected height, equivalent to 'on (top of)':

Lo dejé sobre el estante en la cocina.
I left it on the shelf in the kitchen.

Está escondido encima/arriba [LA] del armario.
It is hidden on top of the cupboard.

Se ve allí encima de la chimenea.
You can see it up there on the chimney.

Note: Note the interesting contrast between **Los vimos en la televisión** 'We saw them on television', and **Lo puso sobre/encima de la televisión.** 'She put it on the television'.

21.10.3 *'Above' and 'over'*

Sobre and **encima de** fit this context with reference to elevation:

Vamos a volar sobre los Alpes.
We are going to fly over the Alps.

¡Mira la nube de humo encima del bosque!
Look at the cloud of smoke above the forest!

Both of them may also be used figuratively in the sense of 'over and above', 'in addition to', 'as well as':

Encima de todo critica a la gente que intenta ayudarlo.
On top of everything he criticizes the people who try to help him.

desgracia sobre desgracia
misfortune on top of misfortune

Sobre has other related uses with regard to superiority, precedence, magnitude and approximation:

Sobre todo pide justicia.	Above all she is asking for justice.
Sobre ellos está la junta directiva.	Above them is the board of directors.
una temperatura de 5 grados sobre cero	a temperature of 5 degrees above zero
Llego sobre las dos.	I'll arrive around two o'clock.

21.10.4 'On', 'about', 'concerning'

Sobre is used with these meanings to express formal treatment of a topic:

una conferencia sobre Brasil   a lecture on Brazil

21.10.5 Expressions formed with en

Amongst the many are:

en broma	as a joke	**en lugar de**	instead of
en casa	at home	**en resumen**	in short
en caso de	in the event of/in case	**enseguida**	right away
en efecto	indeed	**en vez de**	instead of

21.11 Enfrente de, frente a

These correspond to 'opposite', 'in front of':

| el hotel enfrente de la estación | the hotel in front of the station |
| frente al museo | opposite the museum |

Frente a is used additionally with the meaning of 'in the face of', 'in opposition to':

| El Osasuna perdió frente a Valencia. | Osasuna lost against Valencia. |

21.12 Entre

Entre generally is equivalent to 'between', 'among(st)':

No pude decidir entre protestar y callarme.
I could not decide between protesting and keeping quiet.

La escritura de la casa se halla entre otros papeles.
The deed(s) can be found amongst other papers.

Compare, however, Spanish and English usage in the following context:

Entre Jorge, Luis y Antonio lograron formar un equipo.
Between them/Together, Jorge, Luis and Antonio managed to form a team.

Notes:

1 **Entre semana** (or **los días de semana**) means 'on weekdays', 'during the week': **Solo se permite estacionar/parquear** [LA] **entre semana** 'Parking is only permitted on weekdays'.

2 See 8.1.2.2 for the use of pronouns after **entre**.

21.13 Hacia, hasta

Hacia indicates direction 'towards' literally and figuratively:

La carretera se desvía hacia Chipiona.
The road branches off to Chipiona.

No comparto su actitud hacia la guerra.
I do not share his attitude towards war.

Hacia also commonly expresses 'around', 'about' with the sense of 'approximately', both of time and place:

Esperan que salga el tren hacia las cuatro.
They hope the train will leave around 4 o'clock.

¿Dónde está Baena? Está hacia Granada.
Where's Baena? It's near Granada.

Hasta generally indicates 'until', 'as far as', 'up to', both of time and place

El libro estudia el tema hasta 1950.	The book studies the topic up to 1950.
La valla llega hasta el río.	The fence runs as far as the river.

Hasta also forms expressions of farewell:

hasta ahora	see you in a minute	**hasta entonces**	see you then
hasta luego	see you, bye	**hasta mañana**	see you tomorrow
hasta siempre	goodbye	**hasta pronto**	see you soon
hasta la vuelta	see you when I/ you get back	**hasta la vista**	so long

For hasta in the sense of 'not until' [LA], see 30.6.3.3.

21.14 *Según*

Según usually corresponds to 'according to', 'depending on':

Hay que montarlo según las instrucciones.
You have to set it up according to the instructions.

Iremos o no según el tiempo.
We shall go or not depending on the weather.

It is also used on its own, especially in speech in reply to a question, with the meaning of 'it depends':

¿Piensas ir mañana? Según.
Do you intend to go tomorrow? It depends.

Before verbs such as decir 'to say', afirmar 'to affirm', declarar 'to declare', it corresponds to 'according to what':

según afirman algunos científicos
according to what some scientists state

Before other verbs it is used to imply **mientras** or **a medida que** 'as' or 'whilst':

Apunta las notas según las voy diciendo.
Write the marks down as I read them out.

Note: See 8.1.2.2 for the use of pronouns after **según**.

21.15 *Sin*

Sin usually means 'without' before nouns and verbs:

Prefiero las hamburguesas sin mayonesa.
I prefer burgers without mayonnaise.

Se fueron sin dejarnos las llaves.
They left without leaving us the keys.

For **sin** + infinitive with the meaning of 'un-' or 'not', see 17.2.5.1.

21.16 Combinations of prepositions

Frequently prepositions can occur in combinations formed using **de, desde** and **por**:

El agua salía de entre las tablas.
The water came out from between the boards.

Desde detrás de la pared se oía música.
From behind the wall music could be heard.

Por is commonly used to add an idea of movement especially to a compound preposition:

El niño se escondió por debajo de la cama.
The boy hid under the bed.

La autopista pasa casi por encima de su casa.
The motorway/freeway passes almost over their house.

21.17 *Cuando* and *donde* used as prepositions

These normally function as relative adverbs (see 25.6.2). However, in everyday Spanish they are frequently used effectively as prepositions:

Venía aquí mucho cuando niña.
I often came here as a girl.

Eso pasaba mucho cuando la guerra.
This happened a lot during the war.

Viven donde Eduardo y Ana.
They live near Eduardo and Ana.

Chapter 22

Por *and* para

The challenge for the English speaker learning to use these prepositions correctly is that although they might appear to resemble one another, in the sense that both translate English 'for', they are in fact rarely interchangeable without changing the meaning of the Spanish. Although the complete range of subtle differences only becomes clear after studying examples of their use, it is possible to establish at the outset one or two fundamental distinctions.

In general terms **por** looks back towards the source of things whilst **para** refers to the destination of things. **Por** states where things come from and **para** where they are going:

> **El documento fue preparado por el consejo para el rey.**
> The document was prepared by the council (its origin) for the king (its destination).

There are parallels when each of these prepositions is used to designate time and place. **Para** once again refers to aim or destination:

> **Debemos terminarlo para mañana.**
> We must finish it by (or for) tomorrow.

> **Mañana salgo para Sevilla.**
> Tomorrow I leave for Seville.

In contrast **por** designates time 'during which' or place 'through which' something occurs:

> **Vamos a París por un mes.**
> We are going to Paris for a month.

> **Va a Sevilla (pasando) por Madrid.**
> He is going to Seville via Madrid.

Unfortunately, it is not possible to establish clearly contrasting uses for most of the contexts in which **por** and **para** are used.

22.1 Uses of *por*

(a) **Por** indicates the agent 'by whom' or 'by which' an action is initiated thereby introducing the agent or 'doer' in passive constructions:

Fue invadido por los romanos. It was invaded by the Romans.

(b) **Por** indicates the *reason* or *cause* which initiated an action. In English this is frequently 'because of', 'on account of', 'through', 'for':

Me gusta por lo fácil que es.	I like it because of how easy it is.
Lo admiro por su paciencia.	I admire him for his patience.
Por estar enferma no pudo venir.	Through being ill she could not come.

Translating 'for'

Spanish sentences such as **Lo hice por ti** sometimes confuse foreign speakers. In fact, it is an example of the above use with the meaning 'I did it because of/on account of you'. For **Lo hice para ti** 'I did it for you', see 22.2(a).

(c) **Por** denotes time during or throughout which an action takes place often English 'for':

Piensa venir por un mes.   He intends coming for a month.

Note: When the specific action of the verb takes place during the whole period of time mentioned, **durante** 'during' (or no preposition) is used. In the example above, **venir** and 'coming' do not take place for a month. The real meaning is 'coming' and then 'staying' for a month. Compare: **Voy a hablar durante una hora** 'I will speak for one hour', **Estuve en Londres dos días** 'I was in London for two days'.

(d) **Por** indicates a place through which movement takes place, 'through', 'via' or 'along':

Tuvimos que salir por la ventana.	We had to go out via the window.
Caminaba por la selva.	I was walking through the jungle.

(e) **Por** refers to imprecise locations and times, corresponding sometimes to English 'around':

Está por ahí.	It's around somewhere.
Nunca se le ve por la universidad.	You never see him around the university.
No se hacía por entonces.	People did not do it at that time.

For **por la tarde** 'in the afternoon' etc., see 23.1.5.1.

(f) **Por** denotes the manner or means by which something is done, 'by' or 'by means of':

por teléfono/carretera/correo electrónico	by phone/road/e-mail

(g) **Por** refers to the exchange of one thing for another:

Lo compré por 500 euros.	I bought it for 500 euros.
Cambió su regalo por otro.	She changed her present for another.

(h) **Por** states 'on behalf of', 'in favour of', 'in support of':

No lo hagas por mí.	Don't do it just for me.
El está aquí por Andrea.	He's here on behalf of Andrea.
Estoy por los derechos indígenas.	I am in favour of indigenous rights.

(i) **Por** expresses a description or designation that is a personal opinion or evaluation (sometimes English 'for' or 'as'):

Lo tomé por otro.	I took him for someone else.
Podrían pasar por hermanas.	They could pass for sisters.

(j) **Por** translates rate and quantity:

Viene siete veces por semana.	He comes seven times a week.
Es más económico comprarlos por kilo.	It is more economical to buy them by the kilo.

(k) **Por** followed by an infinitive indicates what remains to be done:

Me quedan tres páginas por fotocopiar.	I have three pages left to photocopy.
Está todo por discutir.	Everything is still open for discussion.

(l) **Por** after verbs of movement states the objective of the action:

Ha ido por pan.	He has gone for some bread.
Vinieron por la televisión.	They came for the television.

Note: In the Iberian Peninsula **a** is usually inserted before **por** in the above usage: Ha ido a por pan.

(m) **Por** multiplies:

Cinco por dos son diez.	Five times two is ten.

22.2 Uses of *para*

(a) **Para** indicates destination, with reference to a place, to a person as an intended receiver or beneficiary, or to a function:

Mañana salgo para Guayaquil.	Tomorrow I am leaving for Guayaquil.
unos libros para ti	some books for you
Están estudiando para el examen.	They are studying for the examination.
¿Para qué sirve este instrumento?	What is this instrument for?

(b) **Para** refers to a deadline or target in time, corresponding to 'for', 'by', 'until':

Para el domingo estará completo.	By Sunday it will be complete.
Tengo una cita para el sábado.	I have an appointment for Saturday.
Aplazó la charla para la semana que viene.	He put off the talk until next week.

(c) **Para** followed by an infinitive expresses purpose, corresponding to English '(in order) to':

Se necesita mucho dinero para hacerlo.	You need a lot of money to do it.
Lo dijo para impresionar a la gente.	He said it in order to impress people.
un trapo para limpiar cristales	a cloth for cleaning windows

(d) **Para** introduces a comparison of what appear to be inequalities or disparities, in which one member of the comparison appears to be unex-

---

Para + infinitive contrasted with *por* + infinitive

Whilst **para** + infinitive is the safest option for learners of the language, cases will also be encountered in which **por** appears to fulfil the same function. In fact, generally this is done by native speakers as a means of stating *cause* or *motive* rather than, or perhaps as well as, purpose.

Por in this usage at times expresses the idea of **por querer** 'because of wanting to': **Decidieron no salir por (querer) estar conmigo** 'They decided not to go out, to be with me'.

---

pected in the light of the rest of the sentence. The English may be simply 'for', or 'although', 'in spite of', 'despite', 'considering':

Para un francés habla bien portugués.	For a Frenchman he speaks Portuguese well.
Es bastante maduro para lo joven que es.	He's quite mature considering how young he is.
Es mucho palacio para poca justicia.	It is a large palace despite so little justice.

22.3   *Por* and *para* with *estar* – comparisons

Estar para

In Spain this generally indicates what is about to be done, or is on the point of being done, what might otherwise be expressed as **estar a punto de**:

Estoy para salir. [SP]	I am about to leave.
El tren está para partir. [SP]	The train is on the point of departing.

Note: In Latin America **estar por** frequently conveys this meaning.

Estar por

In addition to having the meanings illustrated in 22.1(h) and (k), **estar por** can be used with a personal subject to indicate personal inclination, 'to be inclined to':

Estaba por decir que no se podía hacer.
I was inclined to say that it could not be done.

Chapter 23

Numerals and numerical expressions

Numerals occur in four forms: *cardinals* which count ('one', 'two', 'three', *ordinals* which refer to sequence ('first', 'second', 'third'), *fractions* which specify parts of a whole ('half', 'two thirds'), and *collectives* which specify groups ('a couple', 'a dozen').

23.1 Cardinal numerals

These are illustrated in Table 23.1.

Spanish cardinals are invariable when used merely as numbers. However, when used to quantify nouns some of them adopt different forms, as described in 23.1.1 to 23.1.4.

Notes: The writing and speaking of numerals.

1   With the exception of Mexico which follows UK and US practice, millions and thousands are indicated by a full stop (or period) as in Table 23.1, and decimals by a comma: **3,2** (**tres coma dos**) '3.2' (three point two).

2   In a reversal of English usage, Spanish requires y 'and' *only* between tens and units, and not after hundreds and thousands: **cincuenta y nueve** 'fifty nine', but **doscientos setenta y siete** 'two hundred and seventy seven', **mil dos** 'one thousand and two'. However, although strictly speaking not the correct form, **mil y uno/a** is widely encountered: **dos mil y un pesos** '2,001 pesos', **mil y una líneas** 'a 1,001 lines'.

3   Telephone numbers are read (and often written) in pairs. If there is an uneven number of digits, the first group is often read as hundreds, or the first digit as a single number: **62–49–00 sesenta y dos, cuarenta y nueve, cero cero, 194–26–06 ciento noventa y cuatro, veintiséis, cero seis** or **uno, noventa y cuatro, veintiséis, cero seis**.

4   Apart from **uno/a** numerals are plural, therefore the question ¿**Cuánto es?** 'How much is it?' would receive a reply such as **Son veinte euros** 'It's 20 euros'.

Table 23.1 Spanish cardinal numbers

cero	0		
uno	1	**treinta**	30
dos	2	**treinta y uno**	31
tres	3	**treinta y dos**	32
cuatro	4	**cuarenta**	40
cinco	5	**cincuenta**	50
seis	6	**sesenta**	60
siete	7	**setenta**	70
ocho	8	**ochenta**	80
nueve	9	**noventa**	90
diez	10	**cien(to)**	100
once	11	**ciento uno**	101
doce	12	**ciento dos**	102
trece	13	**doscientos**	200
catorce	14	**trescientos**	300
quince	15	**cuatrocientos**	400
dieciséis	16	**quinientos**	500
diecisiete	17	**seiscientos**	600
dieciocho	18	**setecientos**	700
diecinueve	19	**ochocientos**	800
veinte	20	**novecientos**	900
veintiuno	21	**mil**	1.000
veintidós	22	**mil uno**	1.001
veintitrés	23	**mil cien**	1.100
veinticuatro	24	**mil ciento uno**	1.101
veinticinco	25	**dos mil**	2.000
veintiséis	26	**veinte mil**	20.000
veintisiete	27	**doscientos mil**	200.000
veintiocho	28	**un millón**	1.000.000
veintinueve	29	**cien millones**	100.000.000
		un billón	1.000.000.000.000

5 Cardinal numbers occur as masculine nouns: **Escribí un dos en vez de un cuatro** 'I wrote a two instead of a four'.

Approximate numbers

Approximate rather than exact numbers can be expressed by placing **unos/as** before a cardinal number: **Está a unos cien kilómetros de la costa** 'It's about a hundred kilometres from the coast'.

Alternative methods are to use the following: **aproximadamente, alrededor de, más o menos, cerca de, cosa de, cosa así, como: Es cosa de 25 centímetros** 'It's about 25 centimetres', **cien kilómetros o cosa así** 'a hundred kilometres or thereabouts', **situado como a 6 millas de la costa** 'situated at some 6 miles from the coast'.

23.1.1 Uno

(a) This agrees in gender with a following noun:

una manzana	one apple	**treinta y una páginas**	thirty-one pages

Note: Regular usage has established that even when modifying a feminine noun, the feminine form **una** is no longer widely used before **mil**: **cincuenta y un mil personas** '51,000 persons'.

(b) The masculine form becomes **un** *before* a masculine noun, whether used on its own or as part of a larger numeral:

un diccionario	one dictionary	**sesenta y un libros**	sixty-one books

Note: For reasons of stress, see 1.3, a written accent is required on 'twenty-one': **veintiún años**.

The feminine form **una** is not shortened before feminine nouns, except when it directly precedes a noun beginning with a stressed **a-** or **ha-**:

cuarenta y un águilas   forty-one eagles

(c) **Un** is not generally used before **ciento** and **mil**: **cien/mil libros** 'a hundred/a thousand books'. Exceptions are cases like the following: **doscientos un mil cuarenta** '201,040' (because **doscientos mil cuarenta** is '200,040').

23.1.2 Ciento

Ciento is shortened to cien before any noun (including any preceding adjective) and before mil, but not before numbers less than a hundred:

cien pesados kilómetros	a hundred boring kilometres
cien mil habitantes	a hundred thousand inhabitants
ciento veinte libras	a hundred and twenty pounds

The shortened form is also used when the following noun is omitted but can be understood from the context:

Le di diez pesos y me quedan cien.	I gave him ten pesos and I have a hundred left.

Notes:

1 Ciento retains its full form when expressing a percentage: El/Un treinta por ciento son hindúes 'Thirty per cent are Hindus'.

2 In contrast to English, multiples of ciento cannot be used to express thousands: mil quinientos = 'fifteen hundred'.

23.1.3 Doscientos, trescientos *etc.*

The compounds formed with -cientos, and quinientos 'five hundred', agree in gender with what is being counted:

doscientas mujeres	two hundred women
quinientas plazas	five hundred places

23.1.4 Mil, millón, billón

Millón and billón are nouns followed by de before whatever is counted:

un millón de dólares	one million dollars
varios billones de pesos	several billion pesos

As an adjective mil is invariable, but when used as a noun it is pluralized:

Mil personas la saludaron.	A thousand people greeted her.
Miles de personas la saludaron.	Thousands of people greeted her.

| **23.1.5** | *Uses of cardinal numbers* |

| **23.1.5.1** | Time of day |

Hours are expressed in the form **ser** (when a verb is required) + **la** or **la** (to agree with the usually unexpressed **hora** or **horas**) + a cardinal number

The appropriate tense of **ser** must be selected, in the 3rd person singular for 'one o'clock' and plural for other hours:

¿Qué hora es?/¿Qué horas son? [LA]	What time is it?
Son las tres (en punto).	It is three o'clock (exactly).
Era la una.	It was one o'clock.

Notes:

1 There are less specific phrases: **Eran las doce y pico** 'It was just after twelve' and **Son las seis pasadas** 'It is just after six o'clock'.

2 **Dar** is used to mean 'to strike' and agrees with the hour: **Están dando las do** 'It's striking two o'clock'.

Minutes past the hour are added by the use of **y** + cardinal number **Minuto(s)** 'minute(s)' is not generally used except for units of less than five minutes. **Cuarto** and **media** denote 'quarter' and 'half' past the hour:

las siete y veinte	twenty past seven/seven twenty
la una y trece minutos	thirteen minutes past one
las diez y cuarto	quarter past ten
las once y media	half past eleven/eleven thirty

Minutes to the hour are indicated by the use of **menos** 'less' + cardinal number or **cuarto**:

la una menos venticinco	twenty-five to one
las cuatro menos veintidós minutos	twenty-two minutes to four
las nueve menos cuarto	quarter to nine

Alternatives are: (i) **faltar** 'to be lacking', 'to be short' + **para**, (ii) **ser** + **para**

| **Faltan tres minutos para las cinco.** | It's three minutes to five. |

| **Son diez para las dos.** | It's ten to two. |

Spanish also uses the formula equivalent to English 'six forty three (6.43)', **las seis cuarenta y tres**. This is also adopted for timetables and other similar contexts which employ the 24 hour clock.

It is common to include **horas** when quoting hours alone from thirteen onwards:

las veinte cuarenta y ocho	20.48/8.48 p.m.
las catorce horas	14.00/2.00 p.m.

Temporal divisions within the day are stated as follows:

de la madrugada	in the morning (until sunrise)
de la mañana	in the morning
de la tarde	in the afternoon/evening
de la noche	at night

Por with times of day

When a specific time is not mentioned, **por** replaces **de** in the above phrases: **Fueron <u>por</u> la tarde** 'they went in the afternoon', but **Fueron a las dos <u>de</u> la tarde** 'They went at two o'clock in the afternoon'.

This provides combinations such as: **ayer por la tarde** 'yesterday afternoon', **mañana por la mañana** 'tomorrow morning'.

23.1.5.2 Dates

In contrast with English, cardinal numbers are always used in Spanish for days of the month, with the exception of the ordinal **primero** 'the first' which frequently replaces **el (día) uno**:

¿Qué fecha era? El (día) siete. What was the date? The seventh.

el primero de abril   the first of April

A full date in Spanish consists of **el** (except at the head of a letter) + cardinal number + **de** + month + **de** + year:

Se fundó el 15 de agosto de 1534.   It was founded on the 15th August 1534.

Dates are always read as full numbers: **setecientos once** '711 (seven eleven)', **mil cuatrocientos noventa y dos** '1492 (fourteen ninety-two)'.

Word order in dates

Word order in Spanish is fixed as above and does not allow the English alternatives, 28th March or March 28th.

Decades are probably best referred to in the following manner: **los (años) sesenta** 'the sixties'.

23.1.5.3 Basic arithmetical calculations

The verb **ser** is used in the plural to mean 'equals':

Cinco y/más seis son once.	$5 + 6 = 11.$
Veinte menos trece son siete.	$20 - 13 = 7.$
Diez (multiplicado) por cuatro son cuarenta.	$10 \times 4 = 40.$
Cien dividido por veinte son cinco.	$100 \div 20 = 5.$

Note: The division symbol in Spanish is :.

23.2 Ordinal numbers

primer(o)/a	1º/1ª	1st
segundo/a	2º/2ª	2nd
tercer(o)/a	3º/3ª	3rd
cuarto/a	4º/4ª	4th
quinto/a	5º/5ª	5th
sexto/a	6º/6ª	6th
sé(p)timo/a	7º/7ª	7th
octavo/a	8º/8ª	8th
noveno/a	9º/9ª	9th
décimo/a	10º/10ª	10th
undécimo/a	11º/11ª	11th
duodécimo/a	12º/12ª	12th
décimo tercer(o)/a	13º/13ª	13th
vigésimo/a	20º/20ª	20th

Ordinals are adjectives which agree both in number and in gender with the noun to which they refer. **Primero** and **tercero** drop the **-o** before a masculine singular noun:

la segunda pregunta	the second question
el tercer punto	the third point

They usually precede nouns except in titles: **Carlos V (quinto)** 'Charles V'.

23.2.1 Use of ordinals

Except in extremely formal or technical language, it is common practice to replace ordinals beyond **décimo** with a cardinal number:

el siglo XX (veinte)	the twentieth century
el capítulo quince	the fifteenth chapter

Beyond 'tenth' only **centésimo** 'one hundredth', and **milésimo** 'one thousandth' are well known and regularly used by native speakers.

The formal reference to anniversaries is a rare case where the ordinals are regularly used:

el vigésimo aniversario	the twentieth anniversary

23.2.2 Adverbial ordinals

Occasionally adverbial forms of ordinals are found, though generally not beyond **primeramente** 'firstly'. More commonly an ordinal + **lugar** 'place' is used: **en segundo lugar** 'secondly'.

23.3 Fractions

23.3.1 ¹/₂ to ¹/₁₀

From ¹/₄ to ¹/₁₀ these are the same as the ordinal numbers: **un noveno** '¹/₉', **tres cuartos** '³/₄'. **Un medio** is '¹/₂' and **un tercio** '¹/₃'.

Notes:

1 **Medio** has several uses in non-arithmetical situations: (i) as a *noun* it means 'middle/centre' or 'means': **en medio del cuarto** 'in the middle of the room', **los medios necesarios** 'the necessary means', (ii) as an *adjective* it means 'half', or

'average/mean': **media luna** 'a half moon', **la temperatura media** 'the average temperature', (iii) as an *adverb* it means 'half': **Ella está medio dormida** 'She i half asleep'. In Latin America it also means 'rather': **Ella es medio linda** [LA 'She is rather pretty'.

2 **La mitad** 'half' is used in non-arithmetical contexts: **Le regaló la mitad de su libros** 'He gave her half of his books'.

In everyday use fractions besides ¹/₂ are often expressed by the feminine form of the ordinal + **parte/s** (this can be omitted in some cases):

la/una tercera parte a third   **siete décimas** seven tenths

23.3.2 *From ¹/₁₁ onwards*

In technical language, from ¹/₁₁ onwards fractions are formed by adding -**avo** to cardinal numbers, unless these end in -**a**, in which case only -**vo** is added:

un catorceavo   ¹/₁₄   **nueve dieciseisavos**   ⁹/₁₆
un sesentavo   ¹/₆₀

A hundredth is **centavo/centésimo** and a thousandth **milésimo**.

Note: In Latin America, but still infrequently in Peninsular usage, the fractiona forms ending in -**avo** are used as ordinals: **el doceavo tomo** [LA] instead of e **duodécimo tomo** or **el tomo número doce** 'the twelfth volume'.

23.4 Collective and multiple numerals

23.4.1

Collective numerals are nouns which specify groups. With the exception o **par**, **docena** and **quincena**, they frequently express approximate rather than exact numbers:

una centena/ **un centenar**	a hundred	**un par**	a pair/couple
una cuarentena	forty	**una quincena**	a fortnight, two weeks
una decena	ten	**una treintena**	thirty
una docena	a dozen	**una veintena**	twenty, a score
un millar	a thousand		

The numeral **ciento** is sometimes used as an alternative to **centenar**, for example in reference to quantities of money, or in the singular in expressions of rate:

Cobró cientos de euros esta semana.
He collected hundreds of euros this week.

500 pesos el ciento [LA]/centenar
500 pesos per hundred

Se ven centenares de delfines aquí.
Hundreds of dolphins are seen here.

Note: **Cuarentena** also means 'quarantine'.

23.4.2

Multiple births are stated as follows: **mellizos/as** (or **gemelos/as**) 'twins', **trillizos/as** 'triplets', **cuatrillizos/as** 'quadruplets', **quintillizos/as** 'quintuplets', **sextillizos/as** 'sextuplets', **septillizos/as** 'septuplets'.

Spanish has no exact equivalent of the English ending '-fold'. Only the first three of the following words are used regularly: **múltiple** 'multiple', **doble** 'double', **triple** 'triple', **cuádruple/cuádruplo** 'quadruple/fourfold', **quíntuple/quíntuplo** 'quintuple/fivefold', **séxtuple/séxtuplo** 'sextuple/sixfold':

un examen de elección múltiple	a multiple-choice examination
aparcar en doble fila	to double park (a car)
el triple salto	the triple jump (athletics)

The general alternative is to use the pattern of cardinal number + **veces** 'times': **La población es diez veces más que la de Inglaterra** 'The population is tenfold/ten times that of England'.

Chapter 24

Negation

The rules governing the way sentences are negated in Spanish are rather different from the equivalent rules in English. For example, while negation in English frequently involves the use of the verb 'do', as in 'John doesn't drive' or 'We didn't see anyone', Spanish never makes use of **hacer** 'to do'.

In addition, while so-called double negatives such as 'We didn't see nobody' are frowned upon in English, it is routine in Spanish to combine two negative words: <u>No</u> vimos a <u>nadie</u>.

24.1 No

This the most common negative word in Spanish. It may be used with the meaning of 'no' to give a negative answer to a question, or with verbs and other words with the sense of 'not', or 'don't', 'doesn't', 'didn't'.

24.1.1 No used with verbs

No precedes verbs to form a negative statement or question. In compound verbal constructions formed with **haber, ser** or **estar**, it precedes the auxiliary:

No quieren venir.	They do not want to come.
No has puesto tu edad.	You haven't filled in your age.

In general, the only item that can be placed between **no** and the verb is a weak object pronoun. If a subject is mentioned, it must precede **no** or be placed after the verb:

No lo veo muy claramente.	I can't see it very clearly.

Luis no se presentó/No se presentó Luis.	Luis didn't turn up.
¿No te gusta?	Don't you like it?

One exception is when **no** does not negate the verb, but some other word that appears before it:

<u>No todos</u> podemos tener un sueldo como el suyo.
Not all of us can have a salary like his.

<u>No siempre</u> ayuda.	He does not always help.

The above patterns are maintained in sentences where a previously used verb is later left unexpressed:

Le interesa el fútbol pero no (le interesa) el rugby.
He likes football but not rugby.

24.1.2 No used to negate words other than verbs

The word **no** is commonly used to negate adjectives or the adverb **muy** 'very':

una huelga no oficial	an unofficial strike
una casa no muy grande	a not very big house

However, as a complement to other words, **no** is usually placed after them:

– ¿Vendrá pronto?	'Will he come soon?'
– Mañana no.	'Not tomorrow.'
¡Corridas no!	No (to) bullfights!

24.2 Other negative words

The following words are sometimes used alone before the verb. Alternatively, they are commonly used after the verb which *must* then be preceded by **no**, thereby creating the double-negative construction generally unacceptable in English, e.g. **Nunca viene** 'He never comes' or **No viene nunca**, literally: × 'He doesn't never come'×.

24.2.1 Nadie 'no one', 'not . . . anyone' and nada 'nothing', 'not . . . anything'

Both of these may precede or follow the verb.

Nada is more common as the verb's object and so is likely to follow:

No descubrió nada.	He found nothing/He didn't find anything.
¿No le felicitó nadie ayer?	Did no one congratulate him yesterday?
Nadie quiere ser asociado con ella.	No one wants to be associated with her.

When qualified by an adjective, **nada** takes the masculine gender:

La teoría no tiene nada novedoso.	The theory has nothing new.

Notes: Other uses of *nada*.

1   As an adverb with the meaning of 'not at all', 'by no means': **No me gusta nada** lo que estoy escuchando 'I don't like at all what I am hearing'.

2   As a noun: **La amenaza surgió de la nada** 'The threat came from nowhere'.

3   In phrases such as: **pues nada** 'well then', 'OK'; **de nada** 'not at all', 'you're welcome'; **nada más** 'nothing more/else'.

4   **Nada más,** especially followed by an infinitive, is found as a colloquial alternative to **apenas** 'scarcely', 'barely', or **en cuanto** 'as soon as': **Nada más levantarse salen de casa** 'As soon as they get up they leave the house'.

24.2.2 Nunca and jamás 'never', 'not ever'

Generally with similar meaning, they are frequently used before the verb but can also be positioned after it in the double-negative construction. **Jamás** is considered to be more emphatic and is less common.

As with **no**, the subject cannot be placed between **nunca** or **jamás** and a following verb:

Rocío nunca viene a cenar a nuestra casa.
Rocío never comes to dinner at our house.

No he probado el gazpacho nunca.
I have never had gazpacho.

Notes:

1 **Nunca** (and not **jamás**) is used in comparisons: **mejor tarde que nunca** 'better late than never'.

2 For the strongest negative effect, both words are sometimes used together: **Nunca jamás volveré a prestarle mi diccionario** 'I will never (ever) lend him my dictionary again'.

24.2.3 **Ni . . . ni** *'neither . . . nor'* and **ni (siquiera)** *'nor', 'not even'*

Each of these combinations is possible before and after the verb.

Ni with the meaning of '(not) even' is optionally reinforced by **siquiera**:

Ni el queso ni las cebollas me gustan.
I do not like either cheese or onions/I like neither cheese nor onions.

No fueron (ni) María, ni su esposo, ni sus hijos.
Neither María, nor her husband, nor their children went.

Ni (siquiera) en la clase lo entendí.
Not even in class did I understand it.

Notes:

1 Less common than the above patterns is the emphatic use of **siquiera** alone after a verb: **No me contestó siquiera** 'He did not even answer me'.

2 **Ni** is followed by the negatives **nadie**, **nada** and **ninguno** (*not* **alguien**, **algo**, **alguno**): **No lo dije ni quería que nadie lo dijera en mi nombre** 'I did not say it nor did I want anyone to say it on my behalf'.

3 **Ni que** + imperfect subjunctive expresses an exclamation with a negative implication: **¡Ni que ella fuera la más lista de la clase!** 'As if she was the cleverest in the class!'.

24.2.4 **Ninguno** *'no', 'not any', 'none'*

Ninguno can be used both as an adjective and as a pronoun, on its own or in a double-negative construction. It agrees in gender with the noun with which it is associated and shortens to **ningún** before a masculine singular noun.

It is now rarely used in the plural as an adjective, except with nouns that are always plural in form, see 2.1.8.

Ninguna de las chicas me conoce.   None of the girls know(s) me.

Ya no se ve a ningún hombre vestido así.
You no longer see any men dressed like that.

No encontró ningunos pantalones que le quedaran bien.
He could not find any trousers which suited him.

Notes:

1 **Ninguno** can be placed after the noun for emphatic effect: **No hay razón ninguna** 'There is no reason at all'.

2 **Alguno** 'some' can be placed after the noun for an even stronger negative meaning, see 9.3.

24.2.5 Tampoco *'neither'*, *'not either'*

This can be used on its own before the verb, or after a verb preceded by **no** or **ni**:

Tampoco vino Isabel.	Isabel didn't come either.
No vieron a los jugadores tampoco.	They did not see the players either.

As with English 'neither' and 'nor', the associated verb is dropped in a negative reply to a statement:

–No me gustó nada. –A mí tampoco.
'I didn't like it at all.' 'Nor did I.'

–No han traído la comida. –La cerveza tampoco.
'They have not brought the food.' 'Nor the beer either.'

24.2.6 Combinations of negatives

Two or more negative words may be combined in a sentence. **No**, or another of them, *must* precede the verb to form the typical Spanish double negative construction. The order in which they are used is generally that of English. For stylistic reasons it is better to avoid a string of more than two negatives after the verb.

No me trajeron nunca nada/Nunca me trajeron nada.
They never brought me anything.

24.3 Expressions using *no*

24.3.1 Expressions using no

(a) More emphatic than **no** alone are: **claro que no/desde luego que no/por supuesto que no** 'of course not'.

(b) **No** + verb + **más que/sino** means 'no more than', 'only', 'nothing but':

No hace sino emborracharse. He does nothing but get drunk.

For **nomás** [LA], see 30.6.3.8.

(c) **No . . . sino** is frequently used to deny one idea and affirm a second:

No fue el viento sino el agua lo que lo destruyó.
It was not the wind but the water that destroyed it.

Common also is the pattern **no solo/solamente . . . sino (también)** 'not only . . . but (also)'. **Sino que** is required before a clause:

Vino no solo su madre sino también su abuela.
Not only her mother but also her grandmother came.

No solo va a la escuela sino que va con muchas ganas.
He not only goes to school, but he goes willingly.

(d) Students should be aware that in some circumstances a seemingly super-fluous **no** is used by native speakers when the intention is clearly *not* meant to be negative. This occurs above all after **hasta que** 'until' when the main clause is negative:

No les des nada hasta que no terminen el trabajo.
Don't give them anything until they finish the work.

This superfluous **no** is sometimes used in comparisons after **que**, especially if this **que** would otherwise be followed directly by a clause introduced by **que**:

Es mejor que esperes más tiempo que no que te vayas sin verlo.
It's better for you to wait longer than go off without seeing him.

For the use of **no** in question tags, e.g. ¿**no es verdad?**, see 27.3.

24.4 Spanish negatives with English affirmative meaning

In some cases a Spanish negative word will translate an English word that is not itself negative, as in **sin decir nada** 'without saying anything'. This phenomenon is particularly common in the following contexts:

(a) After **sin, sin que, antes de, antes que,** and **apenas:**

sin afirmar nunca nada	without ever stating anything
Antes que nada debo ver el documento original.	First of all I must see the original document.

(b) In sentences which make comparisons:

Jugó mejor que nadie.	He played better than anyone.

(c) After phrases which express negative ideas such as impossibility, improbability, doubt and denial:

Dudo que nadie viva en este lugar.
I doubt whether anyone lives in this place.

Era imposible que ninguno de ellos lo robara.
It was imposible that any of them should steal it.

(d) In questions asked in expectation of a negative answer:

¿Es que jamás le molestó a nadie?
Did it ever upset anyone?

24.5 Affirmative phrases with negative meaning

Whereas the English equivalent is always accompanied by a negative word, there are seemingly affirmative phrases in Spanish which are used commonly (or optionally) without a negative to convey negative meaning. The most common of these are **en mi/la vida** 'never in my life', **en absoluto** 'absolutely not', 'not at all':

En mi/la vida he estado en un hotel tan malo.
Never in my life have I been in such a terrible hotel.

–¿Vas a consultarla? –En absoluto.
'Are you going to consult her?' 'Absolutely not.'

Chapter 25

Relative clauses

A relative clause plays a modifying role in a sentence. For example, the sequence 'who complain' in the sentence 'They don't like customers who complain' is a relative clause and it qualifies the noun 'customers', since it specifies which type of customers are not liked.

Relative clauses in English are often introduced by words like 'who', 'whom', 'which', 'that', 'where', 'whose':

I haven't spoken to the lady *who* booked the holiday.
The meal *that* we had was delicious.
The house *where* we used to live has been demolished.
I don't know the reason *why* they sold the house.
He is the person *whose* flat we have been staying in.

The clause introduced by these words is referred to as the *subordinate clause*, and the clause that contains the element qualified by the relative clause is called the *main clause*. The qualified element is known as the *antecedent*. For example, the noun 'house' and the pronoun 'one' are the antecedents in the following sentences:

They live in a house that is close to the beach.
I've got one that is broken.

25.1   Differences between Spanish and English relative clauses

25.1.1   *Omission of the relative pronoun*

A relative pronoun in English is often omitted:

The man we saw at the beach   =   The man that we saw at the
is here.   beach is here.

In contrast, a Spanish relative pronoun can *never* be omitted. Therefore, the relative pronoun **que**, meaning 'that', cannot be omitted from the following sentence: **El hombre que vimos en la playa está aquí.**

25.1.2 *Spanish relative clauses cannot end in a preposition*

It should also be noted that while in English a preposition can be 'stranded' at the end of the relative clause, in Spanish it must be placed immediately *before* the associated relative pronoun:

Allí está el hombre de quien hablábamos.
There's the man (who) we were talking about.

25.2 Restrictive and non-restrictive relative clauses

A relative clause may be restrictive or non-restrictive:

Los niños que estaban cansados tuvieron que ir a la cama.
(restrictive)
The children who were tired had to go to bed. (restrictive)

Los niños, que estaban cansados, tuvieron que ir a la cama.
(non-restrictive)
The children, who were tired, had to go to bed. (non-restrictive)

In the first sentence, the relative clause **que estaban cansados** defines a sub-group within the group of children, namely those who were tired. It is only these children who had to go to bed. So the restrictive clause restricts what is denoted by the antecedent: not just children but children who were tired.

In the second sentence the relative clause **que estaban cansados** does not define a sub-group among the children. This can be seen from the fact that the overall sentence implies that *all* the children were tired and *all* the children had to go to bed. So a non-restrictive clause does not restrict its antecedent.

Non-restrictive clauses are sometimes placed in the sentence between commas, and in speech set apart by pauses.

English 'that' can only be used in restrictive relative clauses while 'who' and 'which', for example, can be used both restrictively and non-restrictively.

25.3 Spanish relative pronouns, adverbs and adjectives

An inventory of Spanish relative words is given in Table 25.1:

Table 25.1 Spanish relatives

Pronouns	**que** (invariable)	that/who/which
	quien, quienes	who/whom
	el que, la que, los que, las que	who/whom/which
	el cual, la cual, los cuales, las cuales	who/whom/which
	lo que, lo cual (neuter)	what/which
Adverbs	**donde**	where
	cuando	when
Adjective	**cuyo, cuya, cuyos, cuyas**	whose
Adjective/ pronoun	**cuanto, cuanta, cuantos, cuantas**	as much/many

---

Note: The word **como** 'how' can also be used as a relative adverb. However it only appears in one type of context, namely after **manera** 'manner': **No le gustaba la manera como le hablaban a su esposa** 'He didn't like the way in which they talked to his wife'. In everyday speech, the phrase **la manera como** is usually replaced by **la manera en que**.

25.4 A basic system

Although relative clauses are not one of the more difficult areas of Spanish grammar, they can seem so if an attempt is made to learn all of the alternative forms at once. Therefore, in the first instance it is advisable to learn a basic system and to postpone until later any consideration of alternative forms or patterns of regional variation. Such a system is presented below. Possible alternatives (including **el cual** for **el que**) are discussed in 25.5.

In what follows, it is assumed that English prepositions that are 'stranded' at the end of a relative clause (see 25.1.2) are relocated to the position immediately before the relative pronoun prior to translation: e.g. 'The man that we spoke <u>about</u>' > 'The man <u>about</u> whom we spoke'.

Note also that constructions such as 'it was John who ...' and 'it wa
yesterday that ...' are not included in the basic system. They are dealt witl
in 25.6.

25.4.1 *Translating 'that' (restrictive clauses only)*

Unless used with a 'stranded' preposition, the English relative pronoun
'that' can normally be equated with **que** in Spanish:

La comida que te dan es asquerosa.
The food that they give you is horrible.

Me lo dijo el abogado que lleva el caso.
The lawyer that is handling the case said so.

Note: A phrase such as 'the house that he lived *in*', in which 'that' introduces a rela
tive clause with a 'stranded' preposition, must be re-formed before translation a
'the house in which he lived'. See 25.4.3.1(b) and 25.5.2.

25.4.2 *Translating 'who' and 'whom'*

25.4.2.1 In restrictive relative clauses

(a) 'Who' should be translated by **que** (*not* **quien** or **quienes**):

No conozco a los inquilinos que viven abajo.
I don't know the tenants who live downstairs.

Conozco a una chica que ha estado allí.
I know a girl who has been there.

However, if 'who' is the direct object in the relative clause (a substitute fo1
'whom'), then while **que** is normally acceptable, it is in practice safer tc
use an appropriate form from the **el que** series preceded by the personal **a**
The gender and number of the **el que** pronoun agrees with that of the
antecedent:

Esta es la chica a la que detuvieron.
This is the girl who(m) they arrested.

(b) If 'whom' is preceded by a preposition, then **quien/quienes** or an appropriate form from the **el que** series should be used. The gender and/or
number of the relative pronoun should agree with that of the antecedent:

La chica con quien iba a compartir el piso ha perdido su trabajo.
The girl with whom I was going to share the flat has lost her job.

La persona de la que están hablando es un vecino mío.
The person they are talking about (i.e. 'about whom') is a neighbour of mine.

Translating 'who'

Students should resist the temptation automatically to translate English 'who' by Spanish **quien**. In practice **quien** is unlikely to be appropriate unless it is preceded by a preposition. Sequences such as ×**el niño quien vimos**× or ×**la chica quien quiere hablar**× should immediately trigger an alarm bell.

25.4.2.2 'Who' and 'whom' in non-restrictive relative clauses

The rules given in 25.4.2.1 can be followed:

Ellos, que siempre han vivido en el centro, se han comprado una casa en las afueras.
They, who have always lived in the centre, have bought a house on the outskirts.

Pronto perdieron el respeto a Gutiérrez, al que calificaron de inepto.
They soon lost their respect for Gutiérrez, whom they described as inept.

However, it is also possible, particularly in more formal Spanish, to replace **que** with **quien** or **quienes**:

Al final pude localizar a Pedro, quien en aquella época trabajaba en Sevilla.
In the end I managed to locate Pedro, who at that time was working in Seville.

25.4.3 Translating 'which' in relative clauses

25.4.3.1 In restrictive relative clauses

(a) If 'which' is not preceded by a preposition, then **que** should generally be used:

No sé dónde he metido los pendientes que me compraste.
I don't know where I've put the earrings which you bought for me.

(b) If 'which' is preceded by a preposition, an appropriate form from the **el que** series should be used:

Son cosas con las que la mayoría de la gente solamente puede soñar.
They are things about which most people can only dream.

Era un tema al que echaban poca importancia.
It was a matter to which they attached little importance.

If the antecedent is a genderless word like **algo** 'something' or **nada** 'nothing', or an adjective preceded by **lo**, then the neuter pronoun **lo que** should be used:

No hay nada por lo que tienes que estar preocupado.
There is nothing about which you need to be worried.

Lo único con lo que está contento es con sus trenecitos.
The only thing he is happy with is his toy trains.

25.4.3.2 'Which' in non-restrictive relative clauses

The rules are essentially as in 25.4.3.1:

Todavía recuerdo esos sermones, que tuvimos que aguantar durante una semana.
I still remember those lectures, which we had to put up with for a week.

Había dos cómodas antiguas, en las que guardaban toda suerte de trastos.
There were two antique chests of drawers, in which they kept all kinds of clutter.

In addition, neuter **lo que** and **lo cual** can be used on their own or after a preposition. They are required when the antecedent is the preceding main clause itself:

Han retrasado todos los vuelos, lo que hace pensar que hay un problema grave.
They've delayed all the flights, which makes you think there is a serious problem.

Les han dado permiso para construir, con lo cual no estamos muy conformes.
They've given them planning permission, which we aren't very happy about.

25.4.4 Translating 'when' in a relative clause

25.4.4.1 In restrictive relative clauses

Unlike its English equivalent, Spanish **cuando** cannot be used as a relative adverb in a restrictive relative clause. Instead the preposition **en** followed by **que** should be used or, more colloquially, **que** on its own:

El mes (en) que más llueve aquí es octubre.
The month when it rains most here is October.

Incluso las noches que refrescaba no podía dormir.
Even on those nights when it got cooler I couldn't sleep.

25.4.4.2 'When' in non-restrictive relative clauses

Here **cuando** is normal:

Lo haremos la semana que viene, cuando vengan los primos.
We'll do it next week, when your cousins come.

25.4.5 Translating 'where' in a relative clause

Spanish **donde** is used to translate English 'where' in both restrictive and non-restrictive relative clauses. Depending on the associated verb, a preposition may precede **donde** to indicate destination (**a, hacia**), origin or source (**de, desde**), or location (**en, por**).

A + donde > adonde:

¿Cómo se llama la tienda donde compramos tus gafas de sol?
What is the name of the shop where we bought your sunglasses?

Como él era del pueblo adonde iba, ofreció llevarme en su furgoneta.
As he was from the village I was going to, he offered to take me in his van.

Por fin llegamos a la cima, desde donde había unas vistas espectaculares.
We finally reached the summit, from where there were spectacular views.

25.4.6 Translating 'why' in a relative clause (restrictive clauses only)

To translate English 'why' used as a relative adverb, a combination of **por** and **la que** (for antecedent **la razón**) should be used:

No se sabe la razón por la que se fue.
The reason why he went away is not known.

25.4.7 Translating 'whose' in a relative clause

In careful Spanish, English 'whose' is translated by **cuyo**, which functions as a possessive adjective within a relative clause (restrictive or non-restrictive).

Cuyo agrees in number and gender with the item possessed, or if there are several items only with the first.

Unlike 'whose', which some speakers do not use with non-human antecedents, **cuyo** occurs with both human and non-human antecedents:

El dueño, cuyo mayor interés era no ofender a la clientela, no pudo oponerse.
The owner, whose main concern was not to offend the customers, could not object.

Vi varias casas a cuyas ventanas les faltaba el cristal.
I saw several houses the windows of which had no glass.

La policía ha detenido a un hombre cuya identidad y domicilio se desconocen.
The police have arrested a man whose identity and abode is not known.

Note: The phrase **en cuyo caso** means 'in which case'.

Relative clauses introduced by **cuyo** are replaced in informal speech by full clauses introduced by **que** + possessive adjective:

Este es el chico que su padre es un ministro.
Literally: 'This is the boy that his father is a minister.'

Instead of:

Este es el chico cuyo padre es un ministro.
This is the boy whose father is a minister.

25.4.8 *Translating 'what' in a relative clause*

See 3.4.4.

25.5 Alternatives to the basic system

25.5.1 El que *and* el cual

The **el que** and **el cual** series of pronouns are virtually identical in terms of their grammatical functions. They differ however in terms of their frequency of use, although there is also a regional bias. In the Iberian Peninsula **el cual** is notably less common in speech than **el que**, although in many parts of Latin America the reverse situation is true. Therefore depending on the formality of the context or on the region in which one finds oneself, the **el cual** series can replace the **el que** series in all the uses exemplified in 25.4.2.1(b), 25.4.2.2, 25.4.3.1(b) and 25.4.3.2:

¿Cómo se llama el hombre con el cual hemos hablado esta mañana?
What is the name of the man we spoke to/with this morning?

Hubo un intento de calmar a los manifestantes, muchos de los cuales desconfiaban de la policía.
An attempt was made to pacify the protesters, many of whom distrusted the police.

Hojeé las páginas del libro, entre las cuales encontré una postal escrita por ella.
I flicked through the pages of the book, among which I found a postcard written by her.

25.5.2 *Use of* que *after a preposition*

Commonly in the case of **en**, and to a lesser extent with **a**, **con** and **de**, it is possible to have a preposition directly followed by **que**:

Es una obra de teatro en que nadie tiene un papel agradable.
It's a play in which nobody has a nice role.

Esta es la casa con que llevaban tanto tiempo soñando.
This is the house they had been dreaming of for so long.

However, the safest option, in the Peninsula at least, is almost always to use the **el que** series.

One case in which this practice should not be adopted is after nouns denoting periods of time (e.g. **vez** 'time', **día** 'day', **año** 'year'). In this case, **en** followed directly by **que** or, more colloquially, just **que** will suffice:

La primera vez que la vi fue el verano pasado.
The first time I saw her was last summer.

el día (en) que nació Luis
the day Luis was born

25.6 Focusing on words or phrases

English is able to focus on part of a sentence with phrases such as 'it was John who . . .', 'it was in Segovia/June that . . .'. These are called 'cleft' sentences.

The effect of an English cleft sentence can be achieved in Spanish through the use of the relative pronoun **quien/quienes** and those in the **el que** series, or through the relative adverbs **donde**, **cuando** and **como**.

Essentially, while English says, for example, 'it was John who did it', Spanish says 'the one who (**el que**) did it was John':

El que lo hizo fue Juan.   The one who did it was Juan.

Frequently, however, the verb **ser** is moved to the beginning of the sentence and the **el que** phrase is moved to the end, thereby masking the real structure of the sentence:

Fue Juan el que lo hizo.   It was Juan who did it.

Note also that the pronoun **quien/quienes** is used identically to **el que** in this construction:

Fue Juan quien lo hizo.   It was Juan who did it.

25.6.1 El que, lo que, quien

In this usage, these are best understood as meaning 'the one who/that' or 'those who/that'.

Pronouns in the **el que** series refer to humans or non-humans, while **quien/quienes** can only refer to persons:

Son ellos quienes/los que no quieren pagar.
It's they who don't want to pay.

Es la tuya la que se ha perdido.
It's yours that has been lost.

Lo que is used in this construction with reference to a previously unidentified item:

Es el garaje lo que han pintado.
It's the garage (that) they've painted/What they've painted is the garage.

Notes:

1 Sequences such as ×**Fue Juan que lo hizo**× are considered ungrammatical in Peninsular Spanish.

2 If the subject or complement of **ser** in this construction is **nosotros** or **vosotros** [SP], then **ser** agrees in number with the pronoun: **Sois vosotros los que tenéis que investigarlo** [SP] 'It's you who need to investigate it'.

In Peninsular Spanish, if the focused noun or pronoun follows a preposition (including personal **a**), this preposition must be repeated before the relative pronoun:

Fue con la secretaria con la que hablé.
It was to the secretary that I spoke.

Es a María a la que han nombrado.
It's María they've nominated.

Notes:

1 For an alternative construction in Latin America, see 30.5.

2 With **por eso** 'for that reason', the following pattern is acceptable in all parts of the Spanish-speaking world: **Es por eso que** (rather than **por lo que**) **no quería ir** 'That's why I didn't want to go'.

25.6.2 **Cuando, donde, como**

These relative adverbs are used like **quien** and **el que** in focus constructions. For example, where English says 'it was in June that he was born', Spanish says 'when he was born was in June': **Cuando nació fue en junio** or, more commonly, **Fue en junio cuando nació.**

Fue en septiembre cuando nos casamos.
It was in September that we got married.

Es en Alemania donde se celebrarán los mundiales.
It's in Germany that the World Cup will take place.

Es así como hay que hacerlo. This is how you do it.

For Latin American alternatives, see 30.6.

25.7 **Use of el que and quien to mean 'anybody who', 'those who'**

25.7.1 **El que**

In the appropriate forms for number and gender, **el que** is used as an equivalent to English 'he/she/those who':

El que estudie aprobará.	He who studies will pass.
Los que digan eso son unos reaccionarios.	Those who say that are reactionaries.

25.7.2 **Quien**

Similarly, **quien/es** may be deemed to embody its own unexpressed indefinite antecedent, equivalent to 'anyone who', 'those who':

No hay quien te aguante.	There isn't anyone who can put up with you.

No faltaban quienes envidiaban su buena suerte.
People/Those who envied his good fortune were not lacking.

25.8 *Cuanto* 'as much/many as'

In principle **cuanto** is a quantifying adjective and so agrees in number and gender with the noun it modifies. It is equivalent in meaning to **todo el que**, **todos los que** etc:

Tomaremos cuantas medidas sean necesarias.
We will take all the necessary measures.

Bebe cuanta agua necesites.   Drink all the water you need.

However, the form **cuanto** can also be used as an invariable neuter pronoun with general reference (in this use it is occasionally reinforced with **todo** 'everything', 'all that'):

Hice cuanto pude.   I did everything I could.

Les dimos todo cuanto   We gave them everything we
teníamos.   had.

25.9 Relative clauses with infinitives

Particularly when the antecedent is an indefinite or negative pronoun such as **algo** 'something' or **nada** 'nothing', a relative clause may have an infinitive as its main verb:

No tengo nada con lo que secarme las manos.
I haven't got anything to dry my hands with.

Esto me ha dado mucho en que pensar.
This has given me a lot to think about.

In some cases the antecedent can be omitted too, in which case a written accent must be applied to the relative pronoun or adverb:

No tengo con qué lavarme el pelo.
I haven't got anything to wash my hair with.

No encontramos dónde dormir.
We couldn't find anywhere to sleep.

Chapter 26

Comparative and superlative constructions

Comparative constructions are used to express *inequality*: 'Peter is taller than John', 'Peter is more/less liberal than John', and *equality*: 'Peter is as tall/liberal as John'.

Superlative constructions establish limits: 'Peter is the tallest/most liberal'.

In Spanish the corresponding words are: **más** 'more', **menos** 'less', **tan** 'as', **tanto/a/os/as** 'as much/many', and the link words **que**, **de** and **como**.

26.1 Comparisons involving adjectives or adverbs

26.1.1 The basic pattern

The basic pattern for expressions of *inequality* involves **más/menos** + adjective/adverb + **que**. For *equality* it is **tan** + adjective/adverb + **como**:

> **Pedro es más/menos alto que Luis.**
> Pedro is taller/shorter than Luis.

> **Pedro es tan alto como Luis.**
> Pedro is as tall as Luis.

> **Pedro conduce más/menos despacio que Luis.**
> Pedro drives more/less slowly than Luis.

> **Pedro conduce tan despacio como Luis.**
> Pedro drives as slowly as Luis.

26.1.2 Irregular comparatives

26.1.2.1 Forms

Single-word comparative forms are available for the following adjectives and adverbs:

Irregular comparatives			
Adjectives		Adverbs	
bueno good	**mejor** better	**bien** well	**mejor** better
grande big	**mayor** greater, older	**mal** badly	**peor** worse
malo bad	**peor** worse		
pequeño small	**menor** lesser, younger		

The adjectives are invariable for gender but have plurals in -es. The adverbs are invariable:

Mi bicicleta es mejor que la tuya.	My bike is better than yours.
Estos niños son menores que los míos.	These children are younger than mine.
Cantan mejor que yo.	They sing better than me.

The regular forms **más bueno/más bien**, and **más malo/más mal** are usually replaced in comparative constructions by **mejor** and **peor**.

Más grande and **más pequeño** are used commonly, though not in an identical sense to **mayor** and **menor**, see 26.1.2.2.

Notes:

1 **Más bien** is found with the meaning of 'rather': **Su mirada era más bien triste** 'She had a rather sad look'.

2 **Más bueno/malo** are found with reference to moral qualities: **ser más bueno que el pan** 'to be very good'.

26.1.2.2 *Mayor* and *menor* compared with *más grande* and *más pequeño*

Más grande and **más pequeño** are used above all to indicate physical size:

Mi casa es más grande/pequeña que la tuya.
My house is bigger/smaller than yours.

Mayor and **menor** are used to refer to age:

Pedro es mayor/menor que Luis.	Pedro is older/younger than Luis.
una persona mayor	an elderly person

Mayor can be used like **más grande** to indicate physical size. However, i normally means 'greater', expressing a higher degree or intensity, or simply importance:

El índice de paro es mayor allí que aquí.
Unemployment is higher there than here.

Estas pastillas tienen mayor efecto.
These pills have a greater effect.

la Calle Mayor
the High Street

In addition to referring to age, **menor** is used for abstract comparisons. I is *rarely* used as an alternative to **más pequeño** to refer to physical size:

Ahora viene con menor frecuencia.
Now she comes less often.

Se vende en cantidades cada vez menores.
It sells in smaller and smaller quantities.

26.2 Comparisons involving nouns

26.2.1 Comparisons of inequality involving nouns

For comparisons of inequality expressing 'more than' and 'less/fewer than', the pattern is the same as for adjectives, **más/menos** + noun + **que**:

Pedro comió más/menos patatas que tú.
Pedro ate more/fewer potatoes than you.

Hace más calor en Sevilla que en Madrid.
It's hotter in Seville than in Madrid.

When the word **mucho** is used in comparisons involving nouns it agrees with its associated noun:

Comió muchas más patatas que tú.
He ate many more potatoes than you.

mucha menos velocidad
much less speed

26.2.2 Comparisons of equality involving nouns

With comparisons of equality, expressing 'as much/many ... as', the pattern is **tanto/a/os/as ... como**:

Pedro tiene tantas camisas como Luis.	Pedro has as many shirts as Luis.
No hace tanto calor en Cantabria.	It isn't so hot in Cantabria.

Uses of *de* after *más* and *menos*

Note: **Tanto/a/os/as . . . + que** indicates a result, 'so much/many . . . that': **Bebió tantas copas que se emborrachó** 'He drank so many glasses that he got drunk'.

26.3 Comparisons involving verbs

With comparisons of *inequality* relating to the action of a verb, the pattern is verb + **más/menos** + **que**:

Susana trabaja más/menos que tú.	Susana works more/less than you.

In comparisons of *equality*, the pattern is verb + **tanto** (in this case invariable) + **como**:

Susana trabaja tanto como tú.	Susana works as much as you.

26.4 Uses of *de* after *más* and *menos*

26.4.1 Before numbers

De must replace **que** as the link word meaning 'than' after **más** or **menos** in comparisons that state 'more' or 'less' than a number or numerical expression (such as 'half', 'dozen'), or before other words that imply an amount or quantity:

No vengas más tarde de las ocho.	Don't come any later than eight o'clock.
Murieron menos de la mitad de los pasajeros.	Fewer than half the passengers died.
Vino menos gente de la esperada.	Fewer people than expected came.

Note: Care should be taken to distinguish between **no más de** 'not more than', and **no más que** 'only': **No distribuyeron más de diez kilos** 'They did not distribute more than ten kilos', and **No distribuyeron más que diez kilos** 'They only distributed ten kilos'. See 26.7(a).

| 26.4.2 | **Más/menos de** *before a clause* |

This usage occurs when the comparative precedes a subordinate clause with its own finite verb.

If the comparison relates to a specific noun in the main clause, the pattern is **más/menos + del/de la/de los/de las + que**, reflecting the number and gender of that noun:

Tiene más dinero del que necesita.	He has more money than he needs.
Hubo menos problemas de los que esperaba.	There were fewer problems than I expected.
Has comprado más carpetas de las que necesitamos.	You've bought more folders than we need.

On the other hand, if the comparison refers to the main clause as whole, rather than to a specific noun within it, the pattern is **más de lo que**:

| **Pedro es más listo de lo que creíamos.** | Pedro is cleverer than we thought. |

Comparisions involving *de lo que*

It may help to think of this as meaning 'than what', where **de** means 'than' and **lo que** means 'what'. In this way, the sentence **Elena gana menos de lo que pensaba** can be thought of as meaning 'Elena earns less than what I thought'.

| 26.5 | *Cuanto más* and *cuanto menos* |

The English construction 'the more/less . . . the more/less . . .' is expressed using **cuanto más/menos . . . (tanto) más/menos . . .**. **Cuanto** and **tanto** agree with any associated noun, although **tanto** is nowadays usually omitted from the second part of the construction.

Irregular comparatives may be used instead of **más/menos . . ..**

Cuantos más trabajos corregimos ahora menos tendremos que hacer esta noche.
The more assignments we mark now, the fewer we'll have to do tonight.

Cuanto más lo pienso menos me apetece.
The more I think about it the less I fancy it.

In speech **cuanto** is often replaced by **mientras: Mientras más lo toques más te va a picar** 'The more you touch it the more it will itch'.

26.6 Superlative constructions

26.6.1 Adjectives

These are usually expressed in English by the suffix '-est' (e.g. 'the happiest') or by using the word 'most' (e.g. 'our most sought-after product').

In Spanish they are typically rendered by the use of the definite article/possessive adjective, a noun and a comparative adjective.

De translates a following 'in':

la montaña más alta de España	the highest mountain in Spain
nuestros productos más solicitados	our most sought-after products
su mayor éxito	her greatest success

If the context allows, the noun can be omitted from this construction:

No compres la más cara.	Don't buy the most expensive one.

Note: French speakers should be aware that Spanish does not repeat the article before the comparative: compare 'le garçon *le* plus intelligent de la classe', with **el chico más inteligente de la clase** 'the most intelligent boy in the class'.

The definite article is *not* used in Spanish to form superlatives with adjectives that are governed by verbs meaning 'to be', 'to seem', 'to look', 'to become' etc:

Es en verano cuando el agua del mar está/se pone más caliente.
It's in the summer that the sea is/becomes warmest.

Así es como queda más bonito. That's the way it looks nicest.

26.6.2 Superlative adverbs

These are formed without the use of the definite article, by either más/menos + adverb, or by one of the irregular comparative adverbs such as **mejor**:

Es Pedro quien conduce más despacio.	It's Pedro who drives slowest.
El que baila peor es Antonio.	The one who dances worst is Antonio.

But if the adverb is qualified by a relative clause or by an adjective, then **lo** is used:

Conduce [SP] lo más despacio que puedas.	Drive as slowly as you can.
Ven lo más pronto posible.	Come as soon as possible.

Note: Lo is used also in phrases such as **lo más temprano/tarde posible** 'as early/late as possible', **lo antes posible** 'as soon as possible'.

To express ideas like 'works hardest', 'eats the most', the word **más** should be used:

Ana es la que más trabaja.	Ana is the one who works hardest.
La que más come es Pepi.	The one who eats the most is Pepi.

Superlative adverbs

Students should resist the temptation to automatically use **lo** with superlative adverbs. This is *only* required when the adverb is qualified. So **¿Quién baila mejor?** 'Who dances best?' but **Hazlo lo mejor que puedas** 'Do it the best way that you can'.

26.6.3 Absolute superlatives ending in -ísimo

The suffix **-ísimo** can be added to an adjective to intensify its meaning, resulting in one corresponding to a strong form of the English 'very + adjective'.

As adjectival forms, they adopt the appropriate endings for gender and number relevant to the noun which they modify. Any written accent on the original Spanish adjective is removed.

Adjectives ending in a consonant simply attach the ending. Those ending in a single vowel drop the vowel:

un juez liberalísimo   a very liberal judge

un tren rapidísimo   a very fast train

Adjectives ending in two vowels drop both of them unless they form two syllables, in which case only the last vowel is dropped:

una superficie limpísima   an extra clean surface

un paisaje feísimo   an extremely ugly landscape

As a result of the above, some adjectives may also require a spelling change according to the general norms of pronunciation and spelling, notably those ending in -**co**, -**go** and -**z**:

poco   poquísimo   largo   larguísimo   feliz   felicísimo

Most adjectives ending in -**ble** change this to -**bil** before adding -**ísimo**:

amable   amabilísimo   very friendly

Amongst the most commonly used irregular forms are: **antiquísimo** 'very old', 'ancient', **jovencísimo** 'very young', **pésimo** 'very bad', 'dreadful' and **fidelísimo** 'very faithful'.

Máximo 'greatest' and **mínimo** 'least', 'slightest', are used as follows: **Su máxima ambición** 'her greatest ambition', **la tarifa mínima** 'the minimum charge'.

Students of Portuguese should note that **óptimo** 'superb', 'excellent' is usually literary in Spanish and not comparable in use with its Portuguese equivalent.

The suffix -ísimo

This cannot be added to all adjectives. Many adopt very different forms, especially in the literary language. For this reason, unless entirely certain, foreign students are advised to adopt other means of intensifying an adjective, e.g. by using words such as **muy, sumamente, extremadamente, altamente, excesivamente: Carmen es sumamente eficaz** 'Carmen is outstandingly efficient'.

Another alternative is to use prefixes such as **re-** and **super-**, see 29.2.4 and 29.2.6.

This may be added to adjectives, although only infrequently, to form an intensified adverb, as in English 'very/most . . . ly':

rápido	**rapidísimamente**	very rapidly
claro	**clarísimamente**	most clearly

26.7 Other comparative expressions

(a) No más que 'only':

Juan no habla más que de política.	Juan only talks about politics.

(b) Nada más que 'nothing except':

No había nada más que dos bollitos de pan.	There was nothing except two bread rolls.

(c) Nadie más que 'nobody except':

No vimos a nadie más que a Pedro.	We saw no one except Pedro.

(d) Cada vez más/menos 'more and more'/'less and less':

El tren iba cada vez más rápido.	The train went faster and faster.
Viene cada vez menos gente.	Fewer and fewer people come.

26.8 Other expressions of equality – 'the same (thing) as'

The English word 'as' is translated using **que** after words meaning 'same'.

These are: **mismo** before *nouns*, **igual** after *verbs* and **igual de** before *adjectives*. Lo mismo is equivalent to 'the same (thing)':

Tiene el mismo televisor que nosotros.	He has the same television set as us.
Ana es igual que su madre.	Ana is just like her mother.
Es igual de antipático que su hermano.	He's as unpleasant as his brother.
Dijo lo mismo que Luis.	He said the same thing as Luis.

Chapter 27

Questions and exclamations

Questions can be direct, as in 'Where is Pedro?', or indirect, as in 'Nobody knew where Pedro was'. A direct question is a complete sentence in itself and usually requires an answer. An indirect question is only part of a sentence and does not in itself require an answer.

Within the category of direct questions, there are two basic types: (i) those introduced by an interrogative word (see Table 27.1) and (ii) those that require a 'yes/no' answer, such as **¿Es difícil leerlo?** 'Is it difficult to read it?'.

In English some form of the auxiliary verb 'do' is often required in a direct question. In Spanish, questions are never formed in this way. Instead they are marked as such by reversal of the usual subject + verb word order, and by a question mark at their beginning (inverted) and their end:

¿Fue Miguel a la cena?   Did Miguel attend the dinner?

A preposition in Spanish cannot be 'stranded' at the end of a question. Instead it must be placed immediately before the interrogative word with which it is associated:

¿En qué habitación estás? (not ×**¿Qué habitación estás en?**×)
What room are you in?

27.1   Subject-verb inversion

In both direct and indirect questions the Spanish subject is frequently placed after the verb:

¿Qué disco ha comprado Javier?   What disk has Javier bought?

Nadie sabe dónde está el hospital.   No one knows where the hospital is.

However, when the interrogative word itself is the subject, or modifies the subject, Spanish like English does not invert word order:

¿Quien ha hecho esto?   Who has done this?

¿Cuánta gente asistió?   How many people attended?

See also 28.6.

27.2 Spanish interrogative words

Both indirect and direct questions, other than 'yes/no' questions, contain (usually at the beginning) one of the interrogative words listed in Table 27.1. They always carry a written accent.

Table 27.1	Spanish interrogative words
¿qué?	what/which?
¿cuál/cuáles?	which one/s?
¿quién/quiénes?	who/whom?
¿de quién?	whose?
¿cuándo?	when?
¿dónde?	where?
¿cómo?	how?
¿cuánto/cuánta/cuántos/ cuántas?	how much/how many?
¿por qué?	why?

27.2.1 Qué 'what'

Spanish **qué** can function either as a pronoun or an adjective.

As a pronoun it can only be used with reference to things and *never* with reference to persons:

¿Qué vais [SP] a ver en el cine?   What are you going to see at the cinema?

| ¿De qué hablaron Julio y Luis? | What did Julio and Luis talk about? |
| ¿Me preguntaron qué hacía. | They asked me what I was doing. |

Me preguntaron qué hacía. shown corrected below.

| **¿De qué hablaron Julio y Luis?** | What did Julio and Luis talk about? |
| **Me preguntaron qué hacía.** | They asked me what I was doing. |

In its adjectival function the above restriction does not apply:

| **¿Qué vestido has comprado al final?** | Which dress did you buy in the end? |
| **¿A qué chica te refieres?** | What girl are you referring to? |

Notes:

1 For the use of **cuál/es** to translate 'what', see 27.2.2.

2 In indirect questions **lo que** commonly replaces **qué**: No sé **lo que/qué** voy a comprar para Charo 'I don't know what I'm going to buy for Charo'.

3 **¿Qué tal?** is common in speech to ask for an opinion or assessment: **¿Qué tal las vacaciones?** 'How was your holiday?'.

| **27.2.2** | Cuál/Cuáles _'which one/s', 'what'_ |

In most varieties of Spanish **cuál/cuáles** is a pronoun that can be used with reference both to persons and things. It agrees in number with what is referred to:

¿Cuáles son los que más te gustan?	Which are the ones that you like most?
¿A cuál vamos?	Which one shall we go to?
¿Cuál de los tres hermanos es el más accesible?	Which of the three brothers is the most approachable?

Cuál/cuáles is also used, instead of **qué**, with the verb **ser** followed by an abstract noun, unless a mere definition is being requested:

¿Cuál es la razón por la que huyó?	What is the reason for which she fled?
¿Cuáles fueron las causas del descalabro bursátil?	What were the causes of the stockmarket crash?
¿Qué es el estoicismo?	What is stoicism?

Note: Particularly in Latin America, **cuál/cuáles** is used also as an adjective, e.g. **¿A cuál hora prefieres venir?** [LA] 'What time would you prefer to come?, as opposed to **¿A qué hora prefieres venir?** The former usage is best avoided in Europe.

27.2.3 Quién 'who', de quién 'whose'

Quién/quiénes is a pronoun that can be used *only* with reference to persons. It agrees in number with the person(s) referred to.

When used as a direct object it is preceded by the personal a:

¿Quién vive allí?	Who lives there?
¿A quién has visto?	Who did you see?
¿Quiénes son los dueños del bar?	Who are the owners of the bar?

De quién/quiénes expresses the direct or indirect question 'whose?':

¿De quiénes son esos asientos?	Whose seats are those?
No sé de quién eran los documentos.	I don't know whose the documents were.

27.2.4 Cuándo 'when', dónde 'where' and cómo 'how'

These are interrogative adverbs. Depending on the associated verb, a preposition may be required before **cuándo** and **dónde** (a + dónde > adónde):

¿Cuándo cerraron el hospital?	When did they close the hospital?
¿Hasta cuándo te quedaste?	Till what time did you stay?
¿Adónde va Juan?	Where is Juan going to?
Se desconoce cómo entraron los ladrones.	It isn't known how the thieves entered.

Note also the special use of **cómo** with the verb **llamar** 'to call':

¿Cómo se llama tu hermana?	What is your sister called?

Note: The rule according to which the conjunction **cuando** (with no accent) calls for the subjunctive when reference is made to future time (see 12.2.2.1) does not generally apply to the interrogative adverb **cuándo**: Cuando <u>vea</u> a Lola se lo diré 'When I see Lola I'll tell her', but No sé cuándo <u>veré</u> a Lola 'I don't know when I'll see Lola'.

27.2.5 Cuánto/a/os/as 'how much/many'

Cuánto is a quantifying adjective or pronoun and so agrees in number and gender with the noun to which it refers:

¿Cuánta gente había?	How many people were there?	
No sé cuántos niños tienen.	I don't know how many children they have.	
¿Cuántos tienen su propia casa?	How many of them have their own house?	

The masculine singular form of **cuánto** can also be a neuter pronoun or adverb meaning 'how much':

¿Cuánto cuesta una habitación?	How much does a room cost?

27.2.6 Por qué, para qué 'why'

These are both translatable into English as 'why', but they are not identical in meaning.

Por qué means 'for what reason/motive', whereas **para qué** means 'to what end/for what purpose'. **Por qué** is by far the commoner.

¿Por qué no me has llamado?	Why didn't you call me?
¿Por qué han cerrado el puente?	Why has the bridge been closed?
¿Para qué necesitas otro perro?	What do you need another dog for?

27.2.7 Translating English 'how' + adjective or adverb in questions

There is no neat way of doing this in Spanish, and so a variety of strategies must be employed. The commonest ones are given below.

Adjectives:

¿Cuánto mides?	How tall are you?
¿Cómo es tu casa de grande?	How big is your house?
¿Cuántos años tienes?	How old are you?

Adverbs:

¿Con qué frecuencia se reúnen?	How frequently do they meet?
¿A qué velocidad ibas?	How fast were you going?
¿De qué gravedad fueron sus lesiones?	How badly was he injured?
¿Cuánto tiempo tardaste en hacerlo?	How long did it take you to do it?

27.3 Question tags

Spanish offers no direct equivalent to the English question tags, such as 'isn't it?' and 'didn't I?' However, the word **verdad** 'truth' can often be used to achieve a tag-like effect:

Hace frío, ¿verdad?	It's cold, isn't it?

The word **no** 'no(t)' can be used on its own in a similar way to **verdad** except that less certainty on the part of the speaker is implied:

El frailecillo es una especie de pájaro, ¿no?	The puffin is a kind of bird, isn't it?

Particularly in Latin America, either **¿no es cierto?** or **¿no es verdad?** may also be used:

Prefieres hablar primero, ¿no es cierto?	You prefer to speak first, don't you?

27.4 Exclamations

Exclamations in Spanish have an exclamation mark at their beginning (inverted) and their end. Exclamatory words always carry a written accent.

27.4.1 Qué

Qué + noun usually translates 'what (a)' (without the indefinite article in Spanish). A qualifying adjective after the noun is usually preceded by either **más** or **tan**:

¡Qué lío!	What a mess!
¡Qué mala suerte!	What bad luck!
¡Qué viaje más/tan horrible!	What a horrible journey!

Note: In phrases in which a noun in Spanish corresponds to an adjective in English, qué translates 'so' rather than 'what': ¡Qué vergüenza me da! 'I'm so ashamed!', ¡Qué calor hace! 'It's so hot!'.

With adjectives and adverbs **qué** corresponds to 'how' or 'so' in English:

¡Qué tozuda es Lola!	Lola is so stubborn!
¡Qué despacio va este autobús!	How slowly this bus is going!

Qué + de can be used with the meaning 'what a lot', although **cuánto** is the commoner alternative (see 27.4.3):

¡Qué de regalos has tenido!	What a lot of presents you've received!

27.4.2 Cómo

Used only with verbs as an adverb, **cómo** means 'how':

¡Cómo trata a sus amigos!	How he treats his friends!

27.4.3 Cuánto

Cuánto + verb stresses the intensity or extent of the action, 'how (much)', 'what a lot':

¡Cuánto hemos escrito!	What a lot we've written!
¡Cuánto pesa la maleta!	This suitcase is so heavy!

As an adjective **cuánto/a/os/as** + noun means 'how much/many', 'what a lot of':

¡Cuánta gente lo felicitó!	How many people congratulated him!
¡Cuántas cosas ocurren en la ciudad!	What a lot of things happen in the city.

Notes: The now archaic **cuán** 'how' may be encountered before an adjective or adverb in literature as an alternative to **qué**: ¡Cuán bella es! (= ¡Qué bella es!) 'How beautiful she is!'.

Chapter 28

Word order

Word order in Spanish is very flexible in comparison to English. In particular, the positioning of the subject in relation to the verb is governed largely by factors such as emphasis and focus rather than rigid grammatical rules. For example, the English sentence 'Many people attended the party' obeys a fixed rule according to which the subject precedes the verb and the object or complement follows the verb. In Spanish however, three different word orders are available, depending on where the emphasis is intended to fall:

Asistió mucha gente a la fiesta.	×Attended many people the party.×
A la fiesta asistió mucha gente.	×The party many people attended.×
Mucha gente asistió a la fiesta.	Many people attended the party.

This chapter highlights some of the main principles that govern word order in Spanish. However, except where otherwise stated, the guidelines given should be regarded as tendencies rather than unbreakable rules.

28.1 New versus old information

New or important information typically comes at or towards the end of a sentence in Spanish. Compare the placement of the phrase **a las tres y media** in the two examples below:

Los niños salen <u>a las tres y media</u>.	The children come out at three thirty.
<u>A las tres y media</u> salen los niños.	At three thirty the children come out.

The first sentence, with **a las tres y media** at the end, is the obvious vehicle for countering the claim that the children come out at some other time (e.g. four o'clock).

In contrast, the second sentence can only be used for this purpose if the phrase **a las tres y media** receives spoken emphatic stress. In the absence of such emphatic stress the natural focus of the second sentence is the phrase **salen los niños**, i.e. *what* happens and not *when*.

The principle that new or important information comes at the end of the sentence has the following consequences.

28.1.1 The subject often follows the verb in answers to questions

In a sentence given in response to a question asking ¿quién? or ¿qué?, if the subject supplies the answer it will usually come after the verb:

–¿Quien fue a la cena? –Fueron Ana, Lole y Miguel.
'Who went to the dinner?' 'Ana, Lole and Miguel went.'

–¿Qué se ha caído? –Se ha caído el puente.
'What has fallen down?' 'The bridge has fallen down.'

28.1.2 Indefinite subjects often follow the verb

A subject that is a noun preceded by the indefinite article, by a numeral or by an indefinite adjective (e.g. **mucho** 'many', **alguno** 'some') is very likely to be the main bearer of new information in a sentence. Therefore the subject often follows the verb in this type of case:

Llegaron un montón de policías.	A load of police showed up.
Faltaban tres chicas.	Three girls were missing.
Han desaparecido unos cuantos libros.	Several books have disappeared.

Note: If the focus of the sentence is the verb or verb phrase itself, an indefinite subject will usually come first: **Mucha gente se fue** 'Many people left'. This puts the focus on the idea of *leaving*, in contrast to **Se fue mucha gente**, which puts the focus on the *quantity* of people who left.

The use of a direct object pronoun normally implies that the item to which the pronoun refers has already been mentioned and so is 'old information'. In such cases it is often the subject that supplies the newest or most important piece of information and so it is likely to come after the verb:

–¡Qué cuadro más bonito! –Lo compró Carlos.
'What a beautiful picture!' 'Carlos bought it.'

–Me gusta tu pelo. –Me lo cortó Silvia.
'I like your hair.' 'Silvia cut it for me.'

28.2 Item under discussion at beginning of sentence

A typical strategy involves mentioning a person or a thing and then saying something about that person or thing, as in the English sentence 'As for Jones, he's emigrated to Australia'. This usage is called 'announcing a topic', the topic being the person or thing about which something is said (in this example, Jones).

The practice of announcing a topic is very common in Spanish and can be achieved merely by placing the relevant words at the beginning of the sentence:

<u>Las cañerías</u> las instalo mañana.   I'll install the pipes tomorrow.

A <u>Manolo</u> lo he visto esta mañana.   I saw Manolo this morning.

Similarly, a phrase referring to a place or to a time can be introduced as a topic:

En esta fábrica trabaja Andrea.   Andrea works in this factory.

Ayer vinieron los primos.   Yesterday the cousins came.

28.3 Emphatic stress

Words and phrases that receive an unusually heavy stress for emphatic effect are often placed at the beginning of the sentence, despite the fact that they are not really topics but the bearers of important information:

<u>Esos</u> zapatos me quiero poner.   It's those shoes I want to wear.

A <u>ese</u> hombre han detenido.   That's the man who has been arrested.

28.4   Specific constructions

The following guidelines apply to specific constructions.

28.4.1 *Subjects with no article must follow the verb*

When the subject is a noun on its own, it must be placed after the verb:

Entra luz por la persiana.	Light is coming in through the blind.
Viven lobos en aquellas montañas.	There are wolves in those mountains.

28.4.2 *Subjects of reflexive passive constructions*

Typically in this construction the subject comes after the verb, unless the subject constitutes the topic of the sentence:

No se veían las caras de los niños.
You couldn't see the faces of the children.

No se comentó la gravedad de la situación.
The seriousness of the situation was not mentioned.

But:

Esos platos se ponen aquí.	Those plates go here.

Una deuda tan grande no se liquida fácilmente.
Such a big debt can't be paid off easily.

28.4.3 *Long subjects tend to follow the verb*

Long subject phrases, particularly those that contain a relative clause, are normally placed after the verb, especially if the verb has no object:

Habló uno que es experto en antropología.
Someone who is an expert in anthropology spoke.

28.4.4 *The subject of a relative clause tends to follow the verb*

If a relative clause contains an explicit subject, this tends to follow the verb if placement before it would leave the verb at the very end of the clause:

¿Has visto la casa que se han comprado Pepi y Juan?
Have you seen the house that Pepi and Juan have bought?

He perdido el libro que me regaló Pablo.
I've lost the book that Pablo gave me.

28.5 Position of adverbs

28.5.1 *Qualifying adverbs and adverbial phrases*

These are most common immediately after the verb. However they can also be placed after the verb's object, if any, or in some cases before the verb (for emphasis of the verb):

Ganaron fácilmente a los ingleses.	They easily beat the English.
Ganaron a los ingleses fácilmente.	They easily beat the English.
Fácilmente ganaron a los ingleses.	They easily beat the English.

28.5.2 *Adverbs of time and place*

Words such as **aquí** 'here', **anoche** 'last night' come at the end or the beginning of the sentence, depending on whether they encapsulate new information (see 28.1) or whether they constitute the topic (see 28.2).

28.5.3 *Sentence adverbs*

Adverbs that modify the rest of the sentence in its entirety and not just the verb usually appear at the beginning:

Afortunadamente dejaron de interesarse por el asunto.
Fortunately they lost interest in the matter.

Note: In contrast to English usage, a Spanish adverb cannot be inserted between the auxiliary verb **haber** and a following past participle: **Siempre lo he dicho** 'I've always said this' or **Lo he dicho siempre** (not ×Lo he siempre dicho×).

28.6 Subject-verb inversion in questions

In several types of question the subject is placed after the verb.

28.6.1 General rules for subject-verb inversion

When there is an explicitly mentioned subject, subject-verb inversion is *obligatory* in all direct questions, other than 'yes/no' questions:

¿Dónde está el teatro?   Where is the theatre?

¿Mario sabe nadar?/¿Sabe Mario nadar?   Can Mario swim?

In indirect questions inversion is in most cases optional but likely to be preferred:

No sé cómo lo aguanta Beatriz/No sé cómo Beatriz lo aguanta.
I don't know how Beatriz puts up with him.

But inversion is *obligatory* in indirect questions in the following instances:

(a) After **dónde** with verbs like **vivir** 'to live' and **estar** 'to be':

Pregúntale dónde vive Marisa.
Ask him where Marisa lives.

(b) After **cuándo** with verbs of arrival and departure:

Hay que enterarse de cuándo sale el vuelo.
We need to find out when the flight departs.

(c) After **qué** when this functions as direct object:

No sé qué le dijo Nicolás.
I don't know what Nicolás said to him.

28.6.2 Subject-verb inversion with infinitives and gerunds

In questions in which an infinitive or gerund is used with a finite verb form, the subject after the verb can usually be placed either between the finite verb and the infinitive/gerund or after the infinitive/gerund. The latter case is appropriate if the intention is to focus on the subject.

¿Está Mercedes cantando?	Is Mercedes singing? (focus on verb)
¿Está cantando Mercedes?	Is Mercedes singing? (focus on subject)
¿Qué tienen ellos que hacer?	What do they have *to do*?
¿Qué tienen que hacer ellos?	What do *they* have to do?

Chapter 29

Word formation

The purpose of this chapter is to offer some insight into the structure of words in Spanish and the meaning of some of their components. This is done principally through a discussion of suffixes and prefixes that can be added to base words, and of the ways in which words can be combined.

The objective is to encourage learners of Spanish to think about how words are constructed, detect common patterns in them and even come to understand the meaning of words they have not previously encountered. What follows constitutes no more than a guide to some of the issues foreign learners might consider as their study proceeds.

29.1 Suffixes

A suffix is a unit that is added to the end of a word to form a new word, for example to convert 'care' into 'careless' or 'careful':

Base word		Suffix	New word	
cama	bed	**-illa**	**camilla**	stretcher
avispa	wasp	**-ero**	**avispero**	wasps' nest

When a suffix is added to a word, the ending of this word is often modified in some way. For example, a final vowel may be altered or deleted: sereno > serenidad. In addition, spelling changes may be necessary according to the general rules on spelling, e.g. pedazo but pedacito, cerca but cerquita (see 1.2).

When the addition of a suffix removes the stress in a word away from a previously stressed **ie** or **ue**, these syllables frequently (but not always) revert to **e** and **o**, e.g. **caliente** but **calentito**, **puerta** but **portezuela**.

29.1.1 Suffixes forming abstract nouns

A number of suffixes create abstract nouns that are feminine in gender.

Some such as -ancia, -dad, -dumbre, -encia, -ez, -eza, and -ura typically transform adjectives, whereas -anza changes verbs into abstract nouns. Usually the base word is slightly modified before these suffixes are added. For example, the final vowel may be changed or removed.

Base word		Suffix	New Word	
arrogante	arrogant	**-ancia**	**arrogancia**	arrogance
curioso	curious	**-dad**	**curiosidad**	curiosity
manso	gentle	**-dumbre**	**mansedumbre**	gentleness
inocente	innocent	**-encia**	**inocencia**	innocence
rígido	rigid	**-ez**	**rigidez**	rigidity
limpio	clean	**-eza**	**limpieza**	cleanliness
largo	long	**-ura**	**largura**	length
desconfiar	distrust	**-anza**	**desconfianza**	mistrust

Note: -ura also forms words translated into English with the suffix '-ure', e.g. **super-estructura, arquitectura**.

29.1.2 Suffixes that indicate places

The forms -al and -ar denote a grouping or abundance of whatever the base noun denotes, or the place where this is found. These suffixes are frequently applied to names of plants and trees:

chaparro	dwarf oak	**chaparral**	dwarf oak thicket
pino	pine tree	**pinar**	pine grove

The suffixes -**era** and -**ero** indicate the place where something is put. The related suffix -**dero** often indicates where something is done:

llave	key	**llavero**	key ring
papel	paper	**papelera**	waste-paper basket
desembarcar	to disembark	**desembarcadero**	landing stage

However, -**ero** is also frequently used to designate a person who is in charge of, owns, makes or trades whatever the base noun denotes:

pescado	fish	**pescadero**	fishmonger
rancho	ranch	**ranchero**	rancher

In some cases the suffix -**ía** can be further added to indicate the place where these activities take place, e.g. **fruta** 'fruit' > **frutero** 'fruit seller' > **frutería** 'fruit shop'.

29.1.3 Suffixes forming adjectives

The forms -**oso** and -**udo** create adjectives which express the possession of whatever the base noun denotes, sometimes in the latter case to an exaggerated or excessive degree:

cariño	affection	**cariñoso**	affectionate
pelo	hair	**peludo**	hairy/shaggy
talento	talent	**talentoso**	talented
barriga	belly/paunch	**barrigudo**	pot-bellied

The suffix -(**d**)**izo** forms adjectives which express the idea that someone or something is susceptible or likely to act in the manner indicated by the base verb or adjective:

pegar	to stick	**pegadizo**	sticky/catchy (of a tune)
enfermo	ill	**enfermizo**	sickly
escurrirse	to slip/slide	**escurridizo**	slippery

29.1.4 Action suffixes

The suffixes -**mento** and -**miento** are applied to verbs to form nouns denoting an action:

| **hundir** | to sink | **hundimiento** | sinking |
| **salvar** | to save | **salvamento** | rescue/salvaging |

The suffixes **-ador**, **-edor** and **-idor** (corresponding to **-ar**, **-er** and **-ir** verbs) are used to form nouns denoting persons who perform the action denoted by the verb:

navegar	to sail/navigate	**navegador**	mariner, (internet) browser
beber	to drink	**bebedor**	drinker
seguir	to follow	**seguidor**	follower/fan

Note: The feminine form of **-dor** is often used for machines and household appliances: **secadora** 'tumble dryer', **licuadora** 'liquidizer/blender'.

Another common process for deriving nouns from verbs consists in deleting the **-ar/-er/-ir** of the infinitive and adding **-a**, **-o**, or **-e**, but not according to any definable rule:

cerrar	to close	**cierre**	closing/closure
pagar	to pay	**paga**	payment
volar	to fly	**vuelo**	flight

The feminine form of a verb's past participle (suffix: **-ada** or **-ida**) can often be used to denote an action or the result of an action:

| **llegar** | to arrive | **llegada** | arrival |
| **lavar** | to wash | **lavada** | wash |

The suffix **-ada** is applied to nouns to produce others denoting a blow or other action with an instrument: **puñal** 'dagger' > **puñalada** 'stabbing', **peine** 'comb' > **peinada** 'combing'.

It also specifies the amount contained in an instrument: **cuchara** 'spoon' > **cucharada** 'spoonful', or a period of time: **tiempo** 'time' > **temporada** 'season'.

The suffix **-azo** is often used like **-ada** to indicate a blow or action involving an instrument: **espalda** 'back' > **espaldazo** 'pat on the back', **teléfono** 'telephone' > **telefonazo** 'call/ring'.

It is also used with names to denote succinctly significant political events: **pinochetazo** (Pinochet's coup in Chile, 1973), **fujimorazo** (the **autogolpe** by President Fujimori of Peru, 1992).

29.1.5 International suffixes

A number of Spanish suffixes have equivalents in other European languages. The most common of these are **-aje** (English '-age'), **-ción** (English '-tion'), **-ismo** (English '-ism') and **-ista** (English '-ist'):

pasaje	passage
estación	station
turismo	tourism
socialista	socialist

29.1.6 Affective suffixes

In Spanish certain suffixes are attached to *nouns* to convey smallness or lesser importance (these are called *diminutives*), or largeness and greater importance (*augmentatives*). Many of these suffixes can also convey an emotional quality such as affection or they can express scorn (*pejorative* or *depreciative suffixes*).

Although less commonly, these suffixes may also be used in Spanish with other parts of speech such as *adjectives* and *adverbs*.

The following suffixes are a rich and distinctive feature of contemporary Spanish, with considerable regional variations in their use within the Iberian Peninsula and throughout Latin America. Except in cases where a diminutive or augmentative form has become an established word, learners of Spanish should only use them when experience has given them the knowledge and confidence to be able to do so appropriately.

29.1.6.1 Diminutive suffixes

(a) -ito, -illo, -uelo

These are the most common diminutive suffixes, with feminine forms in -a. They occur in slightly different forms depending on the word to which they are added.

The simple forms **-ito, -illo** and **-uelo** are added to the base word after removing the final vowel (-o or -a):

clavo	nail	**clavito**	small nail
cera	wax	**cerilla**	match

bolso	bag	**bolsillo**	pocket
pollo	chicken	**polluelo**	chick

There are exceptions, e.g. **mano** 'hand' gives both **manita** and **manecita**.

The forms -**cito**, -**cillo** and -**zuelo** are used if the base word has more than one syllable and ends in -**n**, -**r**, or -**e**:

ladrón	thief	**ladronzuelo**	petty thief
autor	author	**autorcillo**	small-time author
peine	comb	**peinecillo**	fine comb

Note that **señor** 'gentleman' (diminutive: **señorito**) does not follow this pattern.

The forms -**ecito**, -**ecillo** and -**ezuelo** are added: (i) after removing the final vowel -**o** or -**a** from two-syllable words whose first syllable is **ie** or **ue**, or (ii) to single-syllable words ending in a consonant or **y**:

nuevo/a	new	**nuevecito/a**	nice and new
vieja	old lady	**viejecita**	little old lady
piedra	stone	**piedrecita**	little stone/pebble
flor	flower	**florecita**	nice flower
rey	king	**reyezuelo**	petty king

Rarely, after removing the final vowel, the forms -**ececito**, -**ececillo** and -**ececuelo** are added to single-syllable words ending in a vowel: **pie** 'foot' > **piececito** 'tiny foot'.

Of all diminutives the several forms of -**ito** are by far the most frequent and varied in their use. They are much used by children and when speaking to them. In the conversation of adults they express a tone of friendliness and on occasions of affection.

With nouns they can signify 'little', but often convey the idea of 'pretty', 'nice', or 'dear', with or without the notion of smallness:

abuela	grandmother	**abuelita**	granny/grandma
nieto	grandson	**nietecito**	little grandson
cerveza	beer	**una cervecita bien fría**	a nice cold beer

The -**ito** forms can be attached to first names (**Ana** > **Anita**), and to other words such as adjectives, adverbs, adverbial expressions, and even past participles, sometimes with the sense of 'nice', or 'quite':

¡habla bajito!	speak quite low!	
ahora mismito	right now	
cerquita	quite close	
ayercito	just yesterday	
tempranito	nice and early	
un poquito	a little bit	

The several forms of -**illo** are used above all simply to make smaller whatever they are attached to, often without expressing any emotion, feeling or evaluation. This may be smallness not simply in respect of size, but an expression of lesser importance or of insignificance. In many cases the addition of this suffix has resulted in a change in the meaning of the original word. The -**illo** forms are especially common in parts of Andalusia:

ensalada	salad	**ensaladilla**	potato salad
ventana	window	**ventanilla**	window in a vehicle/ticket office
boca	mouth	**boquilla**	mouthpiece/nozzle
mano	hand	**manecilla**	pointer/hand on a clock

The several forms of -**uelo** can express smallness or insignificance but are often pejorative. They are generally only used with nouns:

paño	cloth	**pañuelo**	handkerchief
joven	young person	**jovenzuelo**	youth
pintor	painter	**pintorzuelo**	second-rate painter

Between very close acquaintances or members of a family they may be used mockingly rather than seriously.

(b) Other forms of diminutive suffixes

Some diminutive suffixes are mainly regional in their use: -**ín** is Asturian, -**ino/a** is Estremaduran and -**iño/a** is Galician.

When used more widely in the Spanish-speaking world they can indicate smallness and affection, but they may also modify the meaning of the base word.

The form -**ín** changes the gender of feminine nouns to masculine.

calabaza	pumpkin	**calabacín**	courgette/zucchini
langosta	lobster	**langostín, langostino**	king prawn

| **botella** | bottle | **botellín** | small bottle of beer |
| **tesis** | thesis | **tesina** | dissertation |

The various forms of -ico, originally mainly Aragonese in usage, are now not common in Spain except to indicate sarcasm or irony. In Central America and Colombia, however, -ico is more common as a standard diminutive:

| **vaso** | glass | **vasico** | small glass |

The suffixes -ete/-eta used with nouns are diminutive in effect, but on occasions they may also have pejorative intent:

avión	aeroplane	**avioneta**	light aeroplane
historia	story	**historieta**	short story
libro	book	**libreta**	notebook
camión	lorry	**camioneta**	pick-up/van

The form -ejo is used to suggest smallness, sometimes with a hint of unimportance or scorn:

| **papel** | paper | **papelejo** | a scrap of paper |
| **animal** | animal | **animalejo** | nasty little animal |

29.1.6.2 Augmentative suffixes

Augmentatives are used to indicate large size, or the increased and exaggerated possession of a particular characteristic, e.g. not just **grande** 'big', but **grandote** 'huge'. Moreover, in most instances there is an implication that clumsiness, awkwardness and ungainliness derive from this.

In fact, some augmentatives always express *pejorative* connotations such as ugliness, contempt and scorn. Occasionally, however, they change the meaning of the original word without denoting large size.

The most commonly used augmentatives are -ón/-ona, -azo/-aza and -ote/-ota. These denote large size, sometimes with a pejorative connotation.

(a) -ón

When this suffix is attached to feminine nouns they often change gender and take the masculine form. It can also be added to adjectives:

| **cuchara** | spoon | **cucharón** | ladle |
| **pimienta** | pepper | **pimentón** | paprika |

cintura	waist	**cinturón**	belt
oferta	offer	**ofertón**	bargain
dulce	sweet	**dulzón**	sickly sweet
fácil	easy	**facilón**	dead easy

A characteristic usage of the -ón suffix is to attach it to the stem of a verb after removing the infinitive ending, thereby creating a noun or an adjective expressing the action of the verb to an excessive degree:

faltar	be absent	**faltón**	regular absentee
mirar	look	**mirón**	starer

Note: As an example of the pitfalls awaiting foreign users of Spanish suffixes, -ón in some cases denotes a *diminutive* (rather than an augmentative) meaning: **rata** 'rat' > **ratón** 'mouse', **torre** 'tower' > **torreón** 'turret'.

(b) -azo/-aza

As an augmentative, this suffix increases the size of what a noun or adjective denotes. It adopts the gender of the noun or adjective:

cupón	lottery ticket	**cuponazo**	special lottery
bueno/a	good	**buenazo/a**	very kindly

In some parts of Latin America, -azo is used as an alternative to the superlative suffix -ísimo: **feazo** 'very ugly', **cansadazo** 'very tired'.

For other uses of -azo, see 29.1.4.

(c) -ote/-ota

This suffix can imply excessive size and often coarseness:

libro	book	**librote**	boring tome
palabra	word	**palabrota**	swear word

Note: In some cases -ote denotes a *diminutive* meaning: **isla** 'island' > **islote** 'islet'.

(d) Augmentatives with exclusively pejorative meaning

These suffixes are employed above all for their ability to convey concepts such as dislike, contempt, unpleasantness and misery. They include: -aco, -acho, -ajo, -astro, -uco and -ucho:

casa	house	**casucha**	hovel
rico	rich	**ricacho**	filthy rich person

| **blanco** | white | **blancucho** | dirty white |
| **cama** | bed | **camastro** | rickety old bed |

29.1.7 Combinations of suffixes

Sometimes suffixes can be used in combination. The practice is not wide-spread but some individual combinations are common:

chico 'small' > **chiquitito/chiquitillo/chiquitín** 'very small'

calle 'street' > **callejón** 'alley'

guapo/a 'handsome/pretty' > **guapetón/ona** 'very handsome/pretty'

puño 'fist' > **puñetazo** 'blow with the fist'

río 'river' > **riachuelo** 'small stream'

In Latin America especially, the suffix is sometimes repeated to stress the effect: **Me han dejado aquí solitita.** [LA] 'They've left me here all alone'.

29.2 Prefixes

The use of prefixes is less common than that of suffixes as a means of forming words. Therefore, learners of Spanish tend to find prefixes easier to master, especially since prefixes are similar in English and Spanish and they perform a similar function in each language.

29.2.1 De(s)-

Probably the most common prefix in Spanish, it is frequently used to indicate a negative or opposite meaning:

animar	to encourage	**desanimar**	to discourage
montar	to assemble	**desmontar**	to dismantle
congelar	to freeze	**descongelar**	to defrost

It can also be used to create verbs which signify that something is removed, even though there is no equivalent verb stating the opposite:

nata	cream	desnatar	skim (e.g. milk)
cafeína	caffeine	descafeinar	decaffeinate
vía	route	desviar(se)	change course/divert
pelo	hair	depilar(se)	remove hair

29.2.2 En-

This generally denotes the idea of 'placing inside' or 'covering'. It occurs as **em-** before **b** and **p**:

cal	lime	encalar	whitewash
cárcel	prison	encarcelar	imprison
bala	bundle	embalar	pack
paquete	package	empaquetar	to package

Notes:

1   The prefix **en-** may simply be used to form a verb from a noun without the notion of 'enclosing in': **encaminar** 'to channel/direct', **enfocar** 'to focus (on)'.

2   The prefix **en-** can be preceded by **des-** to reverse the action of a verb, e.g. **desenterrar** 'to unearth/dig up', **desenredar** 'to unravel'.

29.2.3 In-

This generally negates an adjective (sometimes a noun). It occurs as **i-** before **l**, as **im-** before **b** and **p**, and as **ir-** before **r**:

alambre	wire	inalámbrico	cordless
decisión	decision	indecisión	indecision
lícito	legal	ilícito	illicit
borrar	to rub out	imborrable	indelible
regular	regular	irregular	irregular

29.2.4 Re-

This commonly functions, as in English, to indicate that something is repeated or done again, often forming words from English precedents:

elección	election	reelección	reelection
orientar	to direct	**reorientar**	to redirect

cartucho remanufacturado   re-manufactured cartridge

industria repotenciada   re-vitalized industry

In addition, in popular speech **re-** is used to intensify the meaning of the word to which it is attached, not only in the form **re-**, but with increasing strength as **rete-** (particularly in parts of Latin America) and **requete-**:

rebronceado	very suntanned
un viaje relindo [LA]	a wonderful trip
requetebién/retebién [LA]	brilliant

29.2.5 Sobre-

This commonly expresses an abundance or excess, sometimes equivalent to 'over-', 'super-' or 'extra':

sobrepoblado	overpopulated
sobrehumano	superhuman
una sobrepaga	a bonus, extra payment
sobresaliente	outstanding

29.2.6 Anti-, super-, contra-, tra(n)s-, pos(t)

The increasing popularity of **anti-** in modern English with the meaning of 'against' or 'opposed to', and of **super-** to denote 'extra', 'in addition', or an 'excess of', is reflected in modern Spanish. These prefixes are found increasingly in the Spanish media, especially to form new nouns and adjectives with modern connotations.

Super- is also found as an adverb.

Contra- appears in Spanish as the equivalent of English **counter-** or **contra-**.

Tras- or **trans-** occur in many words and are not always interchangeable.

crema antiarrugas	anti-wrinkle or anti-aging cream
superficie antiadherente	non-stick surface
supercarburante	high-octane fuel

supercola	superglue
super ambicioso	very/over ambitious
contraoferta	counter offer
a contraluz	against the light
traspasar	to pierce/go beyond
translúcido	translucent
postraumático	post-traumatic

Notes:

1 Spanish in general does not use a hyphen to link these prefixes to the following word.

2 Some words formed using **súper-** may be abbreviated to just the prefix: **el súper** 'supermarket', **la super** 'four-star petrol'.

29.3 Combinations of words

29.3.1 Pairs of nouns

English is extremely versatile in allowing *two nouns* to be juxtaposed so that one of them functions as an adjective. These combinations are relatively rare in Spanish. In English the word order is *adjective + noun*. This is sometimes retained in Spanish in imitation of English, but generally in Spanish this word order is reversed:

página web	web page
horno microondas	microwave (oven)
vídeojuego	computer game
satélite espía	spy satellite
placa madre	motherboard

29.3.2 Nouns linked by prepositions

More common in Spanish is the practice of using a preposition to link nouns to other parts of speech (mainly other nouns or infinitives). The commonest link is **de**, but others are used such as **para** to express the use for which something is intended:

jugo de piña	pineapple juice
ropa de playa	beachwear
hoja de cálculo	spreadsheet
jarra para cerveza	beer mug or tankard
mesa para ordenador [SP]	computer desk
expertos en desarme	disarmament experts

29.3.3 Compound nouns

These are formed not only by the combination of nouns but by the combination of a wide variety of different parts of speech.

They are usually masculine if they begin with a verb or preposition, and singular even though the second element may be plural, e.g. **el abrelatas** 'tin/can opener'. They are feminine if they specifically refer to that gender or end in a feminine noun not linked to a verb or preposition.

(el) cortocircuito	shortcircuit
(el) limpiabarros	boot scraper, doormat
(el) paraguas	umbrella
(el) apoyacabezas	headrest
(el) pinchadiscos [SP]	disk jockey
(el) sabelotodo	know-all/smart arse
(el/la) sietemesino/a	premature baby
(la) drogadicción	drug addiction
(los) sinsabores	troubles

29.3.4 Compound adjectives

A number of these exist based on parts of the body + adjective or past participle:

boquiabierto/a	open-mouthed
puntiagudo/a	bony/sharp-pointed
paticorto/a	short-legged
pelirrojo/a	red-haired

Chapter 30

Differences between Latin American and Peninsular Spanish

Although the Latin American and Peninsular varieties of Spanish are mutually comprehensible, they differ in several important respects. It also needs to be borne in mind that significant variation exists within Latin American Spanish itself. For example, in the Spanish that can be heard on the Caribbean and the Pacific coasts there is a tendency to pronounce the letter 's', when it occurs before a consonant, like the 'h' of English 'hat', resulting in pronunciations such as *ehto* for **esto** or *ehpaña* for **España**. By contrast, the traditional Spanish relationship between letters and sounds is fairly well preserved in the Spanish spoken in the mountainous interior of both Mexico and South America, giving these varieties a more 'Castilian' quality. Nevertheless, despite differences of this kind it is possible to highlight several key features that distinguish Latin American Spanish as a whole from its Peninsular counterpart.

In preceding chapters, instances of Latin American usage have been identified and illustrated [LA], as have practices and vocabulary that are considered to be largely Peninsular [SP]. This final chapter collates and expands coverage of American usage to offer a unified overview of its principal characteristics.

30.1 Pronunciation

30.1.1 *Pronunciation of 'z'*

In the Spanish spoken in most of the Iberian Peninsula, with the notable exception of Andalusia, the letter **z** (and also **c** before **i** or **e**) is pronounced like 'th' of English 'think'. This sound is not used in the Spanish of Latin America where it is replaced by the 's' of 'six'.

Accordingly, in Latin American Spanish word pairs such as the following have an identical pronunciation:

30
Differences
between
Latin
American and
Peninsular
Spanish

rozado worn/grazed   **rosado** pink

maza meat tenderizer   **masa** dough

This phenomenon, which is known as **seseo**, is more or less universal in Latin America. It is also normal in much of southern Spain and the Canary islands.

30.1.2 Pronunciation of 'll'

In conservative varieties of central and northern Peninsular Spanish, the **ll** sequence of letters is pronounced somewhat like the 'lli' of 'million'. However, speakers in Latin America (excluding Paraguay and parts of the Andes), as well as in the Canaries and much of southern Spain, universally adopt the more modern practice of pronouncing **ll** like 'y' as in English 'yes'.

This phenomenon is known as **yeísmo** and among speakers who adopt it word pairs such as the following will have an identical pronunciation:

pollo chicken   **poyo** stone bench

halla he/she finds   **haya** there is (present subjunctive of **haber**)

In the River Plate area, i.e. Buenos Aires and Montevideo together with their hinterland, both **ll** and **y** are pronounced like the 's' of English 'pleasure' or, increasingly, like the 'sh' of English 'shut'. Both of these phenomena, which are essentially a distinctive form of **yeísmo**, are referred to as **žeísmo** or **rehilamiento**.

30.1.3 Pronunciation of 'j'

In the Spanish spoken in most of the Iberian Peninsula, with the notable exception of Andalusia, the letter **j** (and also **g** before **i** or **e**) is pronounced like the 'ch' of the Scottish word 'loch'. On the other hand, in large parts of Latin America, particularly in the Caribbean basin and on the Pacific coast of South America, **j** (and **g** before **i** or **e**) is pronounced like the 'h' in English 'hat'. In these areas, the word **paja** 'straw', for example, will be pronounced as *paha*.

30.2 Forms of address

Perhaps the most striking difference between the Spanish of the Iberian Peninsula and that of Latin America relates to the verb forms and personal pronouns that are used when other people are directly addressed. In the first place, neither the standard 2nd person plural verb forms nor the associated subject pronoun **vosotros** are used in Latin America. (**Vosotros** is also absent from the speech encountered in the Canaries and much of southern Spain.)

In their place, 3rd person plural endings are used, together with the pronoun **ustedes**:

Spain (except Andalusia and Canaries)	Latin America
Vosotros habláis	**Ustedes hablan**
Vosotros coméis	**Ustedes comen**
Vosotros vivís	**Ustedes viven**

In addition, in large parts of Latin America, **vos** is used as the familiar 2nd person *singular* subject pronoun, in place of **tú**. This practice, known as **voseo**, is normal in the River Plate area and in Central America. It does not occur at all in Mexico (except for the far south), the Caribbean and most of Peru. Elsewhere there is variation, although better educated speakers, particularly in urban settings, tend to prefer **tú**.

30.2.1 Verb forms associated with vos

There is considerable variation across Latin America in the verb forms used with **vos**. In the most widely accepted pattern, which prevails in the River Plate area and in Central America, the verb forms for 2nd person singular **vos** are identical to the equivalent **tú** forms except in the present indicative and in the imperative.

30.2.1.1 Vos in present indicative

In the present indicative the **vos** verb forms are derived from the equivalent **vosotros** forms. In the case of -**ar** and -**er** verbs the unstressed **i** of the verb ending is deleted: **cantáis > cantás**.

Verbs in the -**ir** conjugation have no unstressed **i** in the **vosotros** verb ending and so, for -**ir** verbs, the Latin American **vos** and Peninsular **vosotros** forms are identical in the present indicative:

30
Differences
between
Latin
American and
Peninsular
Spanish

	-ar	-er	-ir
Present indicative	**vos cantás**	**vos comés**	**vos vivís**

Note also **vos sos** 'you are'.

30.2.1.2 *Vos imperatives*

See 19.1.2.

30.2.1.3 *Vos in present subjunctive*

Some speakers also use special **vos** forms in the present subjunctive. These are formed for all conjugations by deleting the unstressed **i** of the **vosotros** subjunctive form: **cantéis > cantés**:

	-ar	-er	-ir
Present subjunctive	**vos cantés**	**vos comás**	**vos vivás**

30.2.1.4 *Vos in future tense*

Less widely accepted is the use of special **vos** forms in the future tense:

	-ar	-er	-ir
Future	**vos cantarés**	**vos comerés**	**vos vivirés**

30.2.1.5 Other *vos* verb forms

In some areas of Latin America, e.g. parts of Venezuela together with northern Chile and Bolivia, the **vos** forms in the speech of some speakers tend to be identical to the equivalent **vosotros** forms, e.g. **vos cantáis, vos cantabais, para que vos comáis**, although the final -s is often unpronounced. In the imperative the usual **d**-less ending is retained.

When this pattern prevails the ending -**éis**, both in the -**er** present indicative and in the future tense of *all three* conjugations, is often replaced by -**ís**, e.g. **vos comís** (instead of **vos coméis**), **vos cantarís** (instead of **vos cantaréis**).

30.2.2 Object pronouns and possessives associated with vos

In modern usage the weak object pronoun and the possessives that correspond to **vos** are the same as for **tú**, i.e. **te, tu** and **tuyo**:

Acordáte que fue idea tuya.	Remember it was your idea.
¿Creés que venderás tu carro?	Do you think you will sell your car.

But **vos** and *not* **ti** is used as the object of a preposition:

Estaba pensando en vos.	I was thinking about you.

30.3 Le and lo

Many speakers in the Iberian Peninsula, particularly in the central and northern areas, use **le** as the masculine singular direct object pronoun to refer to a man. In Latin America, in contrast, with the exception of Ecuador and Paraguay, most speakers almost always use **lo** instead (as in Andalusia and the Canaries):

Peninsular usage	Latin American usage
Le hice entrar.	**Lo hice entrar.**
I made him go in.	I made him go in.
Le llamé ayer.	**Lo llamé ayer.**
I called him yesterday.	I called him yesterday.

30.4 Uses of tenses

30.4.1 Sequence of tenses with the subjunctive

In some subjunctive constructions in Peninsular Spanish, for example after verbs of influence, there is a strict sequence of tenses. In particular, a verb in the preterite or imperfect in the main clause requires the imperfect subjunctive in the subordinate clause (see 12.4). In contrast, in many varieties of Latin American Spanish, the present subjunctive would be acceptable in this case, even if the action is envisaged as taking place in the past:

30
Differences
between
Latin
American and
Peninsular
Spanish

Les pidió que entraran.   He asked them to come in.
Les pidió que entren. [LA]

Quería que lo hagamos hoy. [LA]   He wanted us to do it today

30.4.2 Use of preterite for perfect

In much of Latin America, with the possible exception of the Andes, the preterite is used in situations in which Peninsular speakers would opt for the perfect. In some cases this can be compared with the contrast between British English 'Have you done it yet?' and American English 'Did you do it yet?'

Todavía no han llamado.   They haven't called yet.
Todavía no llamaron. [LA]

¿Nunca has visto *Lo que el viento*   Have you never seen
se llevó?   *Gone with the Wind?*
¿Nunca viste *Lo que el viento se llevó?* [LA]

Me tengo que ir. He quedado   I have to go. I've arranged
con Luis.   to meet Luis.
Me tengo que ir. Quedé con Luis. [LA]

30.5 El que, quien and que

30.5.1 Mainstream tendencies

A major difference exists between Peninsular and Latin American Spanish in terms of the construction of sentences in which a word or phrase is focused and given special emphasis. These are sentences that correspond to English 'It was John who did it', 'It was in the park that I saw her'. In Peninsular Spanish it is generally the case that **el que** etc., **quien, cuando, donde** or **como** must be used.

In addition, if the emphasized word or phrase is preceded by a preposition, this must (in Peninsular Spanish) be reproduced before the relative pronoun (see 25.6):

Fue <u>con</u> María <u>con la que</u> hablé.   It was to/with María that I
spoke.

In many varieties of Latin American Spanish, however, when the emphasized word refers to a place or time, or it is preceded by a preposition, it
is common for **que** to be used instead of **el que** etc., **quien, cuando, donde**
or **como**, with no duplication of the preposition (if any):

Peninsular usage	Latin American usage
Fue de política de lo que hablaron.	**Fue de política que hablaron.**
Fue en la fiesta donde la vi.	**Fue en la fiesta que la vi.**
Fue ayer cuando llegaron.	**Fue ayer que llegaron.**

30.5.2 Intensive ser

A more geographically restricted Latin American variant of the above
construction is associated primarily with the Caribbean basin, Colombia
and Ecuador. It involves the omission of **donde/cuando/quien/el que** or of
the sequence, preposition + **el que/quien**:

Peninsular usage	Caribbean/Colombian/ Ecuadorian usage
Quien lo hizo fue Pedro.	**Lo hizo fue Pedro.**
Con la que hablé fue con María.	**Hablé fue con María.**
Donde la vi fue en casa de José.	**La vi fue en casa de José.**
Cuando llegaron fue ayer.	**Llegaron fue ayer.**

30.6 Vocabulary

30.6.1 Common Peninsular–Latin American equivalences

Much of the distinctive vocabulary to be encountered in Latin America is
specific to particular regions. However a number of items have a general
or near general currency in Latin America. Some common examples of such
items are listed in Table 30.1.

30
Differences
between
Latin
American and
Peninsular
Spanish

Table 30.1 Common Latin American vocabulary

Latin American	Corresponding Peninsular term	
(alto)parlante	altavoz	loudspeaker
amarrar	atar	to tie up
anteojos/lentes	gafas	(eye)glasses
apurarse	apresurarse	to hurry up
balde	cubo	bucket
boleto	billete	ticket
botar	tirar	throw out
camarón	gamba	prawn
cancha	campo	pitch/field
canilla/chorro/caño	grifo	tap/faucet
carro	coche	car/automobile
chancho	cerdo	pig
computador(a)	ordenador	computer
demorarse/dilatarse	tardar	to be late/slow
descomponerse	estropearse	to break down
durazno	melocotón	peach
estadía	estancia	stay
estampilla/timbre	sello	(postage) stamp
extrañar	echar de menos	to miss
fritangas	frituras	fried food
lana	pasta/tela	cash/dough
lastimar	hacer daño a	to hurt
lindo	bonito	pretty
liviano	ligero	light (not heavy)
manejar	conducir	to drive
maní	cacahuete	peanut
palta	aguacate	avocado
papa	patata	potato
pararse	levantarse	to stand up

playa (de estacio-namiento)/parqueo	aparcamiento	car park/parking lot
pasto/grama	césped	grass/lawn
piso	suelo	floor
plomero	fontanero	plumber
pollera	falda	skirt
prender	encender	turn on (power, TV)
regresar	devolver	to give back
revisar	registrar	to search (through)
saco	americana	man's jacket
timón	volante	steering wheel
tipear	escribir a máquina	to type
vocero/a, personero/a	el/la portavoz	spokesperson
vuelto	cambio	change

30.6.2 Gender and stress alternations

Some words have different genders or stress patterns in Spain and Latin America (or in parts of the region). Common examples are given below:

Latin American item	Peninsular item	
bebe (Andes/River Plate)	bebé	baby
(el) bombillo (Central America/Colombia/Venezuela)	(la) bombilla	light bulb
(el) cerillo (Central America/Mexico)	(la) cerilla	match
chofer	chófer	driver
(el) llamado	(la) llamada	phone call
(el) radio (not Southern Cone)	(la) radio	radio
(el) sartén	(la) sartén	frying pan
video	vídeo	video

313

30

Differences
between
Latin
American and
Peninsular
Spanish

Items that require special attention

The meaning of some words in parts of Latin America has moved away
from current Peninsular usage, in some cases to such an extent that they
can cause misunderstanding and confusion. What follows are merely intro
ductory words of explanation and caution about a complex but often
encountered issue, especially in speech and informal written language.

30.6.3.1 *Mero* (as adjective/adverb)

In Peninsular usage this means 'mere', 'simple', 'only', 'just', 'pure': **la mera
referencia al libro** 'the mere reference to the book', **Es un mero niño** 'He
is only a child', **una mera casualidad** 'a pure coincidence'.

Alternative Latin American uses are widespread and varied, especially in
Mexico and Central America. The most common are:

(a) as an adjective used for emphasis 'very', 'him/her/itself' (comparable
with **mismo**): **en el mero centro de la ciudad** 'in the very centre of the
city', **el mero día de su llegada** 'the very day of their arrival', **El mero
profesor me lo dio** 'The professor himself gave it to me'.
(b) as an adjective meaning 'exact', 'precise': **a la mera hora de su salida**
'at the precise time of their departure'.
(c) as an adverb meaning 'just', 'right' (comparable with **mismo**): **ya mero**
'right now', **aquí mero** 'just here', **Ahora mero llegamos** 'We have just
arrived'.
(d) as an adverb meaning 'almost', 'nearly': **y merito me ahogaba** 'and I
was almost drowning'.

30.6.3.2 *Puro* (as adjective/adverb)

In Peninsular usage this means 'pure', 'sheer', 'simple': **puro algodón** 'pure
cotton', **de puros celos** 'out of sheer jealousy', **la pura verdad** 'the
simple/plain truth'.

Alternative Latin American uses are:

(a) as an adjective meaning 'only': **Hay puras mujeres en el parque** 'There
are only women in the park', **La sopa es pura agua** 'The soup is only
water'.
(b) as an adjective used for emphasis in the sense of 'very', 'him/her/itself'
(like **mero** and comparable with **mismo**): **Es del puro Cusco** 'He is

from Cusco itself', **Tiene el puro sabor de cenizas** 'It has the very taste of ashes'.

(c) as an adverb meaning 'very': **Su hija es puro traviesa** 'Their daughter is very naughty'.

30.6.3.3 *Hasta*

With an evident possibility for causing misunderstanding, in Mexico, Central America and Colombia, **hasta** is found in speech and writing with the meaning of 'not until', rather than the Peninsular 'until': **Hasta las dos almuerzo** 'I do not have lunch until two o'clock', **Hasta ayer vino** 'He did not come until yesterday', **Se puede matricular hasta mañana** 'You cannot register until tomorrow'.

30.6.3.4 *Coger*

This is best avoided unless one is consciously using it with its widespread meaning in Latin America of 'to screw', to 'fuck'. Acceptable alternatives are **tomar** and **agarrar**.

30.6.3.5 *Demasiado*

This is often found in Latin America with the meaning of 'very' (comparable with **muy** or **mucho**) rather than the norm in the Peninsula of 'too much': **Carmen es demasiado inteligente** 'Carmen is very intelligent', **Lo siento demasiado** 'I am very sorry', **Tengo demasiada hambre** 'I am very hungry'.

30.6.3.6 *De repente*

In the Peninsula this can only mean 'suddenly'. In the Andes and in the River Plate area the meaning is 'perhaps': **De repente se durmió** 'Perhaps he fell asleep'.

30.6.3.7 *Despacio*

In place of the Peninsular usage of 'slowly', there is a Latin American meaning 'quietly', 'in a low voice': **Trató de toser despacio** 'He tried to cough quietly', **¡Hablen ustedes despacio!** 'Speak in a low voice'. **Despaciosamente** 'slowly' is used in Latin America to avoid possible confusion.

30

Differences
between
Latin
American and
Peninsular
Spanish

30.6.3.8 *No más/nomás*

Often used to an excessive degree in speech, this phrase conveys several meanings in Latin America:

(a) 'just', 'only': **Fueron al mercado no más** 'They just went to the market', **hace una semana no más** 'only a week ago'.
(b) to strengthen adjectives and adverbs: **Es un jardín lindo no más** 'It's a pretty garden', **Se hace así no más** 'That's just how it is done', **Vino ayer no más** 'He came just yesterday'.
(c) to emphasize verbs, especially commands: **La tierra empezó a temblar no más** 'The ground just began to shake', **Siga no más** 'Please continue', **Siéntense no más** 'Just sit down'.

30.6.3.9 *Recién*

In addition to its Peninsular use exclusively before a past participle (see 7.2.3(c)), **recién** has the following meanings, especially in South America:

(a) 'just now/recently' (comparable with **acabar de** or **hace poco tiempo**): **Recién salió** 'She just left', **Recién me ofrecieron el puesto** 'They recently/have just offered me the post'.
(b) 'only (then)', 'not before/until' (this usage in South America is comparable with that of **hasta** above): **Recién entonces todos concurrieron** 'Only then did everyone agree', **Recién mañana iba a venir** 'He was only going to come tomorrow'.
(c) 'hardly', 'barely', 'no sooner' (comparable with **apenas**): **Recién salía de casa en ese momento** 'He was barely leaving home at that time', **Recién terminó cuando empezó a llover** 'No sooner had he finished than it started to rain'.

Glossary

Definitions of terms relating mainly to one chapter are given at the head of the relevant chapter, e.g. reflexive verbs, relative clauses. Terms in italics below are defined in this glossary.

Abstract noun A noun that refers not to a person, place or thing but to an abstract concept, such as **justicia** 'justice', **pobreza** 'poverty'.

Agreement Refers to (i) number: the correct choice of the singular or plural form of a word, (ii) gender: the correct choice of a masculine or feminine form of a word, (iii) person: the correct choice of ending for a verb's subject, e.g. 1st person singular (**yo**) **habl<u>o</u>**.

Apposition Two nouns juxtaposed so that the second adds further information about the first, i.e. is in apposition: **Lisboa, capital de Portugal** 'Lisbon, the capital of Portugal'.

Auxiliary verb A verb used in conjunction with a following *non-finite verb* form such as a participle or infinitive: **haber** to form compound tenses as in **Han terminado** 'They have finished' (see 10.9), and **estar** to form the progressive (or continuous) tenses, as in **Está corriendo** 'She is running' (see 10.10). For modal auxiliaries such as **deber, poder** before infinitives, see Chapter 16.

Clause Part of a sentence that contains its own *finite verb*. A main clause can usually stand alone as an independent sentence, whereas a subordinate clause is dependent upon a main clause: **Te lo diré** (main clause) **después de que se marche** (subordinate clause) 'I will tell you after he leaves'.

Conjunction	A word which links other words or *phrases*, e.g. **y** 'and', **o** 'or', **pero** 'but'. Subordinating conjunction introduce a subordinate *clause*, e.g. **que** 'that', **cuando** 'when', **aunque** 'although'.
Countable noun	A noun that can be quantified, such as **zapato** 'shoe' or **casa** 'house'. Thus one can say **unos zapatos** 'some shoes', **varias casas** 'several houses'. Compare *mass nouns*.
Diphthong	Two vowels forming a single syllable: **u** and **e** in **pueblo** 'village'. The equivalent with three vowels is a triphthong, e.g. **i**, **a** and **i** in **enviáis** 'you [plural] send'.
Direct object	The noun or pronoun that experiences the direct action of the verb, e.g. **edificio** in **Destruyeron el edificio** 'They destroyed the building' or **lo** in **Lo mataron** 'They killed him'.
Finite verb	A verb form that indicates person, number and, in most cases, tense, e.g. **hablo** 'I speak', **hablaste** 'you spoke', **¡hablad!** 'speak!'. In Spanish, all forms of the verb are finite except the infinitive, the gerund and the past participle.
Gender	See *agreement*.
Indirect object	The noun or pronoun that corresponds to the recipient or beneficiary of the action: **María** in **Se lo dieron a María** 'They gave it to María' or **le** in **Le han mandado un fax** 'They have sent a fax to him'.
Intransitive verb	A verb which does not take a direct object, e.g. **ir** 'to go', **toser** 'to cough'. Some verbs, however, can be both intransitive and *transitive* in use: **La niña duerme** 'The girl is sleeping', and **Durmieron a la niña** 'They put the girl to sleep'.
Invariable	Describes a word that cannot be changed for the purpose of *agreement* of number, gender or person, e.g. **cada** 'each' or any adverb.
Mass (or uncountable) noun	A noun that cannot normally be counted, such as **fango** 'mud' and **lana** 'wool'. These nouns are typically used in the singular. Thus one does not normally say ×**unos fangos**× or ×**veinte lanas**×.
Non-finite verb form	The infinitive, gerund or past participle of a verb.
Number	See *agreement*.

Perception verb	A verb describing how the subject becomes aware of something through the senses (especially sight): **ver** 'to see', **oír** 'to hear', **notar** 'to notice'.
Person	See *agreement*.
Personal *a*	Use of the preposition **a** to indicate the direct object when this is a person, as in **Hemos visto a Rocío** 'We have seen Rocío'.
Phrase	A group of words that collectively convey a meaning but do not include a *finite verb*: **a las ocho**, 'at eight o'clock', **detrás de la puerta** 'behind the door'.
Prepositional object	A noun or pronoun that is dependent on a preposition, e.g. **mi hermana** in **para mi hermana** 'for my sister', or **ella** in **con ella** 'with her'.
Proper noun (or name)	The name of a person, place or object, e.g. **Ricardo, Madrid**.
Psychological verb	A verb referring to a psychological process or state, such as recognizing, thinking, understanding or knowing.
Reciprocal	One of the uses of reflexive verbs with the meaning of 'each other', 'one another' (see 14.3).
Stress	Emphasis placed on a syllable by pronouncing it more emphatically than those around it. For example, **ro-** in the word **rojo** 'red'. In some words, stress is indicated by a written acute accent: **fácil** 'easy'.
Subject	Noun or *phrase* that performs the action of the verb: **la chica** in **La chica cantó un bolero** 'The girl sang a bolero'.
Syllable	A unit bigger than a single sound, smaller than a word and which (in Spanish) contains at least one vowel. For example, **patata** 'potato' can be split into three syllables: **pa-ta-ta**.
Transitive verb	A verb that has a *direct object*.

Index

a 215–20; in idioms 219–20; before infinitive 190, 193, 208; + object pronouns 77–8; after **oler, saber, sonar** 218–19; *see also* personal **a**
a la/lo 219
a por 236n
abbreviations 10
acá 65
acabar de 'to have just' 190n
accents 6, 7, 8–9
-acho/-aco (suffixes) 299–300
acronyms 10
-ada/-ida (suffixes) 294
adelante 66
adentro (de) *see* dentro
adjectives 52–62; as adverbs 69; of colour 54; compound forms 304; cf. English 52; gender agreement 52–6 (no feminine form 53–4, with nouns of mixed gender 54–5); position with noun 57–61 (different meaning according to position 60–1); shortening of 56–7; plural forms 55–6; verb + adjective 62
-ador/-edor/-idor (suffixes) 294
adverbs 63–9; categories 63; invariability 63; in -mente, 63–4; not ending in -mente 65–8 (degree/quantity 67–8, manner 65, place 65–6 [after nouns, use of **por** before 66], time 66–7); omission of -mente in series 64; phrases 68; stress and accents 64; *see also* adjectives, word order

-aer verbs 104–5, 118, 123
afuera 65–6; + de 225
ahí 65
al 27–8, 219; + infinitive 'on . . . -ing' 194
-al/-ar (suffixes) 292
algo 84–5
alguien 85
alguno 85–6; negative after nouns 86; short form 56, 85, 86n2
allá/allí 65
alphabet: ch, ll and ñ 1
ambos/as 93
-ancia/-anza (suffixes) 292
ante 220
antes: + de 220; + (de) que 154
anti- (prefix) 302
apenas (si) 67
aquel/aquella/aquellos/aquellas 44
aquello 46
aquí 65
arriba de 227
articles: el/un before feminine nouns 28; forms of 27–8; before nouns in series 40; *see also* definite/indefinite articles
-astro (suffix) 299–300
atrás 66; + de 225
-azo (suffix) 294, 299

bajo 220–1
bastante: 'enough' 88; 'quite (a lot)' 88n
'become/get/go' + noun/adjective 171–2
bien 269; *see also* más

Made in the USA
Las Vegas, NV
19 February 2021